ESSAYS ON THE CREATIVE ARTS THERAPIES

ABOUT THE AUTHOR

David Read Johnson, Ph.D., RDT-BCT is an Associate Clinical Professor in the Department of Psychiatry, Yale University School of Medicine, and the Director of the *Institutes for the Arts in Psychotherapy*, New York City, a multidisciplinary training center. From 1985-1991 he was the Chairperson of the National Coalition of Arts Therapy Associations as well as the Editor-in-Chief of the *Arts in Psychotherapy*, positions through which he worked toward greater collaboration among the creative arts therapy disciplines. He was a founder of the field of drama therapy and was President of the National Association for Drama Therapy. In addition to his passionate involvement in the creative arts therapies, Dr. Johnson has contributed to the field of posttraumatic stress disorder, and with his wife, Hadar Lubin, MD, codirects the Post Traumatic Stress Center in New Haven, Connecticut. They have two children, Corinda and Adam.

ESSAYS ON THE CREATIVE ARTS THERAPIES

Imaging the Birth of a Profession

By

DAVID READ JOHNSON, PH.D.

Charles C Thomas
PUBLISHER • LTD.

SPRINGFIELD • ILLINOIS • U.S.A.

Published and Distributed Throughout the World by

CHARLES C THOMAS • PUBLISHER, LTD.
2600 South First Street
Springfield, Illinois 62794-9265

© *1999 by* CHARLES C THOMAS • PUBLISHER, LTD.

ISBN 0-398-06973-5 (cloth)
ISBN 0-398-06974-3 (paper)

Library of Congress Catalog Card Number: 99-23247

Printed in the United States of America
CR-R-3

Library of Congress Cataloging-in-Publication Data

Johnson, David Read.
    Essays on the creative arts therapies : imaging the birth of a
profession / by David Read Johnson.
        p.   cm.
    Includes bibliographical references and index.
    ISBN 0-398-06973-5 (cloth). -- ISBN 0-398-06974-3 (paper)
    1. Arts--Therapeutic use. 2. Creative ability. 3. Psychotherapy.
I. Title.
RC489.A72J64   1999
616.89'165--dc21   99-23247
                                                                            CIP

FOREWORD

David Read Johnson's *Essays on the Creative Arts Therapies* takes us on a twenty-year journey through the sometimes treacherous seas of the creative arts therapies field. Homer's Odysseus wanders from peril to peril for twenty years on the way home from the wars, while Penelope never gives up hope even while fending off the pack of suitors consuming the hogs, crops, and winestores. In this modern-day odyssey of an arts therapist, David relates the perils of being an arts therapist in a professional world that poses many threats. Like Odysseus, he never surrenders his passion for the field, like Penelope, his hope that the several arts therapies disciplines comprising it will work more in concert, less in isolation from one another, never dims.

I doubt there is a corner of the field David does not address in this collection of two decades worth of essays. Rather than producing a disjointed effect, they assemble into a mosaic. The collection begins with an examination of why a person opts to be a member of this minority professional community—he discovers it is both an election and a sacrifice.

David looks at the profession from the inside and out, beginning with history ancient and modern. He states we can incorporate, but not rely upon, or origin as shamans. To survive and thrive in the therapy world it is necessary to claim a theoretical base and to speak the lingua franca. In this connection, David highlights the principal theoretical schools from which the arts therapies have borrowed, and he writes a complex chapter using the most current of those tongues—object relations theory—in discussing our profession(s).

It is also crucial to survival to understand how our profession(s) are impacted by current trends in the health and mental health fields—such as managed care, brief treatment, or claims for biological primacy. It is said that when standing on the edge of the sword one has to keep dancing, and David creatively envisions a place for the creative arts therapies on the cutting edge of theory and practice in educational and therapeutic settings. He sees new opportunities for the field, especially in the treatment of trauma and substance abuse.

One unifying theme of David's explorations is that the arts will stand stronger together than separately. If we speak only separate languages in a house of Babel, we are likely to be gobbled up by larger entities.

Unrecognized shame dynamics, he posits, are a force keeping us down and apart. So he amplifies the numerous links amongst us and encourages cooperation. David explores interesting hypotheses, ranging from gender differences to tribalism to object relations theory, to explain why the boards of the professional associations have resisted a closer union, and he proposes forming the National Creative Arts Therapy Association, a model of cooperation based on the approach of the framers of our Constitution.

This is a book of wide-ranging experience. The writing is strong, clear and eloquent. It is immediate and intimate, as in the accounts of a mentoring relationship, a religious conversion, or a letter to his patient. It is urgent, as it surveys the many mundane challenges confronting the field (such as licensure, insurance, salary scales), and offers workable solutions. It captures the quiet essence of "being with" the client in the therapeutic encounter. It is bold in its proposals to secure a future for the arts therapies. It is imaginative in envisioning the growth in theory, practice, and influence the therapeutic arts can offer to our hurting world.

I will require my students to read these *Essays on the Creative Arts Therapies*. I wish a benefactor would place it in the hands of every member of the creative arts therapies associations. Everyone interested in the intersection of the arts and the psychotherapies will be enriched by this important volume.

Kenneth Gorelick, MD, RPT
Past President, National Association for Poetry Therapy
Co-Director, Wordsworth Center for Poetry Therapy Training
Washington, DC

PREFACE

This book is a compilation of my essays, both published and unpublished, concerning the integration of the creative arts therapy disciplines (art, dance, drama, music, and poetry) into one larger organization representing their clinical, scholarly, and public policy activities. These essays span 25 years of my immersion in the practice, study, and politics of the creative arts therapies: treating clients every day as a drama therapist, serving for six years as the Editor-in-Chief of the *Arts in Psychotherapy*, and for six years as the Chairperson of the *National Coalition of Arts Therapy Associations*.

This is a book about rites of passage, about naivete and maturity, about growing up, both my own and my profession's. It is about poetics and politics, about our tremendous potential to contribute to the public welfare and our deep fears of collaboration and dialogue. Throughout this book I take the position that joining together clinically, academically, and organizationally will be beneficial to the health of our field as well as that of our clients; that we are divided only by the nature of our different artistic media, not by fundamental theoretical or political agendas. I speak not only as a creative arts therapist, but as a member of several other professional groups for whom diversity, debate, and dialogue are accepted and productive norms.

Readers outside of the creative arts therapy field may wonder what all the fuss is about, for the "together we stand, divided we fall" position reiterated here has proven its worthiness during many diverse times and situations. However, creative arts therapists have yet to heed this message and, in my opinion, remain ensconced in relative isolation from each other as well as from the wider mental health fields. This is very unfortunate, for the creative arts therapies have much to contribute to mental health in general, and even more to each other's disciplines.

This book's criticisms of my own profession are embedded within a deep respect for the work and for the creative arts therapists with whom I have been fortunate to collaborate. Many of these essays attempt to highlight the power and poignancy that are reliably evoked by the use of the arts in healing. I remain profoundly aware of my own journey, for I entered college as a student of advanced physics, and there is not a day now that I do not thank God for my stumbling into drama therapy, where spontaneity and beauty combine with service and the intellect.

I hope these essays stir you; they variously offer personal meditation, polemical argument, practical advice, serious theorizing, and some comic relief. Throughout, you will sense my struggle to express simultaneously my love for and impatience with this, my dear profession, being too quietly born.

D.R.J.

ACKNOWLEDGMENTS

Who is responsible for a passion? Certainly those who believe in you, who see the nascent vision inside and encourage it. Foremost among these is Susan Sandel, a highly talented dance therapist who directed the creative arts therapy department I began my career in, and who, through the many years of our partnership, was always my guide and greatest supporter. Many others deserve mention: Ken Bruscia, my "older brother" who by sheer strength of character managed to carry us through the successful 1985 NCATA conference. Peter Jampel, Renee Emunah, Arlynne Stark, Sandra Graves, Ken Gorelick, Art Lerner, Judy Bunney, Dale Buchanan, Paul Fink, and Sylvia Halpern in particular advised and nurtured me through many a difficult time. Sally Kondziolka, Lynn Temple, Cindy Briggs, Robin Gabriels, Peggy Heller, Connor Kelly, Susan Kleinman, Cay Drachnik, Linda Gantt, Richard Scalenghe, Peter Rowan, Vivien Marcow, Cheryl Maranto, and Stephanie Katz were among many colleagues who worked with me in the interests of the creative arts therapies. Eleanor Irwin, Art Robbins, Bob Siroka, Shaun McNiff, Penny Lewis, Robert Landy, Myra Levick, Adam Blatner, Claire Schmais, and Joan Chodorow all have made significant contributions to my understanding of the creative arts therapies. I have had the opportunity to meet so many wonderful creative arts therapists, dedicated clinicians and spirited people, who made the time spent on their behalf seem so worthwhile. Thank you.

Yet there would be no need for passion if there was no resistance! And yes, there have been many who have served this crucial function and have kept my will keen with passion. To all those who have stood in the way of the creative arts therapies becoming a stronger unity, I thank you, for by pressing up against your intellect, political talent, and deep fears, I have learned much indeed.

Finally, to Hadar, my wife and partner in work and love, for your encouragement and advice, and to Corinda and Adam, who have given me a new and welcoming course for my passions.

CONTENTS

Section III. Clinical and Theoretical Contributions

Section IV. Epilogue

ESSAYS ON THE CREATIVE ARTS THERAPIES

Section 1

PROLOGUE

Chapter 1

A COMMUNITY OF CREATIVE ARTS THERAPISTS: MY OBJECT OF DESIRE

My reluctant agreement to convert to Judaism turned into outright hesitation when I learned that I might have to be circumcised. True, I had been circumcised at birth, but a "proper" circumcision was required for conversion, especially if one day I might live in Israel. My Israeli fiancé had requested my conversion as much out of deep nationalism as religious preference, and faced with unthinkable alternatives, I submitted. My love for her prevailed over personal preference. Besides, I could handle this, I said to myself! Take a few classes, memorize a few blessings, do a ceremony.... no problem. But that was before I learned that a moyle would have to actually draw blood! A symbolic passing of a scalpel over my organ would be bad enough, but real blood *? This assault on my autonomy was surely too much to bear.*

I was an unlikely candidate for a career in the creative arts therapies, for my upbringing was entirely consumed by science and mathematics. Unforeseen pressures and chance events in high school and college fortunately guided me toward theatre. I entered Yale in advanced physics, but my distress over my father's alcoholism and the deterioration of my family life made the impersonal world of mathematics deeply unsatisfying. By mistake I wandered into a rehearsal of an improvisational theatre troupe, and was easily recruited. My studies quickly turned to theatre and psychology. In the theatre I found myself in ensembles of artists, incorporating drama, dance, poetry, art, and music in the productions, bound together by the press of opening night. My first job after college was at the Yale Psychiatric Institute, where I joined a team of creative arts therapists: dance, art, music, and video/photography. They quickly explained to me that what I was doing was drama therapy. My own knowledge and experience of drama therapy was profoundly affected by their mentoring and colleagueship. Over the years, I have developed long-term relationships with other creative arts therapists, both at the VA Hospital where I have worked, and in the wider New Haven community. For many years we met for monthly luncheons to share our woes and accomplishments. We have witnessed each other growing up. Living in one place for a long time provides these advantages. These relationships have offered me a productive arena to explore the boundaries between, and similarities among, the different arts modalities.

These collaborative experiences gradually laid the foundations of my belief that creative arts therapists should unite in a larger organization in order to wield greater influence on social policies that will serve our clients and preserve our survival as a profession. These economic and political reasons I found, and still find, incontestable. Nevertheless, as external pressures on the profession, forcing either compliance or resistance, they have not provided creative arts therapists an inner motivation to join together.

I grew up as a Unitarian. The Unitarian Church is an ironic structure, almost an oxymoron, for though its name derives from the desire to "unite" people by advocating the basic principles of goodwill, peace, and faith, its members are dedicated iconoclasts, individualists, and agnostics. My mother told me that Unitarians were skeptics who went to church, just in case. For her, this contradiction was evidence of a basically scientific orientation, which was highly valued in my family. Converting from Unitarianism has little meaning, for the Church professes no specific dogma. I was taught that God was who I thought he/she/it was, and that the principle of religious freedom transcended any one set of beliefs. Given this background, it is curious that I allowed myself to convert to Judaism in my forties.

I cannot remember when my passion for a united creative arts therapy profession began; perhaps in 1981 or 1982. Until then I was consumed with forming and sustaining the newly created National Association for Drama Therapy, and establishing the integrity of my own modality. I do remember my first meeting with the presidents of the other creative arts therapy associations in Philadelphia in 1982, where I was instantly made aware of the numerous political and economic advantages to our collaboration, and also was confronted with the profound hesitations among the friendly parties. For example, the financing of a few hundred sheets of letterhead for our coalition was problematic, and eventually unsuccessful. The meaning of our location in Philadelphia, yards away from where our Constitution was framed, was not lost on me, and I became ever more inspired by the obstacles our founding fathers must have encountered in bringing together a nation of thirteen autonomous states. For creative arts therapists, however, the task of uniting in a more powerful union has remained a daunting, and as yet unfulfilled project.

I spent the next decade devoting the majority of my time to this effort, and this book is a record of my dutiful strivings. In the summer of 1984, Myra

Levick convened a creative arts therapy conference in Philadelphia, where leaders in the various fields were allowed to dialogue freely with each other. This conference was very stimulating to me, and resulted in my first article on the subject (Chapter 2). A close colleague known for her iconoclasm read the article and wrote me a note, commenting simply, "almost inspiring." Torn between being flattered and annoyed, I read the paper again and agreed with her view that I had been holding back. Thus began my attempt to inspire, which is reflected in Chapters 3 through 6. By this time, NCATA had planned the 1985 Joint Conference in New York, and I had been selected both as the next Chairperson of the Coalition, and the Editor-in-Chief of the *Arts in Psychotherapy*, the primary interdisciplinary journal in the field. For six years I served in these highly visible and influential positions, both politically and academically, and the work consumed me. My passions coalesced in the pursuit of one aim: advocating for the creative arts therapies as a profession.

By 1990, the second Joint Conference in Washington, DC had been organized, and though the Conference was highly successful, or perhaps because it was so successful, the member organizations of the Coalition soon stepped back from pursuing a formal organization. In 1991, I left the Coalition, and in my writing shifted from inspiration to direct suggestion for a multi-divisional organization (Chapters 7 and 8), and then interpretation of what I detect as underlying shame dynamics within the field (Chapter 9). Chapters 10 and 11, not previously published, address the serious challenges we face from managed care.

> *I have quite an independent spirit, which I attribute entirely to my family, since independence has been in my family's blood for a long time. For example, my great grandfather, John Lewis, who was the mayor of Oak Park, Illinois at the turn of the century, was also known for his independence: it was said that in Oak Park there were eleven religious denominations, and John Lewis. Or at least that is what the independent members of my family told me they said. The message was clear. So for me to agree to convert to Judaism had only one meaning: submission, and submission was bad. Thus, I decided that if the conversion was to be tolerable, I needed to discover something of myself in Judaism, and I set out to do that with the help of a rabbi. This rabbi served me well, and when I learned that he was a Reform rabbi in a long line of Orthodox rabbis, I was comforted.*

It has been a great challenge to convince creative arts therapists that we share a sense of mutual identity. Though from an external view, the arts therapies seem clearly related and members of the same class, creative arts therapists do not often share such a view. The most significant reason for this discrepancy is that though the arts lie within the field of aesthetics, each individual art form (music, drama, dance, art, or poetry) calls upon distinct talents, sensibilities, and personalities. Proficiency is attained through highly specialized and concentrated practice. The acts of painting, singing, reading poetry, dancing, and acting involve different parts of the body, and different modes of expression. Therefore, training in these art forms, a prerequisite for arts therapists, usually involves little contact with each other. Unlike medicine or psychology, creative arts therapists are not educated in one body of knowledge (such as aesthetics), only then to branch out into specialty training. The creative arts therapies were not originated by one founder, and then differentiated into separate orientations, as in many other forms of psychotherapy (e.g., psychodrama, psychoanalysis, Gestalt, Reichian). Instead of branching out, we seem to be reaching in, seeking the common trunk to our professional tree.

The arts therapies are therefore united in an *abstract communion*: that is, we are viewed as members of a class by those outside of the class. This form of grouping is called a *serial* group, in comparison to a *pledged* group, in which members jointly hold a representation of their group, and feel identified with each other (Sartre, 1960). Creative arts therapies are currently a serial grouping, and those of us advocating unification hope to achieve the level of the pledge. This has been difficult, because the major impetus for coming together are external threats: financial and political pressures from managed care, not internally felt needs. Therefore, some of our members have felt that they have been collectively defined as a family by others, not unlike African tribes, for example, who found themselves haphazardly organized by European colonizers into The Congo, or The Sudan.

I learned of the Jews' deep distrust for leaders, which is reflected in their use of multiple judges and ruling councils rather than single authorities, of majority rule rather than unanimity. In fact, I was amazed to discover that the Sanhedrin, an ancient judicial body of 70 rabbis, followed a principle that if someone brought to trial was convicted by all 70 judges, he would go free, for they believed that truth cannot be monolithic, and occurs only in a state of disagreement! My Rabbi shared a story of one Yeshiva where a rabbi proclaimed himself the Messiah, and upon his word thunder and lightning, floods, and rainbows were made to appear. The other rabbis said they would not follow him, so he ordered a lightning bolt to strike the Yeshiva. Still they did not submit. Finally, a great voice from above called out, "I am God. Why do you not believe that this rabbi is the Messiah and carries my Word?" The most learned rabbi of the Yeshiva replied, "Because we do not follow individuals, we follow only the teachings of the Torah through our study and discussion." I understood then why there were so many former Jews in my Unitarian church.

Serialization can be overcome through contact with each other. Creative arts therapists often work as colleagues in hospital therapeutic activities departments, and a number of articles have described joint clinical activities (see Selected Bibliography, Clinical Section). The two joint conferences were also significant interfaces for members. Several graduate programs have integrated more than one arts modality (Dulicai et al., 1989) and one book has been written on the education of all the arts therapies (McNiff, 1986). Scholarship on the creative arts therapies has been increasing as academic conferences have brought scholars together (see Bibliography, Theoretical section).

Another dimension of professional contact is public debate and dialogue about the relationship among the creative arts therapies. I remain bewildered that such a volatile, important issue in our profession has received so little public discussion (see Bibliography, Professional Issues). The issue of unification, or even collaboration within the structure of NCATA, must still be threatening; even association newsletters have tended to avoid it. Yet I believe that open discussion can only deepen and enrich our understanding of our profession, and need not be threatening. Indeed, in some sense this book is intended to sustain this nascent dialogue, a creative arts therapies version of The Federalist Papers (Madison et al., 1788).

Increased professional contact will reveal that we share a common body of knowledge. If an integrated profession is to develop, then core theoretical concepts need to be identified and articulated. Clinical and theoretical commonalities among the modalities need explication. As the editor of the *Arts in Psychotherapy*, I was frequently exposed to parallel formulations of theory and practice across the different modalities, though rarely did authors make reference to similar scholarship in the other modalities. The pervasive commonalities are evident in the philosophy of art (Langer, 1953), the psychology of aesthetics (Ehrenzweig, 1967), psychoanalysis and object relations theory (Freud, 1920/1966; Jung, 1954; Klein, 1955; Kohut, 1971; Kris, 1952; Mahler et al., 1975; Winnicott, 1971), developmental psychology (Piaget, 1951; Stern, 1985; Werner & Kaplan, 1963) and theories of healing (Frank, 1962; Harner, 1982). In Chapters 12 through 20, I make my contributions to this rapidly growing body of knowledge (see Bibliography). Greater dialogue among creative arts therapy scholars will stimulate theory development in all modalities.

What a discovery it was for me to find that Jews do not prescribe what one should believe about God, for they believe that the transcendent is not knowable in the usual ways. They insist, however, that one engage in the process of discovery through study and debate. I was amazed to find the dialectic discourse of the Talmud, in which commentary follows commentary in a presumably endless process. Truth is sought through dialogue and shar-ing one's perspective; through confrontation of differences.

How, I wondered, could a group such as the Jews, who embrace debate, disagreement, and suspicion of monolithic authority, have survived as an integrated culture over so many years? Why does debate draw them together, when so often I have witnessed it push people apart?

This book is about these same issues: submission vs. assertion, debate vs. silence, autonomy vs. isolation, integrity vs. humiliation, within the creative arts therapies, which in many ways are faced with strong external pressures to join together, despite their profound reluctance. This book is my attempt to convince my colleagues of the greater good to come from uniting togeth-er, or, perhaps is a record of my still uncompleted journey toward under-standing why such a step will not take place.

Perhaps the metaphor of conversion is apt, for conversion brings up deep threats to identity and submission to the Other. Yet, as I found in my own personal case, it is possible to join a larger community without giving up one's fundamental rights to autonomous thinking, belief, or practice, to embrace diversity and debate, and to begin the enriching dialogue among colleagues that we so deserve. The feared surrender and loss of control imag-ined by the reluctant convert can be transformed into delight in participation in a more diverse community whose values can be admired. I have no ques-tion that the values supported by a unified creative arts therapy profession will be those of creativity, autonomy, and relationship, only in larger mea-sure. If, indeed, one function of the creative arts therapies is to make the evanescent present, by embodying spirit in the art form, then surely, over time, with patience and humility, we can bring this nascent community into being. That is my hope, and my desire.

The moyle's knife made a small incision on my foreskin, as two rabbis witnessed the ancient rite; I felt peculiarly held by their presence, and not so frightened. Naked, I entered the ritual bath, and spoke the blessings that announced me as a Jew. The process of conversion had taken place, but not so much through these symbolic actions, as with-in myself. The miracle was that I had transformed my submission to the Jewish religion into an assertion of my individuality. The circumcision and ritual bath had not dimin-ished me through humiliation, as I had feared. Rather, I had extended myself through space and time by joining a cultural heritage of greater power, that I knew would fuel my creativity. I remembered my resentment when initially confronted with the necessity of conversion, but now, emerging dripping wet from the ritual bath, and hearing the rab-bis' exultant "Mazel tov," I felt proud of myself.

Section II
ESSAYS

Chapter 2

ESTABLISHING THE CREATIVE ARTS THERAPIES AS AN INDEPENDENT PROFESSION

It is always a difficult moment for me when another creative arts therapist leaves the field. But when my good friend and colleague left, all of my own doubts arose in even greater force. She said, "I've had it. I'm put down and paid poorly. I'm an *adjunctive* therapist. Sure they respect my work, but will I ever get promoted? Where is this leading to?... I've decided to get a M.B.A." For others it is a M.S.W. or Ph.D., or back to performance. I ask myself: where are we now as a field, after 15 to 30 years of development? What significance and respect have music, dance, art, and drama therapies achieved in our society?

And if indeed the answer to that question is a sobering one, what are the obstacles which lie in our path?

Having just returned from a working conference on the future of the creative arts therapies, sponsored by the Creative Arts in Therapy Program at Hahnemann Medical College in Philadelphia, I found myself both excited and concerned by the debate among leading creative arts therapists and the invited psychiatrists and psychologists. Excited because the discussion again, as always, illustrated the remarkable power of the arts in therapy, the strength of the creative process to unlock crucial human feeling and thought, and the essential need for these modalities to enliven our constricted institutions. Yet I was sobered by the all too apparent reality that, despite our efforts, we are barely known by the health care industry, not to mention society at large, and that as a profession we are still sorely lacking in sophistication, effective organization, financial security, and independence.

It is difficult to face how dependent we still are upon these institutions of psychiatry, education, and business, which we experience so ambivalently. Even those of us who have managed to construct a private practice in a cre-

Reprinted from the *Arts in Psychotherapy, 11*, 209-212, 1984 with permission from Elsevier Science.

ative arts therapy do so as colonists in someone else's homeland. It is true that artists have often been supported by the legitimate authorities in the land, be it kings or government grants. Fine Art developed in palace court-yards and throne-rooms, a tolerated antithesis to the values of conformity otherwise prescribed by those in power. How can we separate the greatness of Michelangelo's painting from the grandeur of the Sistine Chapel? Everyone respects fine art—though few wish their children to be artists. If the creative arts therapies are to be more than valued decoration on the great edifice of modern psychiatry, then I believe we must focus our efforts on three important tasks: We must be able to *articulate our unique contributions* both to the mental health community and to society at large. We must be able to *differentiate a wide range of professional roles* within our profession so we are not narrowly defined. Finally, we must be able to *provide the conditions for mature leadership* to create a safe environment for that diversity.

Identifying Our Unique Contributions

The creative arts therapies cannot expect to achieve the respect and understanding of established professions unless our unique contributions to society are clearly articulated. It is no longer sufficient for us merely to demonstrate that a psychological theory borrowed from psychiatry or psychology also describes processes in a drama or art therapy session. We have established that the creative arts therapies are psychotherapeutic events. But what have the creative arts therapies contributed to our understanding of personality development, divorce, depression, or child abuse? What *new* information has been produced that others deem useful? Unless we are capable of answering these questions, we can be considered no more than an extension of the great tide of psychotherapy into yet another area of experience.

Our profession is slowly developing a body of knowledge in what I see as a three stage process. First, in a stage of *exploration*, creative arts therapists have invented techniques, and have observed their effects on a variety of patients. Many articles in the field are of this purely descriptive nature. The next stage involves *categorization*, in which these various techniques and processes are analysed according to basic elements and then compared. Articles in this stage consist of assertions that certain exercises work better in one situation or with one population than other exercises. Authors have emerged in each modality who provide this essential service. The third stage is *conceptualization*, in which the various categories of events are organized into meaningful relationships to each other through a theory. Thus Viola Spolin categorizes numerous improvisational structures, but does not provide a theory of improvisation, and Laban's Effort-Shape Analysis is a descriptive system, not a theory of dance therapy. Initially, theories previously developed outside of our field by other professions have been imported or borrowed from as models of conceptualization. Thus, each of the creative arts therapies have psychoanalytic, developmental, Jungian, Gestalt, and behavioral versions. Many articles in the field currently reflect this stage of professional development: a creative arts therapy session is analysed according to an accepted theory. Predictably, we prove again that the theory is also applicable to the art therapy medium. As a result, we confirm the theory, not the contribution of arts therapy.

A more sophisticated level of conceptualization will emerge when knowledge gained from a creative arts therapy is used to enhance or improve these theories. Thus, a creative arts therapist's clinical work will be used to advance knowledge of psychoanalytic theory, Piaget's stages of development, or Jung's conception of individuation. Articles will not repeatedly focus on what we *do*, but what we *discover* about people, groups, or society. We will add to society's knowledge about schizophrenia, reactions to trauma or the impact of adoption on children. Contributions of this kind emanating from our field will ensure a significant role for the creative arts therapies in the health care professions.

I firmly believe that we do have unique contributions, and that each of the creative arts therapies have something to offer in specific areas. However, I do not think these contributions have been effectively articulated. For example, many creative arts therapists believe, as I do, that their work (1) allows cognitively impaired and nonverbal patients to communicate more effectively with a therapist, (2) that the arts media encourage access to affect more readily than verbal techniques, and (3) that interpersonal bonding and a therapeutic alliance is established more quickly. These points are made over and over again. Yet are they not also true for other nonverbal therapies such as Gestalt, bioenergetics, and psychodrama? And are they equally true for all of the creative arts therapies? Though drama therapy and dance therapy differ in many ways, are these differences significant enough or relevant to our basic contributions? If they are, who has articulated them? The relatively small output of published articles in the field is an ominous sign, suggesting that these questions are not being sufficiently addressed.

The importance of identifying and describing our contributions in a persuasive manner is increased by the fact that we do not have a possessed technology upon which we can lay claim to survival. Psychiatrists prescribe medications, psychologists give psychological tests, social workers see families. Regardless of the effectiveness of psychotherapy, these professional groups are required in a setting to perform these activities. There is currently no similar activity for which a creative arts therapist is required. We are therefore more vulnerable to criticism that questions our "effectiveness." Being a beneficial service is not enough to protect our position. While I am not optimistic, perhaps one day we may establish a procedure, activity, or population for which we are a necessity.

Differentiating Roles within the Profession

A second obstacle to our profession's growth is our dependency upon other professional groups. This problem, I believe, is sustained by having defined ourselves too narrowly. Most, if not all, of us entered the creative arts therapies in a clinical role, as a therapist of patients. We continue to view ourselves fundamentally as clinicians. A negative consequence of this limited definition has been that those creative arts therapists who wish to become teachers, researchers, or administrators, are often subject to indirect skepticism by colleagues, and by themselves. Becoming an administrator is experienced as leaving the field, or worse, as going over to the "other side."

We need to embrace a definition of a creative arts therapist that can be an administrator, researcher, lobbyist, or scholar, and still be a creative arts therapist. Otherwise, we will maintain ourselves in a dependent position vis-a-vis these other functions, which are currently held by other professions. Perhaps we cling a bit too much to the view that we are the empathic, nurturing, and creative clinician, who is misunderstood, put down, and controlled by the cold, distant, and rigid psychiatric administrator or researcher. Students in other fields are told that they have a number of equally legitimate options for their career: research, clinical work, administration. Students in our field need to have these options, too, and to be encouraged to take them if they are interested. We need to legitimize the full range of roles: clinicians, teachers, researchers, inspirationalists, theoreticians, fund-raisers, and administrators; and create a diversified professional community characterized by mutual respect and unified purpose.

Providing the Conditions for Mature Leadership

The third achievement necessary for our development is stability and security among the leadership of our professional associations. The vulnerability of our profession can be seen in the knit brows of our leaders, whose hesitance and caution reflect the strong pressures being brought to bear on them from within and without their organizations.

First, leaders in the creative arts therapies need to be able to represent our interests forthrightly and with confidence, taking increasingly assertive stands in relation to other professional groups and legislative agencies. The national health care industry is in a period of significant restructuring, requiring constant monitoring and strong action on our part to assure our survival. Mature leadership involves the balancing of this strength with collaboration, achieved through the seeking and development of networks, joint ventures, and coalitions based on areas of mutual concern. This collaboration will require compromise, and even subsequent internal restructuring of our own associations. I predict that we are entering a period of intense political conflict. The structures we have devised have been the result of years of compromise between internal factions within our fields. Yet we must now attend more to the necessary compromises with external forces, which will revive these past internal conflicts. For example, if we need to bring greater consistency to our registration standards across the creative arts therapies, then certain associations may have to upgrade, and others downgrade, their previously established standards. The difficulties this presents are obvious. Our leaders will be at the locus of the ensuing conflict. A major arena of this conflict, expressing both its maturity and vulnerability, will be the National Coalition of Arts Therapy Associations, which has been able to bridge enough differences to sponsor a joint conference of five associations in 1985 in New York, but which remains a tentative Alliance unable at the present time to represent the Creative Arts Therapy field with one voice.

Mature leadership will also mean being able to steer a course that respects both the autonomous, antiestablishment spirit which those in the artistic community have long cherished, and the need to accommodate ourselves to the established power hierarchies in the interests of survival and growth. The paradox lies in the perceived conflict between the values of creativity and spontaneity on the one hand, and order, power, and structure on the other. Our national associations are organizations of spontaneous people; how is that possible? How can one organize spontaneity? My answer is that creative arts therapists do just that in their sessions, when they provide a structure for a person or a group that will maximize the opportunity for a spontaneous response. This in fact is one of our potential contributions to society: we know how to create flexible structures that encourage growth. Nevertheless, within our professional associations, leadership, management, and hierarchical control are often experienced as being at odds with the essential values of our work. Why is it that in the middle of a tense or boring Board meeting I often feel the pressing need to jump up and offer a reassuring, if token, nonverbal exercise? Our leaders are particularly vulnerable to the criticisms of members, and to their own doubts, around these issues of authority. In this unfortunate way the struggle between the creative arts therapies and psychiatry may sometimes be transferred to a struggle between our members and their own leaders.

The potential for success lies here, however; for if a sufficiently secure leadership develops which can convince its members that the fundamental values of the creative arts therapies: play, spontaneity, creativity, and freedom of expression, will not be threatened by collaboration and integration with larger social agencies, then we will be well on the way to contributing greatly to our culture and its people.

To be able to accomplish this, mature leadership must actively demonstrate tolerance of diversity within the profession. Our leaders need to be able to represent the entire field, and to encourage toleration of different techniques, approaches, and theories. The pressures on specific leaders to be seen as loyal to one approach and antagonistic to another are tremendous, and need to be minimized. Just as we need to learn to appreciate different roles for creative arts therapists, so too we need to appreciate the development and articulation of a multitude of theories and techniques. Unlike some therapies (such as Psychodrama, Gestalt, Psychoanalysis, or Bioenergetics), we are not associations with *one* theory, created by one man (Moreno, Perls, Freud, or Lowen). We are defined only by our common link to the awe-inspiring and healing power of an art form.

Our survival and adaptation is enhanced by such diversification, in that our future will not be dependent upon the rise and fall of a particular orientation. If the creative arts therapies are seen as a subspecialty of psychoanalysis or dependent upon the concept of the unconscious, for example, then jobs will be lean in the institutions where a behavorial perspective is held. My point is that all of us as creative arts therapists will benefit from intelligent and effective presentations of widely divergent theoretical and technical views. It is leadership's task, in my view, to encourage the expansion of the creative arts therapies into new areas, including those with behavioral and even biological perspectives.

Conclusion

It is possible that the creative arts therapies will remain as an adjunctive, secondary form of psychotherapeutic treatment. Perhaps we will become identified as valued specialists, who are referred especially difficult or perplexing cases, as in medicine. Or perhaps we will be able to have a more pervasive impact on psychotherapy, education, and the quality of life in our institutions. I fervently believe that such an impact is possible, if we can identify our unique contributions, diversify our roles, and develop mature leadership. Dependency is a necessary step in the development of a profession, as well as a person. We currently have much to gain, and much to learn, from those more established professions. They protect us and offer us great opportunities, even if they appear not to value us. We need not squirm too forcefully in their embrace. After all, Gandhi studied Law in England before leading India to independence.

My good friend, the creative arts therapist, will be finishing her M.B.A. in two years and she will be looking for a job to do. . . . I think we've got one for her.

Chapter 3

ENVISIONING THE LINK AMONG THE CREATIVE ARTS THERAPIES

The official at the government agency was on the phone and she was confused. "Who is this? A drama therapist? The National what? Are you an arts therapist?" I replied, "No, we are drama therapists." Her irritation was evident. "You people are entirely fragmented. Do you realize that I have talked to nine or ten of you in the last week. Some art. Some dance. Music. Now drama. Presidents have called. Committee chairs have called. Everyone asking the same questions. I don't get it." I explained, "You see, we are all creative arts therapists." She sounded relieved. "Ohh! Good! So tell me about your position on the bill." "I can only represent drama therapists," I muttered. She moaned. "You mean you don't have an organization?" "Organization?" "That's right. You don't have any chance of being included in the legislation until you're organized. Surely you know that!"

Economic, legal, and professional necessities are making it extremely clear that only through organized collaboration will art, dance, drama, poetry, and music therapies survive and grow. Licensure, third party payments, inclusion in JCAHO standards and federal legislation are the stuff of myth and dreams for an individual association. Our growing awareness of this reality has lead to a series of joint conferences such as the *Looking to the 90s* symposium at Hahnemann University in Philadelphia (June, 1984), Legislative Affairs conference in Washington (July, 1984), creative arts therapy conference at Concordia University in Montreal (April, 1985), and the NCATA joint conference in New York (November, 1985).

These political and economic realities are sufficient to bring us together. We will probably do so within this decade through the further development of the National Coalition of Arts Therapy Associations. The question is, on what basis will we join together? Solely for political and economic reasons, motivated by survival? Or for more central philosophical reasons, authentically felt, that enrich our professional identity? I believe that now is the time,

Reprinted from the *Arts in Psychotherapy, 12*, 233-238, with permission from Elsevier Science.

when our collaboration is being conceived, to articulate the reasons why the creative arts therapies form a coherent profession.

For years there have been calls for combining the arts therapies and legitimizing the notion of the expressive arts therapist, who is capable of facilitating the client's expressions in all media (Naitove, 1980; McNiff, 1981). What is now being sought, however, is a consolidation of the professional groups, not a fusion of the therapies themselves. Each modality has had time to define itself, reassure itself that it exists, and develop reasonable standards. Now we are ready to create a larger unity while preserving the individuality of each medium.

We need to diversify our professional roles in order to survive in the mental health field (see Chapter 2). We need researchers, scholars, managers, and publicists as well as clinicians. We need a strong and sophisticated understanding of the contribution of each media. Yet diversification without an integrated core identity will lead to fragmentation of the field. Thus, we are under pressure to consolidate in order to establish that identity, to acquire a jointly held vision of who we are.

We are faced with a difficult task. We have been both defined and divided by our allegiance to our particular art media. Unlike the fields of psychology or medicine, whose students study a common body of knowledge for several years before specializing, the arts are differentiated from the start. Artists do not begin with a core curriculum and then specialize in an art form. Creative arts therapists are more apt to have had similar courses in psychology and therapy than in aesthetics or artistic development. Our media are so engrossing, and require so much training in the craft, that specialization precedes an understanding of general aesthetic principles and the artist's creative vision. Though medicine also identifies its specialty areas according to various criteria, such as body organ (cardiology), state of the body (pathology), or technical procedure (radiology), the presence of the physical human body gives the field a definable cohesion. What is the "body" of which art, dance, drama, music are a part? What would a core curriculum be? The list of courses we often propose includes psychology, liberal arts, fine arts, research methods, anatomy, neurology, a little bit of this, and a little bit of that. Are the creative arts therapies really a tossed salad of the major intellectual fields of the twentieth century? If we arise from the same source, and our similarities are not merely apparent on the surface—if we are indeed siblings—then who are our parents?

The creative arts therapies are certainly not united by an agreed upon set of techniques. While there are similarities in types of technique (e.g., improvisational, structured, performance-oriented), they are used in many different ways by each practitioner and in each media. Nor are the creative arts therapies united by a theory of therapy. Currently theories are borrowed from established fields, such as behavioral, psychoanalytic, gestalt, and

Jungian. Many therapists may have a greater allegiance to other therapists of the same theoretical school, than to other arts therapists. There is not even agreement among creative arts therapists about what is the primary therapeutic agent in our work: is it participation in the arts media itself, the insight derived from reflecting on the art work, or the therapeutic relationship with the therapist?

If it is neither our techniques nor our theories that link us, perhaps it is simply the media of expression we use? Are the creative arts therapies those therapies in which the client utilizes the creative arts, as the verbal therapies are those in which the client uses words? Unfortunately, this is too often the position we fall back on when we cannot articulate a more fundamental link. We then constrain the definition of ourselves to what we do, rather than representing an attitude concerning healing and human interaction. The problem with this utilitarian definition is that it marginalizes the act of talking with the patient. We ask ourselves, "If a creative arts therapist spends a whole session talking with the client, is he doing creative arts therapy?" The answer is **No** if creative arts therapies are defined by our activity, but could be **Yes** if it is defined by a more basic principle.

The common source of the creative arts therapies is therefore more likely to be found at a different level than that of technique or theory or media, at the level of basic perspective on the human condition, such as creativity, play, or aesthetic knowing. Let me review several of these perspectives.

The Brain

Imagine how reassuring it would be for our colleagues, and perhaps for some of us, to be able to locate the creative arts in a portion of the brain! If it is in the brain, then it is real. Recent neuropsychological research has indeed indicated that the skills required for artistic expression, such as spatial awareness, analogical reasoning, and identification of musical forms, are more often performed by the right or nondominant hemisphere, while verbal, logical, and sequential learning is performed by the left hemisphere (Gardner, 1980). According to this perspective, the creative arts therapies are linked because they all utilize processes mediated by the right hemisphere and thus are valuable as nonverbal, nondiscursive innovations in treatment, providing access to the thoughts and feelings unavailable through verbal means alone. The discovery that aphasic patients with damage to the left hemisphere from a stroke can speak with less impairment if they sing the words (since singing is processed by the undamaged right hemisphere), or the observed importance of music and song with Alzheimer's patients, are two examples of therapeutic applications of a neurological understanding of the arts.

The research on hemispheric differentiation is often extended to imply that the arts, creativity, or spirituality are located in the right hemisphere of the brain. From a metaphorical perspective, this is major progress, since in most other theories, the arts are located in *lower* regions, e.g., lower developmental levels, down in the id or unconscious, in contrast to verbal processes that are in higher areas. Now at least we are *alongside* verbalization, (even though we remain nondominant)! Unfortunately, the research is more uncertain and the distinctions between hemispheres less clear than orginally thought. Though specific artistic skills and cognitive processes might be *localized*, there is no evidence that something as abstract and complex as creativity or artistic vision is contained in a specific location in the brain.

In the present environment we will be increasingly tempted to justify our profession with a biological basis, despite the fact that our roots are clearly elsewhere. Nevertheless, we should not retreat from using these biological incantations of "right hemisphere" to appease the gods who now hold sway.

Religion

It has now become a cliche for descriptions of the creative arts therapies to begin with, "Since the earliest of times, man has used art (or dance, drama, music) to express his deepest fears and greatest wishes....." The hope is, of course, to establish that artistic expression is fundamental to humankind. This often romanticized attempt to articulate our roots from so far back reveals how alienated we feel from the current culture and recent historical times. If our "parents" were primitive tribal shamans, then we truly are orphans, for they have long been gone.

It is not clear to what extent early art was characterized by aesthetic principles. At that time, religion, the arts, and healing were not differentiated, as they are today. Shaun McNiff and others have carefully explored the similarities in role and function between the creative arts therapist and the shaman, and our techniques with those of ritual. He states the religious perspective most clearly: "I believe that our work in the arts is more closely allied with the larger continuities of religious belief and faith. The arts can, in this sense, be viewed as sacramental actions that symbolically represent the mysteries and intensities of inner experience. They are 'sensible signs' of the psyche's efforts to become transcendent and this kinship with religious ritual explains much of their potency" (McNiff, 1981, p. xxii). The basic concepts of this view of the creative arts therapies include faith, devotion, communion, acceptance, and the sacred. Ritual and ceremony become the central frameworks for action.

In contrast, Susanne Langer supports a purely aesthetic view: that the arts were linked to religion only temporarily. "The arts were never bound to ritual or morals or sacred myth, but flourished freely in sacred realms as long as the human spirit was concentrated there. As soon as religion becomes prosaic or perfunctory, art appears somewhere else" (Langer, 1953, p. 402). It is a natural impulse to look back to find our roots in an early, original, attribute of mankind. However, we must assess in what ways our heritage lives on in us now. The challenge for McNiff and others is to envisage a role for the creative arts therapies that integrates our roots in the past with the current developments of our society. If we are to be shamans, then we must discover how we are shamans of our time, and for the future.

Aesthetics

Arthur Robbins in his reply to my article (Chapter 2) describes the unique identity of the creative arts therapies as aesthetic understanding (Robbins, 1985). "As we understand science in a different context, beauty becomes a means of discovering scientific truth. It is also a means of understanding meaning and truth as communicated from one individual to another. As creative artists, we indeed provide a frame for the exploration of truth, truth that is framed within a theory of aesthetics and presented either in artistic, dramatic, or poetic form." (Robbins, 1985, p. 68). Certainly many authors have seen aesthetics as underlying and unifying the perspective of the creative arts therapies, though I am not aware of many creative arts therapy programs that actually have courses in aesthetic understanding and its relationship to therapy (Levick, 1980; McNiff, 1986). If an aesthetic theory of therapy is to develop, (and Dr. Robbins is one who is approaching such an achievement–see Robbins, 1980), then the concepts of beauty, harmony, rhythm, resonance, brilliance, dynamic tension, and balance will have to be applied to psychological states of persons. The goals of therapy will be described in terms of increasing beauty, balance, or harmony in the person.

Each therapy envisons the client through a guiding metaphor. For psychoanalysis, the client is the dreamer; for behaviorism, a hungry animal; for primal scream, a crying infant. The creative arts therapies envision the client as an artist, who creates his own self and life. Susanne Langer describes art as the "creation of forms symbolic of human feeling" (Langer, 1953). Each art form creates an "essential illusion" through which the art work symbolizes an aspect of human life. In the creative arts therapies, the "essential illusion" is the self. The artwork–be it a painting, song, or dance–symbolizes the essential creation: that of the self-in-the-world. In an aesthetic theory of therapy, the self is consciousness' artwork-in-progress. Instead of id, ego, and superego, perhaps its central concepts will be the three modes of artistic reality: the creator, the performer, and the audience. Since the artist produces something that is both a self-expression and a communication to others, she/he must constantly shift back and forth from an internal source of creative vision to the viewpoint of the audience, and at the same time translate these perceptions into the actual artistic materials in the performance. The actor, for example, must both *be* the character and remember to face the audience. For the arts are not direct expressions of feelings, they are the artist's ideas about feelings (Langer, 1953). This state of *aesthetic distance* has important implications for health and healing that are only recently being explored (Landy, 1983; Scheff, 1979). Aesthetic distance is therefore one possible artistic metaphor for well-being.

Thus, while the goals of psychoanalysis become to dream as freely as possible, of behavioral therapy to achieve success in coping, for creative arts therapies they are to create a meaningful symbol of oneself that captures the beauty of one's soul.

Play

Despite the clear intimacy of the creative arts therapies with artistic principles, the aesthetic perspective does not explain well the centrality of improvisation in creative arts therapy work. We tend not to treat our patients as we train artists. Artistic training involves a step by step, disciplined process of modeling basic forms, which are repeated many times. Whether the plié in dance, the still life in art, or the scales in music, the artist-to-be is trained in the rigorous refinement of basic forms. A creative arts therapy session takes another shape, reflecting another influence. Something more than the aesthetic underlies the creative arts therapies, something involving play. We engage in play with our clients, and value flexibility, humor, and spontaneity in our relationships. The play perspective images the client as the child, exploring, growing, having fun (how different an image from that of the shaman or the artist!). Creative arts therapists who view their work within a play perspective are inclined to emphasize developmental notions, even in their descriptions of "adult" forms of improvisation (Irwin, 1977; Jernberg, 1979; Johnson, 1982).

Improvisation is a relatively late development in the arts, and seems to have emerged in all art forms in the twentieth century, in jazz, expressionist painting, modern dance, and improvisational theatre. The stretching and altering of the rigid artistic forms seems a characteristic of this century's art, and clearly created the conditions under which the creative arts therapies could develop. Yet we still know very little about the similarities and differences in improvisation across the arts media.

In religion, the artist hopes to be possessed by the inspiration of God, the Creator. The creativity is attributed to a transcendent source. In art, the artist owns his creativity, but seeks to create within high artistic standards, for a public and for a culture. The artist is very much aware of this reference group, and hopes to speak to it. In play, the artist seeks to please him/herself and instead of accommodating to a God or a culture, assimilates them into his/her own world (Piaget, 1951). The products of artwork within a religious context are seen as sacred, and preserved at all costs. Within the artistic context, they are highly esteemed and exhibited in special places. Within the context of play, the artworks simply pass on, turning into something else. Because the Self is not a ritual or a script, but a living, changing entity, the element of play will always be relevent to the process of therapy. When we attempt to define ourselves vis-a-vis psychiatry, we tend to emphasize our artistic values. With "pure" artists, on the other hand, who often view us as taking the art less seriously, we find ourselves defending the values of play.

Conclusion

The unifying link among the creative arts therapies surely lies in one of these areas or in some combination. Or is it possible that all of these, biological, religious, aesthetic, and playful, are the specific expressions of something even more basic? I believe so, and I suggest that it is a transformational perspective.

To the extent that life involves the continuous transformation of self and world, then religion, art and play are means by which we attempt to structure these transformations to answer in new ways the basic question, "How and why did we come about?" The creative moment begins with the representation of the void: the empty stage, the blank page, the moment of silence. The artist pauses before creating the world again. And in creating the world, the self is again recast. For what fills the stage or page or silence is not a design, or prearranged model, it is the spontaneous expression of one's inner spirit. As this inner impulse emerges it is altered, and then, as it is understood and taken in, one's internal world is changed. In filling the canvas, the artist deals with the void, with death, and seeks another answer to "What is the point?" Langer said that the pleasure of beauty is the perception of a life wholly significant. The creative arts therapies offer a way toward a life of significance, one entwined in feeling. A successful artwork is so powerful because it reassures us that significance and meaning can emerge from nothing.

The specific media and skills of expression are secondary to this basic transformational, creative urge. Why then do we hold so much allegiance to our specific media? Why, in our efforts to establish our profession, have we so emphasized training in the specific arts media, when such emphasis keeps us apart? The answer may be that though there are many paths to authentic expression, each of us must take one path at a time, and to be helpful the guide must know the way.

The creative arts therapies have not developed in the mid 20th century by accident. They are the result of historical processes, and serve some function for our culture now and in the future. We must understand that function and find a way to articulate it meaningfully. I believe that we have emerged as a healing force that serves the urge for transformation and meaning in a society that is aware of its capacity for self-destruction, and is seeking more and more desperately for a reason to exist. While other humanistic approaches seek the sacred, the spiritual, or the transcendent, the creative arts therapies seek the beautiful and the playful in us. True, it appears that the values of the creative arts therapies conflict with those of the wider culture, whose major interest seems to be weapons. There is more consumer interest in handguns than in artistic works; more government funding in missiles than health care. Perhaps sports, which are also a form of play, receive more support due to their imagery of aggression, success, and defeat. Yet does not this highlight even more strongly the role of the creative arts therapies? From an intergenerational program linking a nursing home with an elementary school, to the Live Aid concert, the arts have a healing role to play within our communities (see Chapter 12).

The creative arts therapies must move into the future together. We cannot do so merely by locating our links in the romance of the past, in pristine artistic standards, in the innocence of child's play, or in impassive neurons of the right hemisphere. We can acknowledge our mutual interest and our mutual vision of human relationships. We have a powerful vision, and we have emerged for a reason; a reason and a vision that can unite us all.

Chapter 4

MELODY AND RHYTHM OF THE CREATIVE ARTS THERAPIES

Rhythm and melody are essential elements to music; but what about to the creative arts therapies in general? In this time when creative arts therapists are joining our energies, skills, and creativity, and exploring the music we make together, perhaps it is appropriate to examine our melody and rhythm. First, let me say a word for the melody. After all, most people remember the melody of the song: it's what's up in the treble clef, what the right hand plays. While the rhythm provides a stable ground for the music, the melody dances to and fro, expressing the *striving* of the music.

So let me propose to you that the melody in today's society is the achievement of status, in the sense of improving our position in relation to other professions, that is, our standing or stature. Imagine this scene: you arrive at the best restaurant in town and approach the maitre'd: "Good evening, I am Dr. Cynthia Briggs, I have a reservation for two." *"That will be an hour and a half wait, M'am."* "Oh, I don't know if you fully understood...... Dr. Cynthia Briggs, **MT-BC**." "MT-BC ? *Oh, yes, of course, well, actually I see we do have a table for two, come right with me."*

Imagine this on the six o'clock news: "Headline: The Governor of the state of Pennsylvania signed a bill today that allows all creative arts therapists to use the special automobile license plates with the letters CAT so that the public will be able to identify a creative arts therapist in an emergency."

Fantasies? Yes, but such sweet ones, for gaining status is the melody of our American song. The main constituents of status among health care professions are money, power, degrees, awards and titles, and technology. Let me say a word about each.

Fundamentally, in America, the measure of status is money. How much money did you make last year? This more than anything else tells you where

Invited Address, Joint Conference of the American Association for Music Therapy and the Mid-Atlantic Region of the National Association for Music Therapy, Cherry Hill, New Jersey, April 1989.

Reprinted from Music Therapy, 8, 8-16, 1989 with permission by the American Music Therapy Association.

you stand. How many of you are satisfied with the amount of money you are paid? How many of you feel you deserve to be paid more? There seems to be general agreement about this. So let's get some feedback. Ask one of your colleagues how much money they made last year. Now, why is that so difficult? If salary is so important to us, why are we so hesitant to make it public? Why so much embarassment? Shame that your salary is so low, or shame in the other person when they find out how much more money you are making. Why does it generate that much envy? People protect the privacy of their salary as if it were an intimate part of their body. There is something so unarguable, so immutable about money.

So how much do creative arts therapists make? The answer is between 15 and 70 thousand dollars a year. That leaves quite a range for shame, doesn't it? We actually don't know very well, since it is difficult to get people to report this information. But this question is probably the number one question I am asked by CATs, employers, and governmental agenices. As a result, NCATA is developing a national survey that will be sent out simultaneously by all our associations at the end of this year to gather this and other job-related data. Our impression is that beginning salaries range between 20-25,000 dollars, though we are seeing an upward trend due to an increased demand for CATs. Many employers are having a difficult time finding CATs. I predict our salaries will be rising relative to other professions.

Status is also given based on power, largely in terms of numbers and organization. Obviously we are stronger as a united NCATA with 12,000 people than we are divided into seven smaller associations. On the other hand, we are currently better organized at the association level than we are at the NCATA level. Those of us working with NCATA are attempting to change that, and we have made progress. NCATA is not only planning the joint conference, but has committees, a brochure, FACT SHEET, national policy on licensing, model licensing bill, representation at JCAHO, liaison with mental health counselors, and other professions, and is increasingly acting as an efficient, coordinated structure. We will need this structure, since we must have a well-working NCATA in order to act in unison with even larger coalitions of health care professions and state governments to get what we need. Power and influence have already been wielded in a number of cases where creative arts therapists have utilized the organization of NCATA. It helps to have me call up an administrator or legislative aide and say, "Hello, this is Dr. David Read Johnson, Professor of Psychiatry in the Yale University School of Medicine. I am the chairperson of NCATA, which represents all 12,000 creative arts therapists in the country. *How do you do?* We have become aware of the situation at your hospital and are very interested in the decisions your administration is making. We will be monitoring them closely since they are of such great interest to our 12,000 members. *How can I be of service to you?*"

Much of our organizational power will be derived from strong state coalitions, and here we are making rapid progress. Only a few years ago we had five state coalitions. Now we have fourteen. Licensure for creative arts therapists as licensed professional counselors is already a reality in several states. Licensure as creative arts therapists is literally around the corner, I predict within one to five years. Our first breakthrough may very well occur in the Mid-Atlantic region, in New York State. The New York State Coalition of creative arts therapists has been working for years in collaboration with other professional groups, and each year has seen progress toward a generic licensing bill.

One organizational challenge we are facing is establishing the integrity of state boundaries. Licensing and civil service regulations are determined by states, not regions. Unfortunately, creative arts therapists are often organized into regions or several chapters within one state or even chapters that cross state lines. The result is that state coalitions of creative arts therapists often must represent individuals, chapters, subchapters, and regions, all at the same time. This makes raising money very complex. In those associations with strong regional structures, the problem arises as to how to give differential amounts of money to different states, without appearing to be unfair. Ulitimately, if we are to be effective, we will need to establish strong state-based organizations for each of the creative arts therapy disciplines.

Status is also based on *degrees*. A.A., B.A., M.A., P.h.D., M.D., and ultimately, the M.B.A. It is clear that for licensure, the masters degree will be the minimum educational degree. For work in certain institutions, the bachelor's will continue to be sufficient, largely due to the continued commitment of occupational therapists and physical therapists to B.A. education. However, once licensure is established, pressures will build within institutions to have employees licensed, giving preference to Masters level clinicians. Nevertheless, music therapists, burdened by your great fortune to have been integrated within schools of music so many years ago, cannot ignore 80 undergraduate programs and several hundred faculty. The solution will be not to undo or devalue undergraduate education, but to build more Master's programs. Clearly, within the next decade, music therapists will need to have Master's degrees for licensure, for job promotion, and for third party reimbursement.

Status also means *awards and titles*. To be a registered, chairperson, professor, certified, licensed, clinical, honorary life, uh, person, does something for any real American. For example, I am an Eagle Scout. That means I earned 21 merit badges. 21. Really. Thank you. 21. More than you have, I'll bet. I can't really remember what they were, but boy am I proud. And so we all should be proud of our awards and titles: being a registered or certified music therapist is an achievement. Being licensed and board certified would even be greater. I am reminded of Mr. John Sanguine, who is 97, and a patient in the VA nursing home where I work. He wears his World War I outfit with all of his medals most everyday. He was in the cavalry in 1916 and chased Poncha Villa into Mexico. I think. As you know, men like long heavy things that dangle off their body. The more the better. Joe's uniform and medals give him status. He only has one leg, which he says he lost in the war, but didn't, but no one questions him, not with those medals. Can you picture me at 85, my RDT credential pinned to my chest?

For a developing profession, awards and titles must initially be self-generated. For example, registration is a means by which we give recognition to ourselves. A group of people get together and decide to give themselves initials based on some basic criteria that they all have fulfilled. Licensure is really a version of the same, only we convince the state to give its name to our recognition of ourselves, since our members constitute the board. After awhile, these awards take on an objective status all their own. I'm pleased to say that our credentials, whether RMT, CMT, ADTR, or RDT are being increasingly acknowledged and respected by other people. By meaning something to others besides ourselves, these letters achieve a measure of objective reality.

So status emanates from the group, but is perceived in the recipient, often the leader. In several African tribes, for example, a king is selected and for an entire year he is carried around, given whatever he wishes to eat, has access to all the women in the village, and rules without opposition. At the end of the year, well, the tribe eats him.....in order to take in his greatness. We do this with our presidents, who are ushered in with great fanfare only to be eaten alive by the media and Congress, and to some extent with every leader, who absorbs our esteem, and then must relinquish it. I must say that, as the NCATA Chair, I've even felt a few nibbles myself!

Yet another source of status is *technology*. Give us a machine to work and our jobs are seen as more important. The more complex and space age the machine, the more status we accrue. To give you an example, many nursing homes are having problems with wandering by their Alzheimer's patients. The solution to this problem is to provide direct supervision or monitoring by a person, who can be with these confused patients and help them participate in activities, talk, or just sit together. The cost of this can be kept relatively low. Instead, in the nursing home market today, technological solutions abound, including locking an electronic bracelet around the ankle of the confused person, and having alarms go off if they pass invisible detectors in doors or walkways. Complex electronic systems with television scanners are being devised. One administrator felt it was inhumane to restrain his patients so he spent many thousands of dollars constructing an outdoor garden for them to walk in. However, since they could fall there too, he thought he might set up television cameras throughout the garden, with the monitors in his office, so that he could ensure their safety! That is, he could watch them fall down, as they wandered alone through a garden maze.

Take for example the need for people-oriented educational and treatment programs to address the drug abuse problem in our country. Instead, our government has been attracted to the high tech solutions of Coast Guard radar surveillance, helicopters, border electronic scanners, missles, and defoliation.

Just as technological equipment has affected occupational therapy, and biofeedback and computerized test scoring have influenced psychology, so too will the development of assessment instruments, packaged techniques, and video, electronic, and computerized interventions affect our field. Hitech. Hi status.

Are we on the path toward greater status, toward more degrees, more awards and titles, more money, more power, and more technology? Yes, we are. Will this improve our profession? Yes, it will. Just like all the other health care professions before us. This is the melody. Now let me turn to the bass clef and the underlying rhythm of our profession.

At heart, what do we do as therapists? I believe that often it is not our technological interventions, but the power of being with another suffering person, showing a genuine warmth and presence that is solacing. Essentially this is what scientists pejoratively call the placebo effect, that is, the impact of a helpful presence on a suffering person, separate from the effect of a speciic intervention such as medication or surgery. For the creative arts therapies, like all psychotherapies, do not really treat the fundamental disease entity itself, such as schizophrenia, learning disability, retardation, traumatic stress disorder, or personality disorder. We treat the human being's sense of courage, esteem, ability to cope and to find meaning in life affected by an illness or disability. Rather than viewing this negatively, as only a placebo, let us not be ashamed of being the placebo, for it can explain anywhere from 10-90 percent of the improvement from the illness.

In the last century, doctors were healers in a full sense. They did everything—gave medicines, nursed, listened, sat, played cards with their patients. As medicine became more technologized and organized in the latter half of the 19th century, they departed from the "being with" part of the task. Thus, the profession of nursing grew out of this need. By the turn of the century, nurses were no longer able to just be with patients and do things with them. The fields of occupational therapy and social work developed out of this need for someone to serve the psychosocial needs of the patients. By the second World War, occupational therapists had put on their white coats, developed their splints and procedures, and could no longer be with clients. That lead the way for the field of activities therapies to grow in the fifties and sixties. Now, we have differentiated and professionalized into the creative arts therapies and recreational therapy, and we now are becoming too busy to just "be with" our clients. Having gained some status, we look down on parties, and sitting, and bingo, and even if we value these things, we are too involved in our clinical assessments, intensive therapies, our degrees, our supervisions, and our scholarly endeavors. And so of course we are now seeing the development of Activities Professionals, and other groups of apparently lower status. Because there is a basic need, like a pulse or a breath, that continues to be felt.

Ironically, professionals in medicine and nursing are full of complaints that they have abandoned good clinical care, which involves an empathic being with the client in time of need. The technologies and the needs for documentation, protection from litigation, and coping with government bureaucracy have undermined the essential healing practice of these groups, and many of their members are discovering they are not doing the things that motivated them to enter the profession in the first place.

Will it be so for us too? Let me say it bluntly: there is no status in merely "being with" another person. Despite the lip service, its real value is ignored. Oh yes, the values of "being with" are raised occasionally as symbols of the shadow side of our emerging culture: Miss Congeniality is given an award for the most people-oriented (rather than most successful) woman in the Miss America Pagent; on the evening news, after 29 minutes of news about brutal, business, success-oriented, aggressive, money makers, and male murderers, we are given the one minute human interest story about some person who bothers to help someone else or who overcomes a handicap.

The shift in values is having its impact: no longer is it sufficient for many women to commit themselves to be with their infant children; more than financial need is motivating mothers to seek higher status activities, more degrees, more money, more power, opening up the need for another profession, day care people who will "be with" children. And we need people to be with the elderly, we need people to be with our family members who are suffering. Yet, this is the ground of our profession; to be with, to witness, to empathize, to acknowledge.

I can think of many patients. Like Ted, a Vietnam veteran who knocked on my door this January 31, unbeknownst to me the anniversary of the Tet Offensive. He was sweating profusely, his large muscles flexing, his jaw tightened, and his eyes all a glaze. Without saying a word he came into my office at the VA, and sat down and said, "It's Tet and I have to show this to you." He opened up a large scrapbook that had pictures and letters he had kept from Nam. He talked about each one as I listened. He told me that the night before he had got drunk, took his four rifles and guns, and drove out into the woods in his truck, shooting at streetlights and trees, not psychotic, not in flashback, just to release the tension. All I said was, Yes, a couple of times. When he left, he said, "thank you."

Several years ago I had Doc Needham in my men's group. He was demented and suffered from advanced Parkinson's disease. He was mute on the ward. His family had abandoned him, and his only brother sent him a shirt in the mail once every year. He had been a respected pediatrician in New Haven. Twice a week for five years, I wheeled him to my drama therapy group for men, where he moved his body, made sounds, sang songs, and after a couple of years, actually responded verbally to questions. We became quite attached. He did not participate in any other organized group in the nursing home. Many times the group spent time being together in silence or listening to music or humming. This was not an intervention. This was not a technique. This was not even an assessment. This was just him and me, being together, for a few minutes each week, for the last five years of his life. Isn't it incredible to think that this doctor, a Yale graduate, who had had a family and career, would spend his last five years in a relationship with me? He left no legacy. I may be the only one who remembers him. Will there be a young drama therapist or music therapist who will be there for me?

Or there is Henry, a 76-year-old patient with Alzheimer's and depression, who is quite agitated and feels he has died and needs to be taken to the undertaker. He actually calls several funeral parlors each day. He calls the director of the hospital, he bothers the staff and patients constantly, and he tries to enter my office unannounced. This was so bothersome that I had to lock myself in my own office to protect myself from his intrusions. Until one day when I decided to let Henry come in and sit. I invited him to sit with me and informed him I needed to do my work. I made my phone calls, wrote my writings, consulted with staff, all with him there, quiet as a lamb. I remember playing on the carpet as a child on Sunday mornings while my parents read the newspaper and listened to the radio. I rarely talked to them, but found solace in their presence. So does Henry in mine.

Imagine one of these Henrys, or Teds, or Doc Needhams whom you have worked with. Perhaps you can close your eyes and see them. And perhaps you might write a mental letter to them, like this:

> Dear Ted,
> I see it in your eyes. The panic. The terror. I am glad that you came to see me. Even though I can't do anything about Nam. I wasn't there. Even if I was there I couldn't do anything to erase what happened to you there. All I can do is to listen and feel and be with you. I worry about you. Someday I may learn you have killed yourself. I know you think about that constantly. I know it may happen. I know you can do it. Yet, it's funny. I don't even feel helpless, since I look forward to seeing you, I feel the gladness you show when we meet. Being together is a success.
>
> Love, David.

Being there has no status. Yet being in tune with our patients is our fundamental act. The thrills and complexities of the melody—our specialized techniques—build upon this foundation of rhythm and harmony. What will be important to you when you find yourself alone at home, your children living far away; when you lie ill in the hospital bed, or in the wheel chair in the nursing home. When you rise from your bed the day after your divorce or miscarriage. Then what will the status of the degree, the money, the power, the titles, and the technology mean, compared to the look, the touch, the glimmer, the laugh, and the shared tear of the one who is with you. Really with you.

Do you hear it? The rhythm of your heart....the rhythm in your relationship......the rhythm of your life.

> "Sing me a farewell song,
> A canticle of life.
> For I am leaving land,
> And taking space to wife.
>
> Into the rising wind
> I'll shout the ecstacy.
> Echoes will answer back,
> I am where I wished to be."
> (Wynne Rettger Lewis, unpublished)

Chapter 5

ON BEING ONE AND MANY

I would like to speak to you about being one, and many.

I am a drama therapist. I seek the interface between theatre and therapy, and attempt to help my clients by bringing out the dramatic and the playful in their experience of life.

I am a creative arts therapist. I belong to a group of professionals who believe in the power of creativity and nonverbal modes of expression as a means of healing. As a creative arts therapist, I am part of a movement toward transformation and meaning in a culture otherwise absorbed in the concrete, the rational, and the self-destructive.

I am a mental health professional. With my colleagues in psychiatry, psychology, social work, counseling, rehabilitation, and nursing, I am trying to defend the importance of the mind, inner experience, and the need for treatment for psychiatric illness, conditions still met with suspicion and denigration from the wider culture, which chooses to direct mass amounts of dollars to "real" illnesses, and provide little support for people suffering from mental illness.

I am a health care provider, a person who has devoted his life to the care of people. My choice to serve, like for many others, is based on my own suffering under the care of people I love. In my case, my commitment to help others was nurtured by my failure to help my father, who suffered from alcoholism.

And I am a suffering person, who constantly struggles to hold onto the good inside me that I let go each time I am criticized, to tolerate the strains that a marriage of depth evokes, to fill a hole inside me left by the emotional unavailablity of my father, to allow myself to succeed despite my doubts that I deserve it.

I am one person, yet I am all of these, a drama therapist, a creative arts therapist, a mental health professional, a health care provider, and a suffer-

Opening Address, Joint Conference of the National Coalition of Arts Therapy Associations, Washington, DC, November, 1990.

Reprinted from the *Arts in Psychotherapy, 18*, 1-5, 1991 with permission from Elsevier Science.

ing person. Each of us faces this challenge, to be one, and to be many. The capacity to integrate experience: our feelings, thoughts, roles, and identities into one whole, while maintaining an appreciation for the diversity and complexity of the parts, this indeed is the challenge of development, of growth, of maturity.

If I ask myself now, "how do I feel?", I check in with my body—and find my knees are tight, my chest is heavy, my mind clear, my eyes filled with you, and then through a mysterious process from body to image to word, I become able to tell you that collectively, I am feeling joyous, for this is a great day for the creative arts therapies.

In this room, here and now, we are both one and many. Many different kinds of people with different training, techniques, life experiences and attitudes. Over the years each of our associations has achieved a sense of oneness despite this diversity within our memberships: so for example dance therapy, or art therapy or music therapy have attained a meaning, a coherence, that gives form to the many types of dance or art or music therapies, and therapists. And all of our seven associations have worked together as the National Coalition of Arts Therapy Associations, and are both many, and one, at the same time.

What kind of association is NCATA? .... I believe that we are a *free* association! By this double entendre, I mean that no one has been forced to come here. Each association has chosen to participate. Each of you has chosen to come. But why? Why are we here? I doubt we are here by accident? Or random coincidence!

Free association and improvisation are dear to us as techniques: we ask our clients to let their imaginations roam, to see what comes out—what is linked to what. From initially disconnected or awkward expression, eventually the client turns toward the source, the wellspring of self. This is also true for us on the professional level. Our *relations* with each other have at first been disjointed and awkward, even seemingly unnecessary. Yet, despite our best efforts to remain comfortably isolated, we keep finding each other. Yes, we keep discovering that we are linked to each other. We *are* here. A free association.

Jacob Moreno, the grandfather of action therapies, would not be surprised. This therapist of vision saw that all the arts have tremendous potential, and when he arrived at St. Elizabeth's Hospital fifty years ago, and did plays with Marian Chace, and psychomusic and psychoart sessions with soon-to-be music and art therapists, he understood their common bonds.

Suzanne Langer would not be surprised, as she saw how feeling interacts with form in all of the arts, a philosophy in a new key.

Donald Winnicott would not be surprised. He saw how the transitional space is a playspace, a symbolic space, an artistic space.

Carl Jung would not be surprised. He understood how the arts are the expressions and celebrations of our collective human experience.

Indeed NCATA is a collective, and each modality, an archetypal form of expression. Though NCATA is a coalition and not the National Creative Arts Therapy Association, we have been acting as one in many ways. We have sent out representatives to other groups. We have developed a number of national policies. We have developed an integrated database. We have jointly held two conferences. We have formed unities at the state level for mutual support and to seek licensure. The presidents and representatives of your associations have met and worked and worried and laughed and played and debated and leaned on each other. Why? To move our professions forward by acting in concert.

Other groups far more disparate than us have sought and achieved a unity that respects diversity. Our own country was merely a coalition for 13 years after the revolution. What led them to decide to become the *United* States? The largest states of New York, Virginia, and Massachusetts, were not so sure it was in their interest to join with the smaller and less organized states. Why did they finally embrace them? —Europe, filled with centuries long enemies, is about to become one. From the Common Market to the European Community, with one currency, no borders. Why are they doing this? Yes, they will become one of the three major economic powers in the world. But won't their traditions, languages, and characters be weakened?

The advantages to integration are obvious: one becomes larger. It is not well known that collectively, NCATA has as many members as mental health counselors, as psychiatric occupational therapists, as other groups who have achieved greater recognition and licensure. The counseling profession, which is actually a group of 12 disparate associations, has via integration made tremendous achievements in the past decade, including licensure in over 35 states and vastly increased third party reimbursements.

Licensure is an area many creative arts therapists feel is a long way off. I disagree. It is true, licensure is an odd business. Many professions have attained it. Perhaps you are not aware that Frog Dealers are licensed in two states, garbage feeders in five. Yes, Maine licenses marine worm diggers; Montana keeps a tight rein on roadside menagerie operators. Tattoo artists in Nevada, and non resident sea moss rakers in Georgia! Two states have deemed it more important to regulate itinerant photographers than creative arts therapists!

Remaining unlicensed poses a risk to our practice. As other mental health professions attain licensure in various states, we may become subject to their regulation. We will also be pressured to alter our training programs in order to meet their equivalency standards. But can we be marriage and family therapists in California, licensed professional counselors in Texas, and social workers in Maryland? Unless we organize together, these forces may sweep us aside and fragment our field.

It is time we act our age, and our size. It is time that we are recognized for our unique contributions, it is time that our professions are mentioned in legislative and regulatory policies, it is time that we are no longer hired under somebody else's job title, it is time that we establish certification and licensure, it is time that creative arts therapists are paid commensurate with their service.

And we deserve this because we are making significant contributions to the health care of our patients. Art therapy is distinquishing itself in the treatment of sexual abuse and trauma, by helping patients access their hidden memories. Dance therapy is discovering new pathways into the treatment of eating disorders and traumatic brain injuries. Music therapy is now well established as critical in the treatment of dementias and Alzheimers disease, and truly exciting discoveries are on the horizon in the treatment of chronic pain and auto-immune diseases. Drama and poetry therapy are being used extensively in the treatment of posttraumatic stress disorders and substance abuse.

Over the past five years, as editor of the International Journal of Arts in Psychotherapy, I have had the opportunity to see these contributions revealed in the 400 manuscripts I have reviewed. Though the specifics of our media—paint, movement, sound, dramatic role, rhyme, are very different— though the theoretical and technical methods we have devised differ greatly- there are basic values, patterns, and rhythms that reassert themselves over and over again in each article—that serve as a basis for our unity:

• that empathy and attunement with the client are essential and can be enhanced through our media.

• that much of our being exists in kinesthetic and symbolic modes rather than verbal ones.

• that fullness of expression in richness, depth, complexity, and dynamics results from our work.

• that aesthetic form can become a way for inner feeling to emerge.

• that concepts of harmony, balance, dissonance, rhythm, tone, climax, and flow are central; indeed, that beauty is a psychological reality.

There was a time I believed that, as professions, "united we stand, divided we fall." I no longer believe that to be true. We can continue on separately if we wish. We are not being forced together. We are free to work with each other. Because the time of the pioneers is over. The foundations have been laid. We thank you, dear Moreno and Chace and Kramer; Schoop and Gaston and Morrison and Nordoff and Robbins; Whitehouse and Leedy and Naumburg and Enneis; Irwin and Lerner and Sears and Schattner; Espenak and Ulman and Alvin, and so many others, whose names you may feel like calling out, whom you want us to remember. Thank you, for you have done your work, you have carved out of the wilderness a space for seven small tribes to practice their professions, with safe boundaries, and with wonderful traditions. It is now time for these tribes to interact with each other in a larger community, to achieve being one *and many* at another level.

There was a time when leaders within our associations saw the board of directors or presidency as the final stage of service to their profession. But it is a different time, and from deep down within our collective body, comes a call to service beyond our specific modality, a call to serve this larger community of ours, with its diverse needs and common visions. And I know that the leaders who will emerge to achieve this vision can hear my voice now.

Such a call to serve, of course, ultimately is given meaning by our patients, who are also beset with the challenge of integrating their various parts. I learned about being a patient from my father. My father actually had three chronic illnesses: TB, alcoholism, and cancer, from which he died this summer. His experience has taught me about living with suffering, and about how to help others.

In 1946, one week after he married my mother, he began his medical residency at the University of Michigan. His routine chest X-ray however showed he had TB, so at 26, he was sent to the sanatarium, where he was to spend most of the next three years lying in bed. The treatment for TB then was complete bed rest, which meant that he had to use a bedpan, not sit up or turn, rest on the side of his illness, and only read or listen to the radio. After nine months, he was well enough to be let out of bed once a day to go the bathroom. After a year and a half, he was discharged, and soon relapsed, and spent another year and a half in the san.

Can you imagine what this healthy 26 year old felt when he was told? Can you imagine what our patients feel when they are told that they have schizophrenia, AIDS, alcoholism, or Alzheimer's and face the burden placed on them by the treatments as much as the illness? Burdens both physical (such as pain) and psychological (such as shame and stigma).

The definition of a patient is bearing illness with equanimity. Equanimity! No wonder over 40 percent of TB patients went AWOL from sanatariums. No wonder most of our psychiatric patients stop their medications as soon as they leave the hospital. No wonder the human spirit rails against the sentence.

My father, like many other physicians who contracted TB, went on to become a specialist in chest disease, and lived to see the dreaded illness conquered. But as he treated his patients, they could see that he had a different look in his eyes than other doctors, a look that recognized the person behind the illness. In offering patients treatments they did not like, treatments that did not work, or treatments they refused, my father understood that his real aim was to help a suffering person cope with their illness. For there is often no cure.

As creative arts therapists, we too, do not directly treat the primary illnesses presented to us: schizophrenia, mental retardation, dementia. No, we treat the person's morale, self esteem, and courage in facing these life challenges, and help them ward off the depression, the hopelessness, the anger that such conditions give rise to.

Our fundamental act is to find a means of *being there* with our clients, and our form of being there involves the miracle of creation—that act available to each of us, to transform suffering into beauty, to achieve meaning out of an empty canvas, or stage, or silence, and in this way conquer fate. For the human spirit can not be constrained, and it is in accessing this existential freedom that we help our patients gain solace and joy in the midst of their suffering. I remember when Daniel, who suffered from catatonic schizophrenia, first wiggled his hips to the music in a dance therapy session. Susan and I bounded out of the session to tell his psychotherapist the good news, only to receive a sardonic, even patronizing look. Few of our colleagues appreciated the momentous occasion. But it was momentous! Not because we had cured Daniel's schizophrenia, but because in that moment Daniel transformed his relationship to his schizophrenia, to not being bound and enslaved by it. How hard this is, acceptance of both reality of the illness and the continued possibilities of being human despite it. Hard and absurd.

How absurd, for example, must it have been for my father, laying in his bed at the san, a doctor and a patient, a husband and an invalid, at the same time?

How absurd, indeed, for my patient Terry, a Vietnam veteran with PTSD, to have been told upon his return from Vietnam, that he was a wimp (by the veterans of WWII) *and* a cold-hearted murderer (by the anti-war protesters), all at the same time. How could he be both a loving and kind father to two little girls, and be the soldier who was forced to kill two Vietnamese children at point blank range? His attempts to integrate these disparate realities only led him to have flashbacks of the torn and bloody bodies as he picked up his own children, forcing him into isolation, drinking, and fits of anger. "Where am I?" his eyes said to me. Being many, he could not find the path to be one.

And there is Bill, whose bout with AIDS lasted four years, without the help of his family, who could not integrate his homosexuality into their sense of family unity. He refused to tell them he was dying, so they did not know. His poems were beautiful, his singing soulful. They did not hear. Finally, with death upon him, a friend could not take it any longer and called his parents and told them. They came out to his home, and there, as Bill looked into his mother's eyes, past all the homophobia, the horror of the cancer, the reality of death, and wasted years of anger and resentment on both sides, all this at once, she smiled and said, "You are mine," and he died, oh so peacefully he died.

Our job as therapists is to hold and nurture this inner image of our patients, as one and as many, and to do that requires us to stay in touch with our own suffering and our own struggle with this challenge. And on the professional level, as separate individuals and separate modalities, with real distinctions, we can still experience the freedom to be together, we can still hold a shared image of ourselves as creative arts therapists; we can be one; just as I hold one image of my father, physician and patient, loving man and insensitive alcoholic, source of my grief, source of my wish to heal. I know him well.

> "So now, dear father, I come back to you,
> my old and weary,
> my cold and feary father
> till the near sight of him makes me swoon
> and I rush, my only, into your arms.
> I see them rising!"[1]

---

1 Adapted from Finnegan's Wake by James Joyce. New York: Penguin, 1939.

Chapter 6

THE NATIONAL COLLAGE: THE POETICS OF THE JOINT CONFERENCES

The joint conference of the National Coalition of Arts Therapy Associations held in New York City in November 1985 was a crucial event in the development of the creative arts therapy profession. Building on a decade of interdisciplinary conferences, workshops, and political discussions, the 1985 Conference was the first formal arrangement among the national associations, involving a major commitment of time, energy, and expense. The 2500 attendees who packed into the luxurious Marriott Marquis Hotel on Times Square arrived with anticipation, experienced with excitement hundreds of workshops and presentations, and learned much from the dialogue with their colleagues in other art forms. The presentations collectively provided a picture of the creative arts therapies as a developing profession, rooted in our past, and reaching into our future, a future we will share together.

What an auspicious conclusion to a tentative beginning six years earlier, when the presidents of the creative arts therapy associations held a meeting sponsored by the Maurice Falk Foundation and the American Psychiatric Association to what would become the National Coalition. Several years later, when I joined the coalition representing drama therapy, I was dismayed by what seemed tremendous hesitance among the participants to engage in joint action; the associations were even reluctant to purchase coalition stationery! Then, quite on his own, Scott Stoner, the executive director of the art therapy association, booked the Marriott Marquis for a joint conference, *a hotel not yet built*, and managed to garner the agreement of five associations. When the presidents were invited to visit the site of the hotel, which was to be the arena for the coalition's finest hour, we gathered on 47th street and peered down into a gigantic hole. "Imagine.....it will be wonder-

---

Revised from the *Arts in Psychotherapy*, "Introduction to the Special Issue on the 1985 NCATA Conference," *14*, 197-200, 1987, and "Introduction to the Special Issue on the 1990 NCATA Conference," *18*, 383-386, 1991 with permission from Elsevier Science.

ful," Scott said, reassuring no one. But he was right, it was wonderful. And we have had to trust in our imagination ever since, risking new ways of being together despite our hesitance and sense of caution.

Ken Bruscia (1986), in his opening address to the conference, asserted that only by working together can the creative arts therapies be an effective contributor to health care in this country. Bruscia also identified the many obstacles to this collaboration and the need for courage to meet them: "in order to face the many developmental challenges that lie ahead–to become separate but together, united but diverse, independent but interdependent–we will need the courage to risk being together. Inevitably individuation requires trust–in ourselves and in each other."

Yet what holds this trust and this courage is an organization, that of the coalition and that of the conference. Is this not a problem? Isn't there a fundamental conflict between all this organizational business and the essentials of creative arts therapies? Perhaps, but I believe art is intimately linked to organization. Many art forms present an organizational challenge: a tapestry, a play, a symphony, a collage, a performance... As a director of theatrical plays, I had to deal with many organizational issues, bring together many different elements (script, actors, set, costumes) into one artistic meaningful whole. Not organization for organization's sake, but for an artistic purpose. Yes, art is a coming-together, an organization of elements that enlivens, enriches, and communicates a vision, balancing feeling with form, as opposed to one that is rote, lacking in dynamics, absent of harmony. Perhaps NCATA would be better named the National *Collage* of Arts Therapy Associations, of the National *Chorus,* or *Concerto* of Arts Therapy Associations! If an aesthetic product is one that balances feeling with form, then the first NCATA Conference was indeed a work of art: for the formal scholarly and organizational structures were infused with spontaneity, brilliance, and life.

After the 1985 conference, NCATA pursued many important tasks in the legislative and political arenas including state licensure, regulatory and accrediting agencies, state job lines, and improvement in creative arts therapists' salaries. Attention also turned to the education of the creative arts therapist, both within each discipline and across the entire field (Dulicai, Hays, & Nolan, 1989; Levick, 1989; Lusebrink, 1989; McNiff, 1986). Though the development of our profession matured through distillations of distinct bodies of knowledge within each modality, many areas of knowledge are common across all the arts therapies. We shared our views of the essential skills required of creative arts therapists, and how methods of training (didactic, experiential, research, internship, thesis) could be employed to effect competencies in these skills. We found significant differences in how the main educational tasks of clinical practice, research, and theoretical scholarship were distributed among our undergraduate, Masters, and doctoral programs.

Yet the balance between the experiential foundations of our professions and the didactic methods of the pedagogical tradition were endorsed by all.

Because our programs were located in departments of creative arts therapies, education, psychology, counseling, marriage and family therapy, and professional art or music schools, we were confronted with the challenge of how to establish an integrated identity amidst the competing influences of these more established fields. Was it possible to find our own homeland, or would we remain scattered throughout many other "nations," never completely accepted?

It was an important time in our development as a profession. Issues of structure, process, and identity were being examined. A dialogue and debate began in earnest over the advantages and disadvantages of a unified vision. As we moved toward 1990, compromise and the capacity for decision sustained the supportive embrace for our essential diversity of opinion.

The second Joint Conference of the National Coalition occurred in November, 1990 in Washington, DC, attended by all seven national creative arts therapy associations. We surprised ourselves by our largeness. We were large in numbers (3333 to be exact), in ideas, in experience, in spirit and vision. A largeness both thrilling and disorienting. Our closely-held beliefs about ourselves as creative arts therapists, as people who were alone, misunderstood, and powerless, found no support in the multitude. The normal scenarios were absent. Where were they who would suppress us? Where were those who did not understand?

The conference demonstrated the progress our field had made in scholarship, clinical interventions, and professional training. We were rapidly approaching the degree of sophistication that other, more established, fields had achieved. The number of books and articles that had appeared on the creative arts therapies was astounding. Each modality had successfully demonstrated that significant psychotherapeutic processes occur within their media. An emerging challenge was understanding the relationship among the arts media, in terms of theoretical concepts, preferred populations, and treatment methods (Blatner, 1991; Lusebrink, 1991). Many of the presentations at the Conference grappled with this challenge. By understanding the whole of creative expression, our understanding of each modality can be clarified. Thus, our journey toward professional individuation, of being differentiated and connected at the same time, continued.

Yes, the meaning of this event was transparent. This, our second joint Conference, could not have been called in order for us to declare our lack of relations! Everyone knew of Winnicott's transitional objects, Jung's archetypes, Freud's unconscious; everyone understood improvisation, play, symbolism, sublimation, and imagery; everyone appreciated the importance of empathy, mirroring, and the holding environment. Everyone believed in the power of creativity and the arts. Everyone.

In this context of synchrony, our differences became highly valued. Political, theoretical, and technical differences served as sources of new insights and questions. It was bewildering, creating a need for a complete reassessment. We did not have to struggle to be heard. We had knowledge. The creative arts therapies had come of age. And yet, as the conference coordinator, Peter Jampel (1991) later reflected, "But perhaps we became too close too fast. This event may have put the national associations into positions with each other that they are not quite ready to assume. More time may be needed for the associations to develop sufficient cultural familiarity to tolerate the degree of interdependence required to move the profession ahead."

Though Jampel's prediction was borne out, these two joint conferences were nevertheless important way stations along our journey as a developing profession, brought to life through the hard work of many creative arts therapists who shared the same vision, articulated so beautifully by Helen Bonny (1987) after the first conference: "The arts forge a bondedness between therapists; healers with sound; maestros of movement, rhythm, and design; and guides of the drama. We are bound by our common love of, and sensitivity to, beauty and by our overwhelming need to share its power and healing source with others." In seeking the roots of our inspiration, we have come full circle: a profession that arises from a desire to heal through beauty, then shapes itself with increasing sophistication, theoretical articulation, clinical toughness, cognitive specificity, and hard-nosed economics and regulations, returns in order to reassess its basic vision. At these moments, most intimate and uncertain, the path is found again in the arts and in the inner pulse of artistic expression.

Being bound together, we experience certain limits; yet by being bound within the creative arts, we are at play in a vast universe of expression with plenty of room for all.

Chapter 7

TAKING THE NEXT STEP:
FORMING THE NATIONAL CREATIVE ARTS
THERAPY ASSOCIATION

It is time for creative arts therapists to take the next step in our profession-al development by forming one national multidivisional association that can more effectively represent the strength of our contributions to health care.

The success of the 1990 National Coalition of Arts Therapy Associations ("Coalition") Conference shows beyond doubt that creative arts therapists are linked to each other out of more than political need (73% of attendees rated it positively). Increasingly, scholarship in this field is turning its atten-tion to the relationships among the various modalities, in terms of theory (Aldridge et al., 1990; Blatner, 1991; Gorelick, 1989; Johnson, this book; Lusebrink, 1991; Robbins, 1985), assessment (Bruscia, 1988; Goldberg et al., 1991), training (Lusebrink, 1989; McNiff, 1987; Robbins, 1988), and profes-sional development (Bruscia, 1986; Dulicai, 1984; Johnson, this book). The trend is clear: creative arts therapists are having increasing contact with each other in clinical, educational, and legislative settings. There is no question that the "creative arts therapies" now exists as a shared concept.

This article intends to further the public discussion of this topic by propos-ing an actual model for this unified association. Debate about this idea has gone on *sotto voce* for many years among the leadership. Now it is time that an open and spirited discussion occur. Nevertheless, I am not writing this article for the purpose of persuading diehard separatists, but rather to engage the growing numbers of creative arts therapists who have become convinced that such a step is the correct one.

We are at a very similar point in development as the colonies of America were after the Revolution. The Articles of Confederation, which had provid-ed a loose coalition of states, were not working. Each state was conducting independent foreign policies that conflicted with each other. Despite signifi-

Reprinted from the *Arts in Psychotherapy, 18,* 387-394, 1991, with permission from Elsevier Science.

cant interdependence, the collective grasp for autonomy was creating chaos. "Each State yielding to the persuasive voice of immediate interest or convenience has successively withdrawn its support, till the frail and tottering edifice seems ready to fall upon our heads and to crush us beneath its ruins," exclaimed Alexander Hamilton in the Federalist Papers (1987, p. 151). How these states were convinced to come together in a federation that respected the states' rights, how the larger states were persuaded to join with the smaller, is, of course, another story. The creation of a federation of creative arts therapies will be our story.

As we will see, the principles of the United States Constitution, in which rights and responsibilities of each level of government are clearly spelled out, and in which there is a balance of power among several branches, are very applicable to the organizational challenge we face.

Rationale

Let me review the basic reasons why a multidivisional national association of the creative arts therapies makes sense.

1. We will increase our power. Clearly, an integrated position taken by an association of 12,000 will be taken far more seriously than one of 3,000. Legislative bodies have been more responsive to coalition positions than those of individual associations, and, as a result, the coalition has been able to achieve representation in a number of important regulatory bodies and legislative hearings.

2. We will benefit financially. The duplication of overhead, offices, committees, staff, and computers is significant, and having one national office will save us hundreds of thousands of dollars a year that can be put to use in legislation, publication, or training. For example, last year's NCATA Conference turned in a profit of $200,000. The year before, the seven national associations collectively had a profit from their separate conferences of only $70,000. With an additional $130,000 each year, and several hundred thousand dollars in savings from office overhead, we could hire several full-time lobbyists, place a deposit on our own building, publish our own books, and much more. Coming together will give us a great deal more financial power.

3. We will avoid undermining each other. Recent events have underscored again that, if not coordinated, the seven associations will interfere with each other's interests. "End-run" maneuvers to achieve listings in bills or policies, when discovered by the other associations, lead to an acrimonious, chaotic competition that undermines the initial effort. Is there any bill, licensure issue, or policy that most of the associations will not be interested in? There is no way for one association to try to sneak in alone, because the other associations have now developed effective monitoring networks. Prior coordination is essential and, without the structures set up by a national federation, this coordination cannot take place.

4. The present coalition is inadequate. The lack of an organizational structure among our associations prevents us from responding quickly and effectively to crises. Confusion as to procedure, panicked conference calls among the presidents, last minute coordination, and tremendous miscommunication have characterized our functioning. Actions are delayed because boards have to be consulted, lack of clear communication networks leads to miscommunication, and then paranoia. Proactive efforts are constantly halted in a paralysis of uncertain procedure. Not wanting to formally recognize state coalitions because there is not a structural relationship between them leads the national associations to undermine our own state coalitions, the critical components of legislative projects!

The coalition is currently governed by equal votes of each association, regardless of size, clearly unfair to the membership of the larger groups.

Finally, the coalition has little contact or input from the membership; information is filtered through association boards. The coalition now speaks for boards of directors, not creative arts therapists.

Principles

By proposing a specific model for our federation, I am hoping that some of the fears expressed by separatists will be allayed. Public discussion of this issue has been hampered by the fact that there has been no model proposed. The one I am proposing is called a multidivisional association, and is based on existing professions, such as the American Medical Association (AMA), the American Psychological Association (APA), and the American Association for Counseling and Development (AACD).[1]

One fear has been that one association will mean a fusion of identity, for example, in the development of a Registered Creative Arts Therapist. The model I am proposing here will not lead to this, as each association will continue to exist as is, only as a division of the larger organization. All training, accrediting, and credentialling would continue as they are now, coordinated by each association's board of directors.

---

1. Now the American Counseling Association.

The principles of these multidivisional associations include:
1. Maintaining relative autonomy of the divisions.
2. Protection of diversity within the organization and between divisions.
3. Centralization of the financial, legislative, publications, and conference planning functions into one national office.
4. Creating a governance structure that ensures multiple inputs into decision-making.

Multidivisional Associations

Unlike the singular focus of our associations, multidivisional associations attempt to maximize the integration and power that are possible in larger groupings of related units. Despite their appearance as large monolithic entities, these groups are actually quite supportive of autonomy among their divisions, and allow for a great deal of variation in standards, regulations, dues, and traditions.

Typically, their structure involves a set of officers elected by the entire membership, a board of directors elected by the divisions, and a senate or council also elected by the divisions. The board of directors usually can only recommend or propose policy to the council, which has the power to act. In this way, the divisions hold the greatest power.

The other element, of course, is that the administrative, publications, and financial components of the profession are centralized in one office. Typically, divisions have their offices in the same building as the central office. Dues are assessed both by the main association and each division (whose dues are often much less because the administrative costs are borne by the main association). Thus, AACD's dues are $85, and each division adds on from $5 to $45 more, depending upon their activities and unique needs.[2]

Each division usually has their own credentialling standards, accrediting bodies, registry committees, legislative committees, and lobbyists.

The Example of AACD. AACD now has 58,000 members, and consists of 15 separate divisions of completely diverse counseling groups, from mental health counselors who have Masters degrees, to rehabilitation and vocational guidance counselors who have bachelor's degrees. Thus, concerns about the variation in educational requirements among creative arts therapists are not at issue.

AACD is governed by a set of officers (president, president-elect, and past president) who are elected from the entire membership, a treasurer and exec-

2. These figures were accurate as of 1991.

utive director who are hired, and four representatives elected by the governing council. Together these nine individuals constitute the executive committee, which serves as the administrative arm of the association, capable only of recommending actions to the governing council as a whole.

The governing council is the legislative arm of the association, and consists of proportional representation from the divisions and the regional associations based on their size, one member per 3000 members (a total of approximately 40 people). Thus, the larger divisions have a stronger voice in the decision-making.

AACD owns a building in Alexandria, Virginia, and has offices for all divisions there. Each division acts as an autonomous association, with its own board of directors, bylaws, and policies. Divisions hold their conferences together at the annual AACD Conference. Smaller conferences are held by region during the year.

There remain extremely strong disagreements and differences in policy and opinion among the divisions, committees, and regions, yet the association remains a powerful and effective union. Since AACD reorganized into this structure, they have gained measurable strength politically and have effected remarkable successes in licensure, third party payments, and salary increases for their members. Figure 1 shows the rate at which they are achieving state licensure.

Figure 1

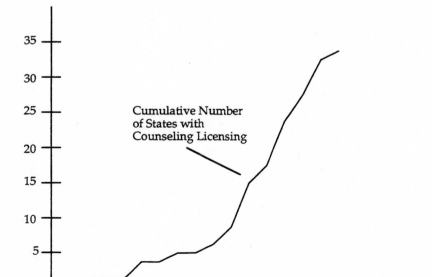

The Power of AACD:
Growth of State Counselor Licensing 1976 - 1990

Cumulative Number
of States with
Counseling Licensing

The Model

Based on a careful review of the governance structures of many large professional associations, particularly the AACD and APA, as well as those of our own associations, I would like to propose the following model for the (newly named) National Creative Arts Therapies Association (NCATA). This model has benefited from the experience of more developed professions, but also recognizes the unique aspects of our own professional needs and traditions, and the current state of organization in each of our associations. I became very familiar with these issues while serving as the chairperson of the coalition for the past five years. There is a need to develop a structure that both reflects the complexity required by a large organization, and respects creative arts therapists' lack of enthusiasm for top heavy, legalistic structures.

Basic Structure

NCATA would consist of a board of directors as the administrative arm responsible for the ongoing operation of the association and its policies; a council of delegates as the legislative arm responsible for determining association policies, amendments, and actions; and an appeals board as the judicial arm to hear appeals and resolve conflicts among elements of the association. The association would consist of the 6 divisions (the current 6 creative arts therapy associations), each with their own board of directors, bylaws, and standards.

The national association would be responsible for the overall governmental affairs, convention, publication, and national office functions. Divisions would continue to be responsible for registry and certification standards, ethical codes, standards of practice, and training programs within their respective fields. All the various certifications, boards, committees, and approval bodies of the current divisions would remain in effect. Nothing would dilute the special requirements for each creative arts therapy discipline.

National Office

One national office would be established, run by an executive director hired by the board of directors. It is possible that our own building could be purchased. Each division would have its offices within this national office. Secretarial, clerical, mailing, and filing systems would be integrated.

Membership

All members would apply to membership in NCATA and pay a fee. In addition, they would have to apply to at least one Division and pay an additional fee set by the division. All membership criteria would be determined by each division. Membership in NCATA would be contingent upon qualifying for at least one division. There may be a need to make the membership category titles consistent across Divisions, but the specific criteria would remain the responsibility of the divisions. Thus, fees that currently are needed for the functions to be taken over by the national association would be paid to NCATA. Division fees would, therefore, likely be less than they are currently.

Conferences

NCATA would have one national conference of all divisions each year, planned by the national office. However, although the conference will take place in one city, I propose that its structure differ from previous coalition conferences, in that there be a greater differentiation among the divisional events. Each division's conference subcommittee would plan workshops limited to its members, in addition to plenary and combined events open to all members. Thus, the national conference would have the form of 6 divisional conferences occurring at the same time. In this way, profitability, collaboration, and autonomy would all be enhanced.

Publications

All publications of the divisions would be centralized in our own publishing house, including all journals, books, and manuals. Rather than each association paying outside publishers to finance their journals, we would reap the profits ourselves, and be able to offer members better services.

Regions and States

In an organization of this size, regional and state groupings become highly valued structures for information sharing and collaboration. However, currently many of our associations are not well organized regionally. Therefore, it will take time for regional associations to form and sponsor conferences. I expect that eventually NCATA would adopt the American Music Therapy Association's (AMTA) regional groupings, since AMTA has the most developed and established regional structure.

State coalitions of creative arts therapists will be encouraged to form, to serve as the impetus for state licensing efforts. These state coalitions would report directly to the NCATA Board of Directors and be coordinated by the government affairs representatives at the national level.

Governance Structure

The proposed governance structure of NCATA follows those principles of other multidivisional associations, particularly in ensuring that the representational constituencies of the board of directors come from a variety of sources, so that minority opinions within divisions or regions have a number of pathways of expression. Figure 2 outlines the overall plan.

Figure 2

Proposed Model for a Multi-Divisional Association

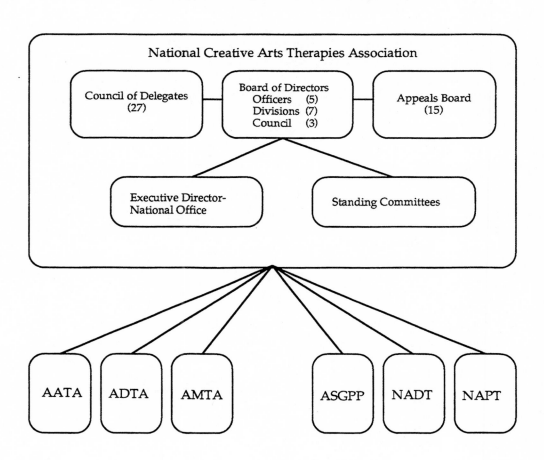

Thus, I propose the following:

1. Council of Delegates. Each division would elect delegates to this body, which is the policymaking body of the association, based on the ratio of 1 delegate for each 400 members. Terms of office would be two years. Given current (1991) figures, the Council would consist of the following delegates:

American Music Therapy Association (AMTA)	11
American Art Therapy Association (AATA)	9
American Dance Therapy Association (ADTA)	3
American Society for Group Psychotherapy and Psychodrama (ASGPP)	2
National Association for Drama Therapy (NADT)	1
National Association for Poetry Therapy (NAPT)	1
Total	27

The powers and functions of the council would include voting on policies and actions of the association based on recommendations from the board of directors, amend bylaws, and establish long range goals for the association. The council would elect a chairperson and two additional members who with the chairperson would serve on the board of directors.

2. Board of Directors. The board would consist of three officers (president, past president, president elect), who would be elected directly from the entire membership for one year terms; two nonvoting officers, executive director and treasurer, who would be hired by the board; three representatives from the council of delegates as described above; and one delegate each from the divisions. Division delegates would be the president of each division.

The powers and functions of the board of directors include: proposing policies and actions to the council, conducting the operations of the association, identifying issues and priorities for the association, and acting on behalf of the council when necessary. The board would hire the executive director, who is responsible for managing the national office, and the board would select the chairpersons and members of the standing committees. In this structure, represented constituencies include the membership (officers), the divisions (delegates), and the council (council delegates). Despite this diversification, in general each division would be represented in proportion to its membership relative to other divisions. The larger associations would have proportionately a greater say in the affairs of the association, though representation by each division is assured.

3. Standing Committees. These might include government affairs, publications, nominations, convention, state chapters, finance, and others as established by the board and the council. Composition of these committees should vary according to the needs of the specific task. Some may be composed of equal membership from each division (e.g., convention), and others by a set number of people based on their expertise (e.g., finance). These would be detailed in the bylaws.

4. Appeals Board. The appeals board would consist of 15 members elected for overlapping three year terms by the council of delegates, based on their experience, stature, and character. At least one member must be from each division. The appeals board would hear appeals of any decision by the board, standing committees, or council of delegates, made by individual members or divisions. A hearing committee of five would be selected on a rotating basis out of the group of 15 to hear each case. Appeals of registry decisions by divisions, however, would continue to be heard by the relevant division appeals process.

5. Process. The addition of new divisions would be by vote of the council of delegates, upon application by an association that fulfills the criteria for membership in NCATA. These are likely to be very similar to the criteria already existing. Likewise, a division could decide to withdraw from NCATA.

This model would engage our members in an exciting process of rapid professional development, as they elected officers to the national board, became engaged in their regional creative arts therapy groups, and came into even more contact with colleagues at the national convention. Nothing in these guidelines would diminish the rigor or values of art therapy, dance/movement therapy, drama therapy, music therapy, psychodrama, or poetry therapy. Nothing would reduce the specific control each division maintains on its own training or credentials. The energy released by this integration of our efforts would lead quickly to advances in jobs for our members, higher salaries, greater public exposure, licensing for our practitioners, and funding for our research.

Implementation

I propose that this plan be implemented in the following manner. After the proposed bylaws of the NCATA are finalized by a working group, a target date is set for transfer to the new structure, perhaps two years ahead, as contracts with existing management firms and publishers will need to be terminated. Then, the proposed entry of each division be voted on by the entire membership of each creative arts therapy association. NCATA would exist once three associations ratify the bylaws.

It will not be necessary for all 6 existing associations to agree for NCATA to be initiated. NCATA will likely begin with a subset of the current 6 associations. Once the new structure demonstrates its effectiveness, the other associations may decide to join.

Nevertheless, I do not expect the boards of directors of the existing associations to be the fountain of advocacy for this plan. The boards of directors will naturally be concerned about maintaining their own sense of power and control. This is why the founders of our country insisted that the Constitution be ratified by specially held Constitutional conventions, rather than the state legislatures. If it had been up to the state legislatures, the Constitution would not have been approved.

No, impetus for this approach will need to come from creative arts therapists themselves, from the teams working together in institutions, from the state coalitions of creative arts therapists, and from individual leaders in the field who write, and speak, and remind us what is needed now. My only hope is that the current boards of directors, who control the information to their membership, will allow an open debate. I believe that if they do, they will find a large reservoir of members who are concerned about the state of their profession, who want to tackle the issues of licensure and better jobs, and who are not afraid of joining together with others toward that end.

The larger creative arts therapy associations are apt to show the greatest reluctance to consider this step; they will feel they have something to lose, as did the larger states of New York and Virginia, who were the last to ratify the U.S. Constitution. Once they realize that their participation will not mean losing control, but actually gaining power within a larger organization, perhaps they will overcome their resistance. The smaller associations have much to gain by being part of a larger NCATA–however, in so doing they agree to a smaller degree of representation in the governance. Thus, each association, large and small, trades something in order to achieve greater success for the whole.

I hope that the membership of this great profession will act wisely, and not allow our loosely formed coalition to meet the same fate as the early American confederacy, becoming, in George Washington's view, "a half-starved, limping government, that appears to be always moving upon crutches, and tottering at every step" (1939, p. 305).

Perhaps we must go through this painful stage of development, driven by our defensive need for control, our fears of being swallowed whole by our friends, our assertions of pseudoindependence and precious insularity, and our suspicions of structure and authority.

Perhaps we must tolerate the humiliating displays of our lack of coordination, the loss of jobs and graduate programs, and the flight of our best to social work and psychology degrees or counseling licenses.

I am told that we must go through this. But it is a great deal of pain. It requires a great deal of tolerance. I propose to you another way, a way that embraces interdependence, individuation, and growth.

Chapter 8

THE CHALLENGE OF MENTORING

I believe that the field of creative arts therapy is suffering from an absence of mentoring. Students are completing masters programs and internships only to find themselves in a void, employed perhaps, but with little guidance through their early professional development. The result is that many graduates are finding it difficult to establish a strong professional identity as a creative arts therapist, and eventually are turning to other professions, institutes, or programs where there is a stronger tradition of mentoring (see Chapter 2).

The training of a psychotherapist, especially a creative arts therapist, takes many years, perhaps well over ten years. The capacity to understand, to hear, and to help other people continues to grow throughout one's lifetime (Irwin, 1986). It is conceivable that a two year Masters program and a six month internship might prepare a student for *doing* creative arts therapy, but it is clearly not enough to prepare a student for *being* a creative arts therapist (Emunah, 1989; Landy, 1982). What will help our graduates achieve this goal is to experience closely-held relationships with senior therapists for several years. Yet, when they leave the embrace of the program and get their first job, too often these creative arts therapists are isolated from a professional community. This leads to what I have often seen in postgraduates: postmasters depression, a serious condition of malaise, uncertainty, and self-questioning. Many times they do not survive this phase, and decide to go to graduate school in another profession where they feel they will be better taken care of.

Studies of mentoring largely support the idea that for young adults, mentoring leads to a more successful integration of self and role (Levinson, 1978). The mentor is usually a half-generation older than the student, not so old to resemble a parent, nor close enough to be a peer. The mentor supports the apprentice in achieving his or her own unique inner vision, in contrast to the tendencies toward possessiveness of the parent, or competitiveness in the peer. The mentor is a transitional figure in the young professional's life, who serves as a bridge between studenthood and fully independent practice. The

Revised from *Dramascope, 15,* 1993 with permission of the National Association for Drama Therapy.

respectful distance maintained by the mentor allows the young professional to integrate an established body of knowledge with his or her own independent aspirations, ideas, and visions. A more extensive internalization of professional identity occurs.

Perhaps our graduates do not understand that they need to be mentored. Perhaps more senior creative arts therapists do not understand that they need to provide mentoring. The situation is serious if creative arts therapists who graduated 4 or 5 years ago still feel that they cannot take on an intern, or if some of our students are still doing internships where there is no registered creative arts therapist! The situation *is* serious, though I remain hopeful largely because the quality of the students we are attracting remains so high.

The heads of major graduate programs certainly do all they can while the students are in their programs, and for the large part are very successful. They cannot be expected to single-handedly continue to mentor everyone once they leave as well! Other creative arts therapists are needed to fill in this gap. Indeed, I believe that those of us out in the field have a responsibility to mentor new creative arts therapists who are emerging from our graduate programs. The whole field needs a consciousness-raising that mentoring is a fundamental professional function. The question, "Who is your mentor?" should become an essential one facing each student.

We do not have a culture of mentoring for several reasons. First, the pioneers in creative arts therapy often did not have mentors. The capacity to reach beyond prescribed roles and boundaries, to discover the uniqueness of the arts therapies, required people who were unattached to previously-defined structures. The independent reach into the unknown may facilitate the beginning of a field, but not its maturing. Many of the creative arts therapy pioneers are still today with few disciples, apprentices, or students. Have we inadvertently created a self-defeating cycle where our students, insufficiently mentored by us, are unable to mentor others? I am no exception to this, as I found it difficult to find and hold onto mentors—in fact, for years I didn't know I needed a mentor. I was creative, unique, discovering new techniques all by myself, unaware of the toll I was paying (in my case due to the disappointment in a father who fell to alcoholism). Now I struggle with my responsibility to mentor other drama therapists.

We may not encourage mentoring because as artists seeking the autonomy necessary for creative expression, we share an antiestablishment sensibility. We hesitate to claim allegiance to a method or theory, or reliance upon a teacher or guide. Yet let us remember the years of disciplined work required to hone one's talent, largely through controlled repetition of basic forms (e.g., character work, still lives, ballet steps, the scales, voice training). Originality usually emerges from discipline, from groundedness.

We may have difficulty mentoring because we are a shamed culture, in which our internalized humiliation undermines our capacity to identify with or idealize our teachers (see Chapter 9). The fact that the creative arts therapies remain so little known and appreciated serves to weaken our self-confidence, leading too often to highly critical evaluations of each other.

The absence of mentoring in the creative arts therapies is evident in many ways. It is rare that presentations at our national conferences are co-led by a senior and junior colleague. Presentations are still too often in the "here is my way of doing things" mode, rather than "here is how I have extended, challenged, or developed my mentor's thinking or technique." Articles are rarely coauthored by a mentor and student, which in other professions is a well-established method for encouraging people to write. Third, many students fail to complete their thesis requirement and may shift into other fields due to a lack of support following their more formal training. Finally, there are almost no opportunities for advanced training, other than isolated workshops. A field with maturity will have institutes and training programs for post-masters therapists.

Now that we are beginning to develop specific "schools of thought," dialogues among creative arts therapists who have trained within a specific theoretical perspective will help each of these schools to mature further. Without this colleagial dialogue, linked by mentoring networks, a field lacks vitality, and falls into fragmentation.

I encourage us to examine our own experience with the mentoring process. I encourage us to think about how to support graduates of our programs. I encourage us to find ways of linking up with each other, so that important beliefs, ideas, and perspectives can be deepened, and then passed on. These are the elements of building a tradition, one that not need be static and constricting, but can transform organically through time, creating a rich context, history, and atmosphere within which we can develop further as creative arts therapists. We need to shift our attention from what we have not been given by those who came before, to what is needed by those who are following us.

Where do I come from? On whose shoulders do I stand? Out of what soil do I grow? Without roots in a nurturing environment, we will produce people without the energy to produce their own seeds. Without effective mentoring, our field will become barren.

Here are two discourses on mentoring, from the perspective of the young professional and from the mentor:

AN APPRENTICE'S EXPERIENCE
Kathryn C. Templeton, M.A., RDT/MT

In January, 1993, my husband and I moved from San Francisco, California to New Haven, Connecticut. We did not move because one of us was offered a fabulous job. We did not move to be closer to family. We moved so that I could join the New Haven Drama Therapy Institute and continue to study with David Johnson. I had been feeling lost and cut off in my professional world. The system I worked in was uneducated about drama therapy, and the burden of educating others while continuing to struggle for my own deeper understanding was stifling. I needed a mentor. I needed a peer group with which to explore ideas, examine theories, discuss fears, and celebrate success.

The past year and a quarter has been at times disillusioning. My fantasy of being mentored and the reality of the relationship have been vastly different. Yet I would recommend the mentor/student relationship.

When I graduated in 1992 after finally finishing my thesis, I worked for about a year. I was supervised by a knowledgeable psychologist but I had never been supervised on site by a drama therapist. I was learning important information on a range of psychological thinking but nothing about how to integrate the information and apply it to my work in drama therapy. Those two worlds were separated. I attempted to create a group of professional peers to gather together and discuss our experiences as drama therapists. Yet I failed, as time was not on our side and I was not motivated enough to tolerate the struggle of starting a group. Finally, I quit my full-time job. I continued in a consulting position with one weekly drama therapy group and went back to acting and teaching aerobics.

One day I found out about a week-long summer intensive in David's developmental transformations method that would take place in New Haven. I decided to go to see if I could rejuvenate my passion for drama therapy, as by this time I felt isolated and my confidence in my work had slipped. The workshop was pivotal for me. It became clear that this was the type of structure I needed to continue in my process. This realization frightened me, because I had been a member of small groups and acting companies with strong mentors, and the experience had not always been positive.

Furthermore, I would have to ask my husband to move across the country for me to join this group—a selfish request with no guarantee. Not to mention that both our families in Nashville would undoubtedly have a problem with us moving without jobs to the cold Northeast for me to study. We agreed to take a one-year adventure and moved six months later.

Initially, I kept myself on the periphery of the group. I was skeptical of David. I was hypervigilant of his words and behaviors. I wanted desperately to become dependent upon this mentor and paradoxically this was my worst fear. I was resistant to letting David help me find jobs or give me advice. I needed to be outside of his world–to keep things separate. The fear of collapsing into a mentor was profound for me. This struggle was played out in my individual transformations therapy with David and became so intense I could not interact with him socially at all. I found myself entertaining the notion of getting rid of him, and indirectly acted this out in transformations. My anxiety was tolerable only because of the support from the rest of the group. My peers in the Institute sensed my ambivalence and actively engaged me, and made it feel safe enough to tolerate my anxiety.

After a year of struggle we finally broke through during a series of transformations sessions. I recall one moment when David acknowledged my internal restriction and I experienced this reflection as giving me freedom. My anxiety has decreased significantly. I no longer perceive my dependence on my mentor as a negative. I cannot articulate the transition at this point, as I am still in the shift. However, I now know the benefit of persevering. Learning to tolerate my own need for dependence has helped me embrace my abilities. My confidence and skill level have grown and this makes it easier for me to learn. David's help is now accepted and paradoxically my need for his help has diminished. My mentor helps me theoretically, strategically, and personally.

So far, my experience in being mentored has been a difficult wave to ride. The wave has not reached the beach, but that's okay because now I am enjoying the ride much more than anything else. I feel the learning has been multilayered and all areas of my life have been touched. In retrospect I do not know if I would have moved to New Haven to be mentored had I known how personally hard I was going to have to work. I am glad I did not have that knowledge. I am glad I had my positive fantasy to get me here. I do not know how else I would have learned so much about myself, drama therapy, teamwork, or teaching.

A MENTOR'S EXPERIENCE
David Read Johnson

Kathryn sat across the table at the hotel, asking me if she could come to New Haven to train with me. She would bring her husband, find a job, work with me at the VA as a volunteer, and then continue her training at the Institute for several years. This was intimidating. What am I promising her? What if it doesn't work out? What if her husband gets mad? What am I doing? Am I worth it? These questions entered my mind then, as they do now, as I contemplate mentoring younger drama therapists.

I had known Kathryn a few years, first as a teacher at California Institute of Integral Studies, then as a supervisor. I remember we took a walk into town at the Pittsburgh drama therapy conference; it was just after the San Francisco earthquake and she wanted to talk about herself and her future. She seemed eager, naive, uncertain, ambitious yet troubled. Now, over breakfast two years later, she was more grounded, though just as eager. Yet I wondered—she's not really coming to train with me, she must have another reason.

Well, she moved and began her training. She found herself among a group of drama therapists who had all moved to New Haven to train—a supportive group for sure—but at the same time she became the "new guy." The excitement of being special, of coming to be mentored by me, was diluted by the sense that I must be more invested in the core members. The magic turned quickly to just plain work.

Yet I tried to maintain the magic. You don't have someone move their family all the away across the country to a town like New Haven for nothing! So I often felt like I had to demonstrate some special attachment, some special bond. This was hard.

I remember when her husband finally joined her. I felt I needed to welcome them and suggested a small restaurant near their apartment. To my horror, when I arrived I found that I had suggested the wrong place—this was just a darkened hick bar—totally tasteless. And worse, Kathryn and her husband were already there. "This is New Haven? Let's go home!" I imagined him saying. To someone who thinks about moving to San Francisco all the time, I thought they were crazy! I remember my relief when I greeted them and he said, "Heh, these appetizers are great!"

Kathryn had a hard time accepting the fact that I was willing to help her out—just to help her out. And that I am interested in the work of drama therapy. Personal and professional dimensions are interwoven in the training which both enrich and complicate our relationships. This is a highly personal process for us all. Each of our vulnerabilities become highlighted. As a mentor, I have had to be open as a person to my trainees—far more than to my clients or colleagues. That is hard. Yet I have to maintain a perspective—there is only so much time I can give to each one. I have to rely on their own sense of place and journey, while at the same time guiding them, giving to them, caring for them.

Kathryn rejected many of my offers. I wondered, "why did she come all the way out here, and then avoid me?" I was disappointed, irritated, and relieved, all at the same time. "She doesn't need me after all," I thought. Nevertheless, I was glad when her deeper concerns finally came out, all of a sudden during the course of her transformations. She finally felt free enough to tell me that she worried that I cared only for the core members, or that I only wanted her to practice the Developmental Method, and she had to hide the fact she did other things too, or that she felt I didn't think much of her work, or that she didn't think everything I said made sense. Could she be critical of me? Could she handle my criticisms of her?

She was surprised and relieved to find that these concerns were not new to me. Other trainees had felt them also. They were both true and not true. And that beyond all of it I am still interested in the work of drama therapy, and in encouraging her development, wherever it may lead.

The task of the mentor is not to indoctrinate the student into one's own vision, but to notice and appreciate the unique vision within the student and to encourage it. What often gets in the way is the fear of bondage, submission, or manipulation and control. I suppose I feel as burdened and controlled by my trainees' attachment to me, as they are by my interest in them.

Recently Kathryn became pregnant with her first child, and she and her husband are looking to buy a house. In New Haven. She has begun to see private clients at the Institute. She suggested we write this article together. I was pleased.

I believe that I have a new colleague.

Chapter 9

SHAME DYNAMICS AMONG CREATIVE ARTS THERAPISTS

In thinking about the difficulties that creative arts therapists and creative arts therapy associations have been having, I would like to propose that many of these problems stem from an underlying dynamic of internalized shame that is now interfering with our progress. In some cases, the experience of shame is the result of a pervasive cultural denigration and disinterest in art, women, and therapy, and in some cases is the result of actual abuse. The attendant alterations in our professional identities lead to diminished capacities to manage the challenges of collaboration and professionalism.

We are a shamed culture. As artists, therapists, and (mostly) women, creative arts therapists have experienced a sizable amount of humiliation in the course of their careers.

First, there is the fact that we live within a culture of the concrete. America is built on the values of the pragmatic, the parsimonious, the undeniably practical. How does it work? What can it do? Show me. Ben Franklin observed, "To America, one schoolmaster is worth a dozen poets, and the invention of a machine or the improvement of an implement is of more importance than a masterpiece of Raphael." One of the founding fathers of our country had this to say: "The arts have been from the dawn of history the product of despotism and superstition and so should be avoided in the new republic." That was John Adams, our second president.

The values of a culture are symbolized by core images of itself as a community or nation. America's sense of itself, its communitas, is in large part based on images of joint, pragmatic action: such as barn-raisings, wagon trains, neighborhood tag sales, firewood stacking parties, and wars, in which the entire community joins together to accomplish a real-world task. A fundamentally masculine, pioneer spirit. In America, the body, the abstract, and the unconscious are all suspect, are all feminine, or worse, homosexual, which is the perceived antithesis of the primary American cultural norms.

Reprinted from the *Arts in Psychotherapy, 27,* 173-178, 1994, with permission from Elsevier Science.

To choose a career as a creative arts therapist often means stretching the tolerance of one's family, and entering a world where one is not understood, or appreciated. We have been so pervasively put down that we tend to take it for granted or joke about it. I have been called an activities therapist, drama specialist, rec worker, nursing assistant, and even, "you, there." Our supervisors may be an occupational therapist, recreation therapist, nurse, social worker, or volunteer. When I say I am a drama therapist, the other person usually develops a haze over their eyes, and then says, "Huh?" I have to repeat myself. In the 60s they thought I said "drumming therapist;" lately people think I said "trauma therapist," or in some circles "dharma therapist." Are these minor slights in the career of a developing professional? or attitudes that form a significant threat to our identity? Let me tell you a few stories about this, all true:

Surely This Could be Rescheduled

I stood in the doorway of the seclusion room, waiting. I was afraid. The patient, Carolyn, lay in the room behind me in wet packs, cold wet sheets wrapped around her body, supposedly creating a womb-like environment, quieting her activity, forcing the cathexis in her body into verbalization so that the psychiatrist could talk to her. Carolyn had yet to talk with him. She had hit him once.

Both of us were quiet. I was waiting for the famous psychiatrist to come because, again, he had scheduled his session with her during our regularly scheduled movement/drama therapy session. Carolyn talked easily and meaningfully to Susan and me, as long as she could move and sway with us to the music. A busy man, the psychiatrist's secretary would call up the nurses' station whenever he could fit in a session. He came down the hallway at last, looking distinguished in his white coat, white hair. I stood in the doorway, but as he came through, not noticing me, I couldn't stand firm, and moved slightly to my side. I spoke: "Dr. F., I'm sorry to delay you, but you see, Susan and I have a regularly scheduled movement/drama therapy session with Carolyn at this time, and we were wondering if you might be able to work around that, since it is confusing to her when everything changes, and we feel we are getting somewhere with her. She talks to us!" Though he stood looking over my shoulder at Carolyn, barely a flicker of an eyelid could be seen as he passed by and closed the door. Not a word. I did not exist.

I Don't Want to Bother You

The session had been going well. The six hyperactive patients had finally agreed to come to the group, the music had started and we were beginning to focus on an important theme. An argument had broken out last week that had made everyone feel less safe. Suddenly, a loud clattering sound came from the windows of the room. Two men, painters, had hoisted themselves up on their platform outside the windows, opened them and began placing paint and cloths on the windowsill. One of them stepped inside the room. He was completely oblivious to our presence, the music, and the six disheveled patients, several of whom now sat down. I was incredulous. I thought, boy are they going to be embarrassed when they find out they have disrupted a therapy session! I went up to them and said, "Excuse me, but we are having a therapy session in here." I smiled. The man, appearing a bit startled, looked around, and in a pleasant voice said, "Oh that's OK, you won't bother us at all!"

The New Member

Her face was beatific. I could have been looking at Mother Mary herself, so confident and self-secure was the face of the Director of Nursing whom I had come to confront. I had been working in this nursing home for four years, and had worked hard to establish the creative arts therapies there with the many elderly patients. This person had never been supportive, but what had just happened was the last straw, and I had come storming down the hall into her office. "David," she said patronizingly, "you have to understand that some things just take priority."

For weeks there had been a fight over space, and the usual activities room had been taken over by the nursing staff as an office and lounge. The only room for activities was the big multipurpose room which had no privacy. Finally, after much cajoling, a patient bedroom was emptied and we were allowed to use it for our therapy groups. Nevertheless, I was prepared for the nurses to try to turn it back into a bedroom again.

And so when I wheeled a patient into the room that day and saw that a patient and her bed had been moved into the room, I was angry. Not wanting to disrupt the group that day, however, I decided to wait until later to confront the nurse, and so my cotherapist and I collected the rest of the patients who easily fit in a circle at the other end of the large bedroom. I then went over to the new patient with the idea of explaining to her that we were going to have this group in her room, and even invite her to join if she wished. She was quite old but had an attractive and thoughtful face. As I sat down next to her bed and addressed her, "Excuse me maam," I felt how embarrassing this was for me and for her, and why didn't the nurses tell me they needed the room for a new patient. As I looked at her more closely, I wondered if her delay in answering me was due to depression, or even dementia, when finally, out of the pit of my stomach, out of the rods and cones of my retina, the realization came that this woman was not a new patient, this woman had not been moved in here to live, Nooo......for this woman was dead.

Suddenly I saw the blue color of her skin, suddenly I knew why the window had been kept open on this cold winter day. Suddenly I heard the other patients cry out, "Oh my god she's dead," and wheel themselves out of the room. Suddenly I found myself looking into the face of the Director of Nursing, and hearing her speak of priority. "But you put a dead person in my drama therapy group!" "David, we had to put her somewhere, otherwise she would disturb the other patients and visitors." "But what about me and the members of the drama therapy group?" "You should have met elsewhere." "But that is our room. It's important for us to have a consistent space each week!" She just smiled and said, "The word for today, David, is *flexibility*."

These three incidents, hopefully more characteristic of the past than the future, are painful reminders of the struggles that creative arts therapists have not infrequently faced in achieving recognition and respect by society and other members of the health care community (see Chapter 2). When I think about my feelings aroused by each of these incidents—beneath the anger, even rage—is shame. I was embarrassed, not at what I did, but for who I was. This goes to the core. Since then I have attempted to avoid these feelings through a series of gymnastic twists of myself and career, anything to rid myself of being subjected to ridicule again. Similarly, I believe creative arts therapists, like other individuals subject to intense shame and humiliation, may have developed alterations in our professional identities not unlike those seen in personality disorders or posttraumatic stress disorder.

Impact of Shame on Personality

There is growing interest in the study of shame and its impact on psychological conditions (Kaufman, 1980; Lewis, 1971; Nathanson, 1987). Shame is a particularly distressing, yet common, affect, in which one's self is highlighted in the eyes of the other in a negative way. Shame is usually differentiated from guilt in that in guilt, one is deficient for what one has done, and in shame, one is deficient for who one is. Shame is therefore a global, overwhelming experience. Behaviorally, shame is demonstrated by bowing the head, blushing, averting the eyes, and wishing to hide or disappear. Many authors identify shame as essentially interpersonal in origin. Kaufman (1980) defines shame as a disruption of the interpersonal bridge to the other, where the person experiences a feeling of complete loss of union with the loved one. The person's sense of trust in others is significantly disrupted. In addition, a process of internalization occurs, in which a new shame experience, however small, kicks off the whole shame sequence, consuming the self again. The person becomes shame prone. The result is that the person quickly turns to a number of defenses against the experience of shame. Most of these lead to disruptions in object relationships. Let me briefly discuss these.

Heightened interpersonal boundaries. Shame leads to a need to protect the self from intrusion from others. This often expresses itself in a fear of exposure, avoidance of scrutiny, exaggerated need for autonomy, and distaste for submission, vulnerability, or dependency. Kaufman calls it righteous self-sufficiency. The shamed individual shows marked guardedness, and a high need for control over situations. The ability to compromise becomes impaired because ambiguity or gray areas are avoided. Organizations of shamed individuals therefore tend to fragment easily. For example, while there remains only a handful of priestly orders, highly stable over centuries, there are many hundreds of orders of nuns, which continue to divide, despite very small numbers.

Transfer of shame to others. Shame is so intolerable that the individual attempts to redirect it to others. When internalized, this defense leads to the development of judgmental attitudes, overly rigid standards, faultfinding, and even contempt as a personality style. Lewis (1971) calls this process bypassed shame, indicated by the person obsessively ruminating about the stupid things others have done, mocking others for minor faults, and developing a self-righteous demeanor.

Compensatory maneuvers. Another method of dealing with shame is to try to compensate for it. The individual strives for perfection, hoping that by being perfect no one will make fun of them. Attitudes of false pride develop, in which one's achievements are overly valued. Often a compensatory fantasy evolves that the self is a misunderstood and unappreciated, but secretly unique, creative person.

Repetition compulsion. Unfortunately, all of these defenses against shame fail to relieve the self from the original pain, and because they disguise the real problem, they lead the person to endlessly repeat similar situations, in which they are shamed again. The result is a development of a shame-prone personality, characterized by rigid interpersonal boundaries, overly judgmental ideas, and susceptibility to compensatory fantasies. These personality alterations are not dissimilar to those seen in people suffering from post-traumatic stress disorder (Stone, 1992).

Empowerment

The pathway out of a shame stance begins with a painful self confrontation: that one has indeed been shamed or abused. This is made possible by the recognition and support of other members of the shamed group. The attainment of a true, modest pride in oneself or one's profession, or of a mature sense of humility and self-respect comes as one focuses on goals for the future rather than the blame for the past, on who we are and what we have to contribute rather than what others think of us. Empowerment also means carrying the burden of past abuse that we do not pass on to those who follow us: to support others, when we were shamed; to mentor others, when we were not mentored; to remain positive when what we experienced was negative. Sacrifices of this order by members of many shamed groups have allowed them to progress and achieve success. I believe such sacrifices are required now of creative arts therapists.

Experience from Alcoholics Anonymous has proven to be very valuable in the treatment of shaming conditions of all kinds. The 12 Step movement is in fact, in many of its elements, a treatment for shame. The first step of the Twelve Steps addresses acceptance: "We admitted we were powerless over alcohol–that our lives had become unmanageable." To be powerless, to be unmanageable, to surrender to the disease of alcoholism is initially viewed as shameful and therefore unacceptable. What is important is that acceptance occurs not as a singular, personal event, but in relation to the group, and with the group's support. The stepping forward and saying, "Yes, I am an alcoholic" is a rite of passage from isolation into the group. Paradoxically, the patient fears the opposite: that acknowledging his/her condition will mean leaving the group (of normal people) and lead to isolation. What a surprise it is for them to be welcomed into the group (of fellow sufferers.)

Overcoming the culture of shame has been essential to many groups' development: the labor movement, the women's movement, the civil rights movement, and now the gay/lesbian movement. Each struggle has involved "coming out" and acknowledging that there is no reason to be ashamed of being a worker, a woman, a black, or gay. All have involved tremendous efforts at organizing disparate elements within the shamed culture to collaborate together (see Chapters 3 and 4). "We must stick together!" has been the rallying call of many a shamed group's journey up from oppression toward meaningful integration into the larger culture. This is because shame separates, shame compartmentalizes, shame silences.

Symptoms of Bypassed Shame among Creative Arts Therapists

I believe that creative arts therapists, due to their experiences as a shamed professional group, exhibit a number of the symptoms of the shame-prone individual. These have hindered our professional development in three areas: (1) internally within each discipline, (2) among the creative arts therapy associations, and (3) in our relationship with other mental health professions.

By far the most obvious symptom of shame dynamics is the inability of the six creative arts therapy associations to join together in a larger multidivisional entity that will save money, increase power, and serve its membership (see Chapters 5 and 7). Despite many warnings and recommendations by government agencies, larger organizations, and others, the National Coalition of Arts Therapy Associations (NCATA) remains fragmented, ineffective, and ill-prepared to deal with the truly major challenges to our existence that are occurring. A decade of work among our leadership has not impacted on the fundamental ideology of autonomy to which each association clings. Collaboration is experienced as merging or fusing: this is a shame dynamic. Joining together is experienced as losing control: this is a shame dynamic. Differences among groups are viewed as irreconcilable hurdles: this is a shame dynamic. The Joint Commission on Accreditation of Healthcare Organizations, congressional committees, state governments, and large influential organizations all have said the same thing: when creative arts therapists can organize to the point of having unified representation, then they will be invited to participate. Despite this consistent message, we continue our parallel and redundant ventures, unable to develop intimate, effective, and efficient structures of collaboration. We have placed ourselves at the mercy of external forces, and are on the road toward a major crisis, which will either finally force us to collaborate, or do us in.

Criticizing or denigrating other creative arts therapy modalities is another shame symptom. Sometimes there is more denigration among creative arts therapists than between them and other professions who are overtly hostile to us. We revel in contacts with the big groups, and belittle efforts to join together with each other. I can well remember as the NCATA chairperson how esteemed members of one creative arts therapy spoke with scorn and derision at the poor education, small size, inadequate degrees, lax standards, or deficient personalities of other creative arts therapies; being far more critical than members of established (and less shamed) professions. Strange as it may be, shamed people will destroy their own communities when shamed again, as illustrated recently in the riots of African-Americans after the Rodney King verdict.

The reverse of this process is the common practice among our associations of inviting (usually male) psychiatrists or psychologists as keynotes, who tell us how wonderful we are, instead of inviting members of our own profession as keynotes. These representatives of the abuser are invited to our gatherings to magically undo the previous or ongoing shame. But this maneuver does not work, because it maintains the assumption that our self-esteem is dependent upon how others view us. Progress will mean experiencing the emergence of power from within our ranks.

Focusing on big public relations projects rather than developing an infrastructure of connection with other groups is another symptom observed among our national and local associations. Shamed people sometimes compensate for their feelings of inadequacy through a display of a prized or ostentatious possession: a car, a stereo, a dress. We may spend tens of thousands of dollars on a one-time hearing or special event, instead of paying for our representatives to travel to the numerous coalition, task force, foundation, and agency meetings that would cement our relationship to the broader health care community. The big event relieves us from the fear that we are doing nothing; but avoids the hard and less glamorous development of networks, procedures and structures we can rely on in an emergency. The result is that many of our impressive public presentations or lobbying efforts have been followed by withdrawal or silence, instead of continued involvement and organization.

Creative arts therapists are known for being overly sensitive to slights at work, in comparison to others, particularly recreation therapists. We sometimes appear to have an entitled attitude. This is generated from shame, of which recreation therapists have less, due to this culture's preference for sports over arts. We are particularly upset if we are asked to help with crafts, parties, or diversional activities, which indicate to us that we are being devalued. We insist on doing only our arts therapy activities, and risk becoming so specialized we can only find part-time jobs.

Striving for perfection and being unable to tolerate variation has sometimes led to particularly rigid, inflexible standards in professions known for their valuing of flexibility. We compensate for the perception of us as flaky, stupid, inept, or boundary-less. We emphasize how strict we are. We create many oversight committees, which double check details other more established professions view more flexibly. We become highly suspicious of the practices of our own members, or engage in overly zealous hunts for therapists who are not properly credentialed. The danger is that the shame/blame process is enacted within our organizations, which members experience as humiliating and rejecting rather than supportive.

Shame also disrupts mentoring, and creative arts therapists often have had difficulty being mentored. Mentoring results from and subsequently strengthens the processes of identification and internalization so important to the maintenance of a profession. The shaming of earlier generations may have prevented them from properly mentoring us. Since mentoring is the glue that allows young professionals to integrate their identity in the early phase of their career, we have suffered from an extremely high drop out rate after training (see Chapter 8). Another sign of inadequate mentoring is the rather low frequency of arts therapists who seek arts therapists as their primary therapist. As long as we tend to see other professionals as the source of power, support, and identification, our own professional development will be undermined.

Finally, another symptom is the surprising lack of attention creative arts therapists have given to gay or lesbian issues, when clearly we are a profession that could provide encouragement and support. I suspect that the environment of shame among creative arts therapists is so pervasive, that gay and lesbian issues have been subtly suppressed, by all parties, out of a need to avoid any additional distress.

Becoming Aware of Shame Dynamics

In order for us to move forward in contributing to American health care, we need to be able to collaborate closely with each other; we need to be able to form a larger entity with greater strength and unity. In order to do that we need to reframe our current perception, that coming together will harm us in some way or be an intrusion. Understanding our need for each other, not being hesitant to ask for help, and giving up our pseudoautonomous stance can occur once we realize how these attitudes have been generated. Then we will be able to sense the larger forces that beset us. We need to recognize our roots in shame, identifying and then modifying our defenses against shame, which are crippling us. What is required is a painful acceptance of what has happened to us.

Oh, Captain, My Captain

I was excited about sailing my new boat. I had not sailed before, but had taken lessons. Finally the big day came, and I sailed out of the harbor, standing at the tiller, of course, because I was the Captain of My Own Ship, a genetically encoded instinct every man has. I would go where I desired, though I soon found out it took twice as long to come back (because I had a tendency to go with the wind, and didn't know much about the tides or tidal currents). Nevertheless, one day I was sailing with a friend off the entrance to the Connecticut River, which comes down from Canada, and we were going very fast, I mean at least 5 knots. At this rate we'd be home in no time. About 45 minutes later, my friend said, "Look at the shore, I don't think we've gone very far." I replied, "Nonsense." Then, turning to look, I saw that we had barely moved 500 yards down the coast. How could this be? Well, as we were moving 5 knots one way, the water beneath us was moving 4 knots the opposite way, due to the currents. My friend got upset, and told me to turn on our outboard motor. Now she apparently did not understand that for the Captain of the Ship, a Sailor, to have to put the motor in the water, was tantamount to failure, and the ultimate humiliation. So of course I refused, "I'll trim the sails." She criticized this move, and made fun of me. I yelled back. Even though at this rate we would get back the next morning, if at all. After another 30 minutes of attempting to outwit the tidal currents of Long Island Sound, I finally realized that there was no other way than to put the motor in the water. I felt angry, tired, and stupid. Yet, as I finally placed the motor into the water, a strange thing happened: I sensed the current for the first time. This was how I learned that a good sailor is not one who goes where he wants, but one who respects the larger forces of nature, the wind, the tides, and the currents, who learns about them, and uses them to his best advantage.

I believe this is what creative arts therapists also have to learn. We can no longer survive unto ourselves. We must sense the currents in health care, for they are strong, and we must rely on each other, depending upon our knowledge of these larger forces. This is the way we can make progress, not by going it alone - as heroic as that may appear.

Yet I do not hear the call from many creative arts therapists. Too many of our less shamed colleagues have left us for the more esteemed fields of psychology, counseling, or social work. Are we so proud that we will let our boat sink before we reach out for help?

Creative arts therapists, hands on the wooden tiller of our small boats—look!—the tide! the wind! Let us not be ashamed to turn to each other; it is not a failure, not a submission; it is the way we will get home. It will be the foundation of our success.

Chapter 10

CREATIVE ARTS THERAPIES AND THE FUTURE OF GROUP THERAPY

Significant forces are at work that will affect the practice of group therapy in the next decade. Group therapy has had a long history, garnering many advocates, theories, and methods. Its existence is not in question. However, significant societal transformations are bound to impact on the character and form of group therapy, not to mention the practice of psychotherapy in general, to whose fate it is tied. How will the practice of the creative arts therapies, so intimately involved in group work, be affected by these forces? Will this be a time for the greater recognition we have so long sought, or another retrenchment that will burden our efforts even more?

First let me remind you of the context within which these transformations are taking place: that context is America. But what is America? America is the home of the individual, of the free and the brave, of stark individualism. As a culture made of immigrants who escaped constricting traditions, governments, and prejudices, we remain profoundly suspicious of groups. Groups are associated with socialism, and socialism with communism. Our capitalist and entrepreneurial spirit values individual achievement, denigrates dependency, and expects us to "do it on our own." Unlike many other cultures, we resist investing our money or taxes in communal spaces such as parks, town greens, environmental cleanups, or even schools. We are more likely to attempt to protect our wealth within our homes, surrounded by a less and less safe town or city: that is, we recreate that quintessential American experience: the cabin in the frontier. The image of grandma with the shotgun sticking out of the window has now become real on a fantastical scale, with random, drive-by shootings. I am amazed that Jules Fieffer's absurd comedy, *Little Murders*, written in the 1960s, which portrays average American families shooting people on the street half out of recreation, half out of fear, is nearly a reality. This cultural background of individualism and pragmatism has and will continue to profoundly influence the types of group therapy likely to flourish here. As I have noted elsewhere (see Chapters 2 and 9), creative arts therapists have always had to struggle against these cultural norms; the arts are a reference to a transcendent world, and thus are met with suspicion, for in America, work, not art, feeds the soul.

Group therapy was developed in the 1940s and 1950s largely as a result of European and British influences and necessitated by the cataclysm of the World War. However, group therapy became a widely available treatment in this country as a result of the unique historical discontinuity of the 1960s, in which psychoanalytic, encounter, and self-help methods permeated the popular culture of our society. A panoply of approaches were explored and integrated into psychiatric treatment settings, training programs, and research investigations. The creative arts therapies were supported by these developments, as attested to by the rapid development of our professional associations and training programs. For the most part, creative arts therapies were viewed as more sober versions of the unconstrained approaches such as primal scream, encounter, and marathons.

However, as the tide waters receded in the 1970s and 1980s, and America returned to calmer and more conservative times, many of these group therapy methods fell from favor. For example, the psychoanalytic approach is viewed as too authoritarian and orthodox, Tavistock as too abstract, encounter groups as too intense, and the therapeutic community too cumbersome. Even some of the leaders of these movements departed from or even abandoned the work. Wilfred Bion, who initiated the study of unconscious group dynamics, declared groups unworkable and moved to Beverly Hills to open a psychoanalytic private practice. Maxwell Jones, who created the therapeutic community concept, tired of London and moved to the Caribbean to study cross-cultural psychiatry. And Moreno, founder of psychodrama and action methods, holed up at Beacon and became increasingly isolated from the mainstream of group therapy, a rift only now being repaired.

We are left with three major approaches that I believe will remain viable in the near future. Interestingly, all were developed by Americans rather than Europeans:

Educational Approach: Originally explored by Joseph Pratt (1922) with tuberculosis patients, then explicated by Jerrold Maxmen (1978) and many others, psychoeducational groups are a rising staple of both inpatient and outpatient mental health programs. Patients are placed in the role of student, minimizing many of the regressive effects of groups. Americans have always believed in education, so the lecture format of the psychoeducational groups, which de-emphasizes free group interaction, is more easily embraced. Indeed, the current popularity of cognitive-behavioral approaches derives in part from their educational, didactic formats.

Interpersonal Approach: Irvin Yalom single-handedly saved group therapy from fragmenting into a Babel of unrelated methods with his book, *Theory and Practice of Group Psychotherapy* (1975). He provided the field with an interpersonal approach to group therapy, which emphasizes dyadic interaction within the group, as opposed to group-as-a-whole interventions. His practical, common sense approach to group therapy asserts that groups are excellent forums in which to explore one's relationships with others. Interpersonal approaches remain the staple of outpatient group therapy.

12 Step Models: What Bill W. was able to create 60 years ago to help alcoholics has now come of age. It is truly an American model, because it (1). maintains a use for God, (2). includes imagery of advancement and progress, and (3). is based on a fundamental notion—so dear to Americans —that something is seriously wrong with us. Like the other approaches, 12 Step models subordinate the group process to another focus, in this case, acceptance of a disorder. The Self-Help concept is perhaps having the most sweeping influence on the group therapy scene, indeed even in the society as a whole.

Of concern to creative arts therapists is that our models of practice do not readily fit into these three prevailing approaches. Our field's reliance on psychodynamic exploration, improvisational forms of artistic play, or even more skill-based, performance-oriented models, seem ill-fitted to the predominant trends in the group therapy field. Therefore, it is likely that we will experience pressure to shape our group methods toward cognitive-behavioral, interpersonal learning, or self-help models. Despite efforts to integrate the creative arts therapies with these approaches, the essential principles of creativity, play, and aesthetic form lead us in other directions (see Chapters 3 and 16). In order for creative arts therapies to remain effective participants in mental health services in the future, we will have to accommodate to these cultural norms, which are changing rapidly. Let me briefly describe some of the larger shifts in our society that may have an impact on the practice of group therapy.

The Withering of the Pledge

The concept and experience of the pledge is weakening. Previously highly bounded family units are now breaking down as we enter a mass culture, filled with information, opportunity, and complexity. A profound sense of fragmentation is occurring as people are having difficulty integrating the mass of stimuli within the highly condensed time frame of our rushed lives (Gergen, 1991).

The weakening of the sense of pledge or commitment has led each of us to look for other bases for attachment, connection, and even identity. To a large extent we are finding these in similar life circumstances or problems, such as being overweight, pregnant, divorced, abused, alcoholic, male, or female. No longer are social bonds as likely to be mediated by family or neighborhood networks, but by similarities in maladies, disorders, or misfortunes. These various parameters are dramatically portrayed in the mass media and fed to us in many ways. Our possibilities for identity are becoming commodities. The newest permutations are defined daily by Oprah Winfrey or in the most recent best selling book.

Thus a shift is occurring in the way society mediates our means of grouping ourselves. Let me review briefly the various forms of social grouping. The *pledged group* is a group in which the members are aware of themselves as a group, who have formed a mutual bond that clearly demarcates those who are in the group from those who are outside it. Pledged groups are those with explicit contracts, entry procedures, and cohesion, such as fraternities, teams, and families. In many ways we attempt to achieve a level of pledged group in our long term therapy groups. Many groups are not pledged, however. The *nascent group*, for example, which we often see with seriously ill patients, is a group that either denies or is not aware of itself as a group (Sandel & Johnson, 1983). Only the leader or therapist holds an internal representation of the group separate from the representations of each of its members. Members do not experience themselves as being a part of a larger entity. They may feel coerced by, disinterested in, or wary of the group process. I recall a colleague who finished an inpatient therapy group one day. She was thrilled by the risks taken by the severely ill patients, the presence of interaction, and the tentative engagement with the topic. Eagerly, she asked the members at the end, "What did you think of the group today?" There was silence. Their faces were blank. Finally, one member innocently asked, "What group?" (Sandel, 1980). Many of us experience the towns in which we live as a nascent group: as a source of frustration, taxes, or inadequate snow removal, the town is quite real; as a group of people to whom one belongs, and to whom one has a bond, it does not exist. We live in and tolerate this alienated social landscape, linked to the lives of characters on a favorite TV show, intimate with anonymous friends on the Internet, yet unknown to our next door neighbors.

An intermediate type of group is the *serial group* (Sartre, 1960). The members of the serial group recognize that they are connected, are in some sense a group, but only in relation to some external life circumstance that joins them. For example, people waiting at a bus stop are linked by the joint act of waiting for the same bus. People in an elevator are aware of each other, and are bound together briefly. Generally, members of serial groups have to exert energy to avoid becoming a pledged group. Thus, even though people on the same airplane may help each other in an emergency, ordinarily they treat each other as if they were merely objects taking up space. In fact, many movies show the transformation of the serial into the pledged group, as individuals board the plane or ship at the beginning of the movie, then bonding as a group after the disaster strikes.

It seems likely that pressures within our society are directing us away from pledged groups and toward serial group formations. Groups are increasingly drawn together by their connection to similar external characteristics. The most important relationship is between the person and the external marker, rather than among the members of the group. Thus, we are witnessing an overall shift in the focus of our attention from personal characteristics to external life circumstances; away from the exploration of unconscious processes and fantasy, toward problematic life conditions such as abuse, trauma, and chronic conditions. This shift to condition-based groups is a symptom of the serialization of people in a mass culture.

Viewing ourselves in terms of discrete disorder-based identifications will lead to more attention to issues of shame, acceptance, and tolerance. The purpose of group therapy will shift from providing psychological insight, to providing support, inspiration, and facilitating the "coming out" process. The creative arts therapies are well-positioned to aid in these therapeutic efforts, for the arts are a vehicle for the expression of inspiration and tolerance, an arena for the confrontation with shame, and a stage for the presentation of self to the world. No better example exists than the therapeutic effect of the AIDS Quilt, whose visual and symbolic force transcended this culture's phobias against homosexuals, illness, and death. Paradoxically, the weakening of the pledge may provide renewed opportunities for the creative arts therapies.

The Withering of Privacy

Group therapy practice is being influenced by a general trend toward openness in our culture. What has previously been seen as intensely private is now open to the public. Revelations of public figures' private lives, day time talk shows, and the National Inquirer, have created a new norm of public scrutiny. The move toward "coming out" of gays, lesbians, and AIDS victims is a parallel (and positive) development. Recently one of my patients turned in his signature sheet from an AA meeting, signed by the secretary of the meeting as "Bob S." I was struck by the fact that this nod to anonymity is now rare. Alcoholics Anonymous is no longer anonymous; it is no longer shameful to admit one is an alcoholic, in fact, it is shameless.

It may even be fair to say that there is hardly room for a private thought anymore. How can my unconscious or shameful secrets compete with the incredible things I see in movies, TV, or other media? Aggressive and sexual acts beyond my imagination are being presented to me everyday, sold on T-Shirts and in video stores. My unconscious has been franchised. More and more we look outward for information about our inner selves. Our inner lives are being shaped by the mass culture. Thus, we will see a shift from the valuing of privacy to valuing public revelations, confessions, and coming out; the code phrase, "breaking the silence," now the subtitle of nearly every book being published, is being applied to many psychiatric illnesses and life misfortunes.

The performance or exhibition tradition within the creative arts therapies are likely to flourish in this atmosphere. In the past during psychoanalytic times, our exhibitionist tendencies were viewed with great suspicion and denigration. Now, our patients' art exhibits, musical and theatrical productions, and poetry readings are embraced by the culture as courageous self-assertion, and therefore are viewed as viable forms of group treatment.

The Withering of the Expert

The consumer movement is changing the way mental health services are and will be provided. The AA, or 12-Step model, after years of being compartmentalized into substance abuse, has now broken into mainstream American society. Self-help groups are everywhere and provide support to innumerable conditions (weight watchers, arthritis, divorce, bereavement). Whereas in the past, groups were formed by a leader or professional for "therapy," the empowerment models are exerting strong influence on group therapists to provide condition-based treatments. They are also indirectly influencing leaders to be a fellow or former sufferer, or if one is not, then to be less opaque. Whereas formerly as a therapist one garnered credibility by the absence of bias, now credibility is more likely to be gained from actual experience, that is, by embracing bias. In fact, therapists without some misfortune to report are increasingly suspect and may even feel somehow inadequate. As consumers increasingly participate in mental health programs, policy-making, and public education, group therapists will find themselves needing to identify themselves more clearly in relation to the disorders they are treating. The role and autonomy of the professional may be significantly altered.

The fact that psychotherapy has been so successful in influencing our society has led, ironically, to its dissemination well beyond the boundaries of the professionals who created it. So familiar are therapeutic techniques (e.g., empathic listening, mirroring, role-playing, hitting pillows, drawing pictures) to us that self-help groups have incorporated many of them into their practice. Clients will increasingly be offered treatments that are outside the control of the professions, or regulation by the government. It is possible to imagine a time when the practice of psychotherapy has become "absorbed" by the society at large: when support groups have replaced the weekly bridge game, or family meetings have replaced the Sunday drive.

In this process, the authority of the group therapy professional will be influenced. The myth of the objective, wise leader will transform into the leader as recovering person; fellow sufferer; not charitable rescuer. For those of us who are not fellow sufferers, only the role of the witness will remain.

Here we confront a paradox for creative arts therapists: On the one hand, creative arts therapists have not generally benefited from the expert role in psychotherapy due to our lower status. On the other hand, the nature of our work is specialized, and training is based on the acquisition of expertise regarding our artistic medium. We tend to be concerned about self-help groups that incorporate arts media "without proper training," not unlike our artistic brethren who cringe at the rise of "Outsider Art." We are therefore very much a part of the culture of expertise. As a profession subject to our culture's shame dynamic, we have had to work hard to prove to ourselves and others exactly how esteemed we are, being particularly critical of our own members who do not meet our standards (see Chapter 9). How ironic that as we finally begin to mature we are confronted with the deprofessionalization of the mental health field! Creative arts therapists are therefore likely to demonstrate significant ambivalence toward the weakening of the culture of expertise.

The Withering of Time and Money

The level of accountability to government, insurance, and regulatory agencies, as well as to clients themselves, is making a significant impact on group therapy. One needs to be able to describe the nature and process of the therapy in explicit terms. Abstract processes such as the unconscious are not recognized. Quality assurance, peer review, and third party inquiries are exerting a strong influence on the practice of group therapy, toward more concrete, behavior-based, common sense thinking. It is the "show me" spirit of America come home to roost. This may have a chilling effect on group therapies that are not parsimonious and problem-focused. Esoteric, complex, and especially procedures "unproven by research" will not be supported by managed care or third party payers. Unfortunately, the creative arts therapies are vulnerable to these criticisms. Having spent three decades attempting to demonstrate how complex and esoteric our methodologies and theories are, so that we could gain the respect afforded other modalities, we are confronted with an antispecialization movement that advocates generic treatments by primary care professionals. At a time when we are finally able to articulate our unique contributions, uniqueness is eschewed.

Economic factors also make time of importance in the delivery of group therapy. With lengths of stay having dramatically decreased in both inpatient and outpatient settings, it is very difficult to do indepth work involving fantasy or unconscious material, and difficult to create sufficient cohesion and commitment in the group. Each group session needs to be self-contained as a therapeutic event. Therapeutic community and supportive group therapies have already been moved to partial hospital programs, nursing homes, and rest homes, where creative arts therapists are still being hired. In inpatient settings, the role of group therapy has been reduced to facilitating patient management through structuring the unit and diffusing dyadic interactions, and only secondarily for education. Creative arts therapy groups have the potential to be used to rapidly bolster the patient's motivation and reduce demoralization, but unfortunately this potential is rarely recognized.

In outpatient treatment, group therapy offers the opportunity for a more efficient use of resources, and indeed at the advent of managed care pundits were claiming a bright future for group therapists. However, group therapy requires some time for the development of group cohesion, and in the incredibly brief treatment reimbursed today, individual treatment provides more opportunity to quickly focus on the presenting problem. As a result, the field in general has begun to retreat into individual treatment. Creative arts therapists are therefore being squeezed from all sides, and increasingly are being pressured to cloak themselves as individual therapists credentialed under another profession (such as counseling, social work, or psychology). The paralysis of the creative arts therapy associations' ability to organize into a larger, multidivisional political entity leaves the individual creative arts therapist with no alternative (see Chapter 7).

Conclusion

The creative arts therapies began largely as group therapies, which has been attributed to their location within mental hospitals for the severely ill, in a climate where the psychiatrist was the only professional allowed to do individual therapy. Yet perhaps the link between the arts and groups is more central. The arts are an attempt at communication; they are a presentation..... to whom? To the community, the audience, the group. What is a poem if not read? A picture if not seen? A play if not performed for someone? And these performances are nearly always expressed in groups: for what else are the orchestra, the cast, the chorus, the mural, the ensemble, except the illumination of the creative spirit of communitas (see Chapter 12). The arts have always been linked to culture of the tribal group, and the retreat of creative arts therapists into individual work would be a tremendous loss.

Group therapy will continue to evolve, from its original obscurity in the 40s, to the excitement and great expectations of the 50s, to the explosion of the 60s, and the retreat of recent times. Nevertheless, the challenges to group therapy are substantially those that challenge our wider culture: how can we balance the expansion of human freedom with our needs for attachment, roots, and meaning? Identity cannot be reduced to the individual. It is inextricably a relationship between an individual and the collectivity of others, whether family, work, or society at large. We are each faced with the burden of defining ourselves in the midst of a culture that presents us with a myriad of ready-made definitions. Against these post-modern pressures to construct ourselves merely as a pastiche of the mass culture, the creative arts therapies offer us an opportunity to rediscover and assert our individuality, invited by the blank canvas or empty stage.

At 41, beset as I am by profound changes in my life, I need not look inward to discover I am beginning my mid-life crisis. My story is described in more detail in countless movies, books, and magazines. I need not introspect in order to learn about myself; I need only look up the number for my local support group hotline.

Yet, I think I will call that number. Because what is available to me on the other end is a group of people struggling with similar issues, each in unique ways. In no other setting but this—a group—can I get feedback as telling, or rediscover my basic humanness as I witness the experiences, the stories, the questions of the others. As I stumble upon my wish to help them, I find that I help myself. This is the legacy of group therapy. Imagine how this is enhanced when I can share myself through visual, musical, or dramatic images that reveal my spirit? There is no solution to my mid-life crisis, no one insight that can grasp it for long. But to have others there for me—in the rough and tumble of my life—as I confront the freedom of every morning, the weight of every act—this would be a blessing.

Chapter 11

THE CREATIVE ARTS THERAPIES IN AN ERA OF MANAGED CARE

I remember arriving at the Yale Psychiatric Institute (YPI) fresh out of college, hired as a "drama specialist." I entered the dark Medical School building, and at the end of a long corridor, the locked door awaited me. On the other side of that door was one of the most prestigious mental health treatment centers for the severely mentally ill. The year was 1973.

The YPI was one of the fortresses of the ambitious project of psychoanalysis, which had been extended into the treatment of psychotic disorders in the 1940s and 1950s by such renowned clinicians as Frieda Fromm-Reichmann, Donald Burnham, Dexter Bullard, Harold Searles, and Otto Will. The project of psychoanalysis was nothing less than complete character transformation, through deep understanding of the person, and therefore the treatment by today's standards was not only long, but incomprehensibly long. After admission, the patient and staff worked together to develop a working alliance and then to develop a diagnostic formulation and treatment plan. That generally took one year. The therapist prepared a 25 page single spaced document and the patient was presented in a case conference. Then at least another year of treatment took place, followed by a "discharge planning" conference to plan the delicate termination of treatment, which usually lasted another year.

All of the significant values of psychoanalysis were present: thoughtful silence, suspicion of action, appreciation of the uniqueness of each person, and embrace of fantasies of aggression and sexuality. The mention of a patient's name on the agenda of a staff meeting was often followed by a minute of respectful silence, as each member savored their image, seeking to find the perfect word to sum up their essence. When such a word or sentence was uttered, the room would hum with the sounds of awed reverence usually only heard at an unveiling of artwork.

It was in this environment that I, and many other creative arts therapists at the time, were mentored and tested. This environment both called out for, and subordinated, the creative arts therapies in the therapeutic arena. We were called upon largely to fill the gap of action, created by the psychoanalytic emphasis on thought, and we were subordinated because like psychoanalysis, the creative arts therapies revealed the inner life, sometimes more fully. In these ways, as our artwork adorned the walls of the hospital, and as our performances entertained, so we gave color to the ascetic practice of the dominant culture; it was, to be sure, a willing symbiosis.

The seeds of change had begun as early as 1960, when the psychiatrist Thomas Detre challenged current wisdom and opened a "short term" mental hospital within a general hospital, two blocks from YPI. Short term of course meant 4 to 6 months. I remember esteemed members of the YPI staff, steeped in the 40 year tradition of that facility, deriding the new hospital treatment as only being able to stabilize the patient.

As the influence of the psychoanalytic frame of reference continued to wane, the treatment of the severely mentally ill has increasingly been subsumed under a business-oriented culture, in which therapists and therapies are now viewed as "product lines" and clients as "commodities." The terms of the new arrangement include rehabilitation, adaptation, and motivational skills training, in distinction from the previously valued intrapsychic, existential, and personal transformation sought through treatment. We have found ourselves reformatting the goals of our work into measurable, adaptive and skill-based elements, entering terrain more familiar to our recreational and vocational colleagues. Paradoxically, the gap in treatment has now shifted to the inner life, for now the field is filled with action, and we are no longer needed for that purpose. Though we were ambivalently supported by the psychoanalytic culture, the issue now is whether anyone supports us!

Length of treatment in both inpatient and day treatment programs have been dramatically reduced, often constituting one group session for each patient. The patients' conditions have of course remained the same: devastating personal, interpersonal, and daily life challenges beyond imagining; enveloped in a culture permeated by stigma of mental illness and renewed desire to rid awareness of the problem. Care of the severely mentally ill, previously the subject of a deep mythology of ambition and even heroism, has now been reduced largely to a warehouse mentality, consisting of the housing, feeding, and medicating of the patient. Therapists' credentials and salaries for the care for these clients have thus been reduced commensurably, approaching those required of other "maintenance" workers, clerical workers, or construction workers. The rejected image of "custodial" care has been replaced by that of "case management," a dubious distinction.

Yet here a new opportunity presents itself. In the midst of these significant transformations, both clients and therapists are asking the same question, "what sustains me?" Being able to accomplish the activities for daily living is often not enough; being able to place clients in supervised housing is often not enough. A new gap has opened, once filled by the psychoanalytic dream, which the creative arts therapies are in an excellent position to fill. There is now a wide opening for inspiration, hope, and meaning in the treatment of severely ill patients, and I believe that the creative arts therapies can and are making a significant contribution to these goals, unconstrained by length of stay, managed care, or case management.

Clearly there are limits to the effectiveness of the treatment of severe mental illness, yet effective treatment does not necessarily need to target the illness. Rather, effective treatment may also strengthen the host of the illness, in this case the patient (Forrester & Johnson, 1995). The negative effects of chronic mental illness are magnified tremendously by secondary processes of (1) demoralization, (2) shame and stigma, and (3) treatment noncompliance, that is, giving up on the self, others, or treatment. The creative arts therapies can effectively impact on all three of these processes.

Therapeutic Effects of the Creative Arts Therapies

The contribution of the creative arts therapies to current treatment efforts is based on three major functions: perspective, substantiality, and reanimation. I will try to point out how these functions effectively impact on the negative effects of severe mental illness.

Perspective. The creative arts therapies encourage clients to gain perspective on their thoughts and feelings about life. Despite the persistently held belief that the arts are somehow connected with the outbreak of impulse, rather than its channeling, the arts are in fact methods of distancing from our emotions, since they are representations of thoughts and feelings (Landy, 1986; Lusebrink, 1991). To illustrate this, please compare the general mayhem of an art exhibit, poetry reading, or theatrical play with that of nearly any popular sport such as football or soccer. The former will reliably cause the average person to numb out completely, if not fall asleep, while the latter may be accompanied by loud swearing, drinking to excess, and physical fighting. The average movie will have explicit scenes of naked people having sexual intercourse, mixed in with overt violence, including images of heads being decapitated, open wounds, and people dying. Yet rarely do psychiatric units view a visit to a movie as anything less than positive, though the art therapy group might be questioned for overstimulating the patients.

Because the arts media provide an opportunity for the client to represent his/her own experience in displaced form, either on a canvas, in a dramatic role, or through a musical instrument, and then be able to discuss it with the therapist or other group members, severely ill clients are given a chance to meaningfully look at themselves, their illness, and their situation. The structuring elements within each art form (rhyme, plot, melody, color combinations) also help to organize and maintain the client's sense of self-control (Lusebrink, 1990).

Transcending the facts of one's immediate situation can take place in a single moment. For example, one client, Sarah, was able to achieve this in her first and only drama therapy session on a short term psychiatric unit. Extremely disorganized and demoralized by depression and chronic suicidality, she reluctantly participated in the drama therapy group, which after some movement warm-ups, proceeded to create a "fable." In this fable, the main character, a small girl, got herself in a lot of trouble in a far away land where she was "lost and confused," "frightened," and "afraid she would never get out." As the members of the group realized the potential parallels with their own stories, they became enthused. Sara initiated the idea that a huge boulder had fallen on the small child, crushing her. "The weight is overwhelming." She cried, 'I'd rather be dead than lie here one second more!" The rest of the group pretended to be a herd of antelope who came to her rescue and pushed the boulder off her. Sara (as the girl) cried, "Thank you so much, but look, I'm all scarred!" The group members then pointed out their own scars, and the story transformed to a competition for the worst scars. After the end of the story, in which the little girl came back home, scarred but with a whole new group of antelope friends, the group discussed the story. Sara said it was her story, and that she was amazed at the strength of the little girl to just go on. She seemed energized, relieved, and talkative. This externalization of her story placed her in perspective to it, reminding her that she was not one with her troubles, that she could not be swallowed completely by her illness. Her attitude toward treatment changed immediately after this session. She was discharged the next day to outpatient treatment, with which she successfully followed up.

Substantiality. One of the problems with the project of psychoanalysis was that its objects were the fantasies of the inner world, highly abstract entities generally not available for direct observation; they could not be touched or held. The result was that after years of treatment, one's object relations might have improved, but the concrete reality of everyday life remained unaddressed, and patients were discharged with inadequate preparation. Of course the current emphasis on rehabilitation and skill-building is the response to this problem. Yet unlike psychoanalysis, the creative arts therapies are inwardly directed treatments that do rely on concrete objects and action: the clay or sound or bodily movement. Connecting to something concrete helps counteract the feeling of so many clients that they are invisible: so deeply shamed that they prefer to disappear; so stigmatized and marginalized that they have been hidden away. From an existential perspective, the clay sculpture or videotaped play they create stands as a monument to their presence, a reassuring statement of their right to be here. In addition, the activation of their bodies that occurs in many of the creative arts therapies counters the feelings of derealization, numbing, and disembodiment present throughout the rest of their lives.

Despite the trend in many settings to spend substantial amounts of money to decorate the walls of the hospital or clinic with professional prints of sunsets or mountains, some units spend the money to properly frame and hang the pictures or poems of their clients. I had the opportunity to run an inpatient psychiatric unit where these framed paintings or poems, signed when permitted by the clients, hung on the walls. One of our patients, Robert, visited the unit whenever he was in the hospital or outpatient clinic, and each time he inevitably looked for his own poem on the wall. He said, "No matter what happens to me out there, I know I am in here on this wall, perhaps helping another patient a little bit." This was deeply reassuring to him, and we believe contributed to his dramatic increase in compliance with other aspects of his outpatient care.

Reanimation. The client has been commodified, turned into an object to be taken care of, placed, and managed. Some clients may even prefer this state, for it reduces the sense of their own free choice, and thus responsibility for the mess of their lives. Yet the deadness that subsequently sweeps through their souls eats at their ability to continue, and retreat and eventually defeat are likely to follow. The creative arts therapies tap into the client's everpresent potential as a source of creativity, humor, and love, evidenced by their creative works in our sessions. The client's role as a recipient or consumer of care shifts into the role of initiator, owner, and creator. In this sense, the creative act is an antidote to death, for it rejects the implications of destiny, and reanimates the doer inside each client. Instead of being talked at in psychoeducational lectures, or done to in a rehabilitation setting, the clients take the active role.

Dean was a deeply withdrawn, psychotic man in his 20s who walked in an extremely rigid manner, like a robot, and barely spoke. He came in and out of the hospital and showed no motivation whatsoever to work on his problems. He was passive to the point where his family had to monitor him completely, for he would not initiate any activity. One day, in a dance therapy group, as a movement was being passed around the group, instead of his usual mirroring of what everyone else was doing, he suddenly swung his hips back and forth in a lively manner. The rest of the group reacted immediately with delight, mirroring the movement back to him. He broke into a wide grin, showing all his teeth, and the group broke into applause. This event was communicated to the inpatient community at large, and soon he was referred to only by the nickname, "Hips." He could no longer pretend that he was dead, and he showed a rapid improvement in his motivation for treatment.

Empowerment is the result of gaining perspective, achieving a sense of substantiality, and reanimating the spirit. Through these steps, demoralization and shame can be countered, leading to an increased sense of hope that supports one's ability to continue with unpleasant or inconvenient treatments. No one can predict when any one of these healing moments can occur. In fact, they can occur over the course of one session, even an initial session, and thus they can be delivered within the timeframe of today's managed care environment. Sparked by a single moment of inspiration, clients may have the strength to enliven the rest of their treatment efforts.

A long time ago at the YPI, these healing processes were provided by the charisma, commitment, and optimism of the personal therapist. The narrowing of the scope of mental health treatment today has eliminated these as potential influences on the client. Surely the creative arts therapies as a means of personal exploration and understanding, of revealing deep intrapsychic material, of transforming character and self, are no longer available to severely ill clients in the current climate of managed care. Yet this should not distract us from other possible functions of the creative arts therapies, which I have briefly reviewed here: gaining perspective, achieving substantiality, and reanimation. The years have required many changes, and I have had to mourn the loss of the many good things about the old ways at the YPI. Yet through these changes and mourning, new opportunities have arisen that continue to give me hope; hope primarily for my clients, and hope, too, for the creative arts therapies.

Section III

CLINICAL AND THEORETICAL CONTRIBUTIONS

Chapter 12

THE ARTS AND COMMUNITAS

The clamoring for governmental recognition, funding, and protection has certainly created a competitive atmosphere in today's educational environment. Arts education is somehow pitted against science, sports, and the humanities, and is all too often the loser. This state of affairs has created a need to articulate the unique contributions of the arts to the individual and to society—a difficult task indeed in a world rushing headlong into the technological and pragmatic. How do we respond to the argument that *everyone* needs to read, and *everyone* will need to be able to use a computer, while only a few need make up our artistic elite? Certainly our educational dollar needs to go to the *basics*.

Eloquent spokespersons for arts in education have identified a number of benefits of an arts education. These can be briefly summarized. First, the arts enrich each of our lives. Second, arts education is necessary to create informed consumers of the arts. Third, the development of professional artists of high quality is dependent upon arts experiences beginning at an early age. The major thrust of these arguments is the signficance of the arts experience to the individual. It is natural in our individualistic culture to focus upon the benefits to the individual, rather than the benefits to groups, families, or communities. How can these effects be measured? In this article, I will attempt to articulate what I think is an extremely important contribution of the arts: namely, their impact on communal relations and societal cohesion. I will describe one community that has used the arts to facilitate its healing environment.

Reprinted from *Design for Arts in Education, 86*, 36-39, 1984 with permission of the Helen Dwight Reid Educational Foundation. Published by Heldref Publications, 1319 18th St., N.W., Washington, DC 20036. Copyright 1984.

Communitas

The feeling of belonging to a community, of recognizing the common bonds that link people together in a unit, with shared purpose, may be termed *communitas* (Almond, 1974). Whether this community is a small one, like a family or baseball team, or a large one, such as a nation or the world, the importance of communitas, in contrast to schism and conflict, cannot be overly stressed. I will describe how the arts have a unique role in the development and maintenance of communitas, though of course they are not the only means by which communitas is established.

Communitas may be established by any kind of joint, pragmatic action: such as barn-raisings, neighborhood tag sales, or community clean-ups, in which the entire community joins together to accomplish a real-world task. The feeling of togetherness that develops during these activities appears to be a direct result of this joint action.

Communitas is also the result of symbolic activities which, like the arts, have no immediate pragmatic value. Instead, the common bond among people is represented by an object or activity which symbolizes some past or imagined communal action. Activities of this type include parades, communion, singing the national anthem, and sports. The tremendous power of sports to evoke communal spirit is evident in the Olympic Games and in its attendant symbols such as the olympic torch and flame. Though sports involve competition, and tend to develop communitas within one group against another, the underlying symbolic meaning of a successful broad jump or fast swimming time is the celebration of human achievement in general. We as a culture are particularly enthralled by these physical means of expressing our communitas—what school is not capable of drawing hundreds if not thousands to its major sports events? Compare the intensity of community feeling at one of these games to that evoked by an art exhibit, a play, or a concert.

The arts as a vehicle for communitas are characterized instead by their transcendent quality. The arts are *representational* forms of expression, not merely symbols that stand for another state. The arts are forms of expression, or communication, and thus a language. Due to their nonverbal, nondiscursive aspects, they are also a universal language. But what does art uniquely represent if not the internal life, the murky, ambiguous, constantly shifting internal world of dream, emotion, and doubt. In this way, art is transcendent, since it speaks of the imaginative world. The power of this language to evoke communitas is not based on observable pragmatic actions, nor on external symbols of achievement or communal identity, but on its power to make manifest our inner being, causing us to recognize the profound similarities among us in emotion and thought; that is, our essential humanness.

The pragmatic, the symbolic, and the transcendent media for communitas each involve the recognition of a common bond; they are each cathartic experiences; and they each involve the production of an object or the achievement of a goal. The arts, however, refer to the profound internal experiences within the self, and are therefore more elusive and abstract. When a barn is raised, the purpose of the communal event is apparent. Few do not understand the excitement of a sports game or feel the stirrings of the heart when the national anthem is sung. Many, though, will say in response to a work of art: "I don't get it. What is it supposed to mean?" This is true, I believe, not because it is bad art, not because the person is ignorant, but because it is a courageous and difficult thing to do to turn one's attention inward, and explore a world so mysterious and evanescent.

Healing Communities

This intimate link between the arts and internal experience gives the arts, unlike pragmatic action or physical competition, their special relationship to healing. Historically, healing, community, and the arts were integrated events. Group singing, dancing, drumming, and dramas were the core of the community's identity and basic to its sense of psychological survival. In modern times, healing, art, and community have become distinct structures, introducing a confusing space between the arts therapies and the arts, and between healing communities and other communities. Another distinction has also developed: the differentiation of the roles of artist and audience. No longer is it necessary for the entire community to participate in the artistic event. The artist is the community's highly trained delegate, or representative, who alone enters the ethereal realms of imagination and then returns to re-create that world for the community (Cole, 1975). Communitas is achieved by each member of the audience identifying with the artist, and then *through the artist*, recognizing the universality of the human condition which all members of the audience share. This recognition and the emotional catharsis with which it occurs, constitute the healing properties of the artistic event.

Nevertheless, the arts therapist today who attempts to use the arts to build communitas within healing communities returns to this earlier structure of total communal participation, rather than relying on the specialist roles of the artist and audience. The emphasis is inevitably on the search for the artist within each member, for the discovery of their own creative moment. Not only does this emphasis bridge the artist/audience distinction, it also conflicts with other heirarchical divisions within the milieu. Communities today are almost without exception organized hierarchically into various strata which are endowed with different attributes (patient/staff; teacher/student). In the healing community these distinctions tend to be openly addressed, but an arts experience that involves total communal participation is apt to stimulate a process of active negotiation between the values of communitas and those of heirarchical control. Therein lies its power, and its vulnerability.

An Example of Communitas: Veterans Activity Milieu Program

The arts have had a significant impact on the communitas of a particular community: the Veterans Activity Milieu Program, a 28 bed inpatient psychiatric unit in a V.A. Hospital in West Haven, Connecticut. A senior staff consisting of a psychiatrist, psychologist, head nurse, social worker, and occupational therapist manage the unit. Other staff include 17 nurses and nurse's assistants, and 5 clinicians (residents in psychiatry and doctoral interns in psychology). The patients are veterans, aged 19 to 60, with severe emotional disorders (schizophrenia, manic depressive illness, posttraumatic stress disorder). Length of stay is between two and six months.

Normally, the environment of a psychiatric ward is rife with anxiety. Many patients arrive on the unit extremely distressed, exhibiting strange and threatening behavior. The hierarchies among the staff are well-established and rigidly maintained. Patients are seen as "sick," the staff as "healthy." The patients' attempts to demonstrate competent behavior are often labeled as "cover-ups" by the staff who, in their efforts to help the patients, require them to discuss their problems openly. Patients feel humiliated by such disclosures, and so resist by finding ways not to talk. Soon after patients' conditions improve, they are discharged, creating a constantly changing social environment. Both due to this flux and the tensions between the staff and patient subgroups, the development of a feeling of communitas is a major challenge.

The Veterans Activity Milieu Program has successfully used the arts media, as well as other activities, to create a powerful feeling of communitas within its membership by using pragmatic, symbolic, and artistic activities in an integrated manner. I will now describe some of these activities, which occur in both small group and community wide formats.

Small Groups: These include the drama, music, poetry, art, newspaper, and video groups. Each of these meets weekly with 4-10 patients and staff therapists. The drama therapy group involves physical warmups and improvisational roleplaying. The music appreciation group consists of listening and dancing to taped music. The other groups each produce artistic material which is presented to the wider community. The poems and artwork are posted on special display boards in the main hallway. The newspaper (consisting of articles, poems, and artwork) and the video "News Shows" are presented in the community meeting and commented on by the community.

The video group consists of the preparation of the ward "News Show," and is in many ways the cornerstone of the community's identity. A patient plays the role of the anchorperson, who reads the news. The news includes announcing ward events, introducing new patients and staff, and highlighting controversial issues (often in an editorial by the "executive vice-president"). Improvisational scenes are then devised about a variety of topics important to the community. These skits are often humorous portrayals of common situations on the ward: psychotherapy, group meetings, staff-patient conflicts. Staff and patients in the video group often reverse roles, or more importantly, stereotypical characteristics. For example, in one skit a doctor (played by a staff person) suggests that his patient will miss him terribly when he leaves. The patient denies having such a feeling, and asks the doctor if *he* has any feelings about terminating. This results in the doctor becoming upset, and tearfully pleading with his patient to admit his feelings of abandonment, since otherwise he will be considered a failure. "Everyone knows that the measure of a good doctor is that all of his patients get worse when he leaves!"

After the news show is prepared, the video group views and discusses it. The video is shown again to the entire community at the end of the week. The show is about ten minutes in length, and is often punctuated by applause or laughter from the community. The video is then used to stimulate further discussion about relevant community issues.

Community Wide Groups

Sports: The ward is structured into two basic groups, each with staff and patients. These two groups engage in ongoing competitions in volleyball, softball, and bowling throughout the year. After each game or series, trophies are awarded and speeches made in the community meeting, in a playfully exaggerated style. Staff and patients are encouraged to accept nicknames (e.g., "Spike Johnson") and banter with each other.

Pragmatic Actions: Community events also take the form of tasks with practical value. The Ward Cleanup occurs periodically. Everyone, staff and patient alike, dress in jeans and old shirts and spend two hours cleaning and scrubbing patient rooms and staff offices. Staff and patients are assigned to small teams. Nevertheless, a playful atmosphere is encouraged by the overly ridiculous costuming of the staff, playing of music, and the role of the Inspection Team, (a nurse, clinician, and patient), who wear white gloves, act mean and nasty, and who paste a large red sticker on each room as it passes inspection. Typically, the offices of the senior staff fail the inspection, to the pleasure of all concerned. Lunch and an awards ceremony complete the activity. The Moratorium Week is another community activity in which the usual schedule is set aside for reviewing the program and individual patient treatment plans, and creating new ideas. These Brainstorming Sessions alternate throughout the week with other special community activities.

Ceremonies and Rituals: These symbolic ceremonies are held during community meetings. For Veterans' Day and Memorial Day, poems are read, songs sung, pledge of allegiance given, congressman invited, speeches orated, and photographs taken. These two days are particularly important for this ward, since they link our veterans to the wider community of veterans. These ceremonies also serve to make the (usually nonveteran) staff aware of the patients' identity as a veteran, and that our work on the ward is linked to the veteran's role in society.

Other symbolic activities include prominently displaying the photographs of each patient "leader" on a special bulletin board, and giving them special roles in small group and community meetings, and in ward ceremonies. When the ward is renovated, there are ribbon-cuttings; when there is a death, there are moments of silence.

Movies and Murals: Periodically, the entire community makes a 30-60 minute movie. The community gathers and warms up by discussing ideas and practicing a communal chant. A title is chosen that reflects a particular ward theme, such as "As the Ward Turns," "Ward and Peace," or "Stop the Ward, I Want to Get Off!" Then people divide up into small groups of 2-6 to prepare completely improvised skits, which are taped one at a time in an adjoining room. A communal lunch follows, at which time the movie is replayed. Both the content and meaning of the scenes are then discussed.

Alternatively, community murals are created. The community gathers, and sits in front of two huge sheets of blank paper taped on the walls of the community room. Often each is labelled (for example: "VAMP the way it is" and "VAMP the way we'd like it to be"). After warmup exercises and discussion, everyone moves to the paper and draws individual or group drawings. Again, at the end, food is served and discussion occurs. The mural remains for a week or two, becoming the subject of ongoing commentary by community members, families, and visitors.

Discussion

These communal activities have had a significant impact on the community and its sense of itself in three principal ways: by addressing the irrational divisions between staff and patient roles, by diminishing the fears of humiliation, and by reassuring members of the community that they have meaningful contributions to make.

It is well-known that institutional processes affect the self-perceptions of each group member. In the case of the inpatient ward, specific attributes and expectations are divided between the role of the patient and that of the staff. The patient is seen as less competent, trustworthy, and intelligent, and more sick and out of control than the staff person, who is seen as more healthy, altrusitic, competent and in control. Unfortunately these institutional projections deplete each person of his/her wholeness, leaving the patient in a position of humiliation and the staff in a position of pretense.

Nevertheless, even on the Veterans Activity Milieu Program, some patients arrive who appear to fulfill our expectations of crazy, hopeless, dirty, and incompetent human beings. The staff typically react with some despair and withdrawal, which reinforces the patient's sense of low self-esteem. When Maurice came to our ward, he had spent three months on the street. Toothless, psychotic, and filthy, he arrived for psychological treatment. He was disgusting. No one talked to him. Despite this welcome, he came to the video group, and spontaneously offered to sing a song. He stood up in front of the camera, and bellowed out a plaintive but melodic version of "I left my heart in San Francisco." When the community viewed this that Friday, applause broke out two times during his song. People were amazed: even *Maurice* was a human being! In one instant, the community's expectations of Maurice changed. People smiled. They congratulated him. He responded by coming the next week to the video group and giving a lecture on the biological causes of schizophrenia. In a few short weeks, his image in the community had been catapulted from derelict to that of community leader. He became the anchorperson and performed that role competently. He organized a special feature, called "The Maurice Donahue Show," in which he interviewed other people on various topics.

While the benefits to Maurice as an individual are obvious, the impact on the community as a whole was extremely positive. Within each and every person on the ward, the part of them that felt disgusting, hopeless, and empty was deeply affected by the community's reaction to Maurice. The success of even one individual in reestablishing his humanness in the midst of a dehumanizing world reinvigorates the community's spirit and confidence in itself.

Being a mental patient involves a substantial degree of humiliation—one's life has run aground, one has acted in strange and self-destructive ways, one is now feared and seen as crazy. In the hospital one is treated as untrustworthy, one's behavior is constantly monitored, and one is required to talk openly to strangers about all of these embarassing events. One way patients attempt to hold onto some degree of self-respect is to deny their problems or refuse to talk about them. This can be a major source of resistance to treatment, which often provokes even more intrusive efforts by staff to "get him to admit his problems." The arts media can be a significant way for the patient to express his problems, if at first indirectly, as well as to express his wishes for retaliation for being subject to such scrutiny by others. The staff also use the arts media to demonstrate to themselves and the patients that inside they also contain foolish and embarassing qualities. In a series of video skits, a staff doctor played the resentful and obnoxious son of a beleaguered but equally obnoxious father, played by an otherwise depressed older patient. The son had been sent to a psychiatric hospital by the father "for no good reason." The son was also enraged that his brother had been sent to college "because you are dad's favorite!" Week after week the community watched this soap opera with rapt attention, appreciating the obvious fact that this doctor had much in common with his foolish character, and that inside this depressed older patient lay a strong, even insulting, personality. The community was able to give these scenes a coherent meaning: that it is human to fear the exposure of one's personal faults, which each of us harbor within ourselves. The open recognition of this issue gave powerful support to the building of a therapeutic norm in the community; in this case, the toleration of personal failings.

The sports activities of the milieu allow patients and staff to imagine: "I can win. I can do it. I can reach my goals." The arts activities evoke profoundly different imagery: "Look what is inside me! I am full, not an empty hole. And what I am filled with is O.K., even good. It isn't a disgusting, shameful mess." (Emunah & Johnson, 1983). To witness a community of 60 people sitting, facing a totally blank sheet of paper, or preparing for a completely unscripted movie, is an awe-inspiring moment. One time I asked what people expected will emerge in the mural. A patient responded, "I see nothing. There is nothing there." Another supported the first, "This is stupid. I can't wait to see the mess that we will make." Despite these dire warnings, which are given each time, the community does take the leap, at first tentatively, then with greater trust. At the end, when they view the mural, or see the videotaped movie, there is wonder. "It's like magic," said one chronic schizophrenic man, "First there is nothing, and then 'Kabaam!', all of this appears. Where did it come from?" "From in there, " I replied, lightly tapping his chest.

Conclusion

We do ourselves a disservice by focusing solely on the benefits that the arts have on individuals. The arts have a significant role to play in improving the quality of life of small groups, families, and larger communities. The unique contributions of the arts and arts therapy technologies to the building of communities are being explored through various model projects, and will increasingly be clearly articulated. These include work within specific communities, such as the V.A.M.P. and others (Geller et al., 1981), between different institutions (Johnson & Munich, 1975), and between different generations (Sandel & Johnson, 1987).

Communitas is fostered in many ways, and all of them can and should be used. In the Veterans Activity Milieu Program all modes of communal relating are utilized to create an atmosphere of common bond and mutual purpose, despite the pressure of our culture to reduce the importance of a milieu to its separate impact on each of the individuals within it. It is not necessary to demean or diminish the effect of sports or science on our society in order to assert the value of the arts. We do not need to enter a race against equally important aspects of human experience, however much we are encouraged to do so. The seeds of our survival do not lie in winning such a race, but in the fertile ground of the human being's need to represent and communicate his inner experience.

What does interfere with the further development of arts education and arts therapy projects is the fear of transcendence, of going beyond overt experience and entering the imaginative world. The suppression of the arts is thus related to the fear of dreaming and self-examination, and to a diminished capacity for vision and hope. Perhaps it is the presence of the nuclear threat which, by making the future uncertain, turns our dreams to nightmares, and keeps our vision constrained to the present. Or perhaps some other historical force is at work.

Nevertheless, our need to know about ourselves, to explore who we are, also seeks expression at the collective level, where I believe the arts can serve as the pathway toward communitas.

Chapter 13

THE ROLE OF THE CREATIVE ARTS THERAPIES IN THE DIAGNOSIS AND TREATMENT OF PSYCHOLOGICAL TRAUMA

Knowledge and interest in psychological trauma has been increasing rapidly in recent years, due largely to the women's movement, the Vietnam War, and a reassessment of psychoanalytic theory. The effects of physical and sexual abuse, rape, war, violence, natural disaster, terrorism, and incarceration are wide-ranging and long-lasting, mimicking many symptoms of other psychological illnesses.

The creative arts therapies have a unique contribution to make to the diagnosis and treatment of these disorders because victims of psychological trauma, like children, schizophrenics, brain-damaged, elderly, and the developmentally delayed, have difficulty expressing their experiences directly and effectively through words.

In this chapter, I will describe the major elements of trauma and its treatment, and then examine the reasons why the creative arts therapies may be a treatment of choice. I will also attempt to show how art therapy has a unique role in the early stages of treatment, and how drama therapy does in later stages.

Nature of Trauma

Psychological trauma occurs as a response to overwhelming personal threat, in which the psychic apparatus surrenders to a situation of terror and the immediacy of death. Since the most basic psychological defenses are used to preserve the survival of the self, the organization of the self is in many cases permanently altered.

First, a basic splitting or dissociation of self occurs, in which those parts of the self associated with the trauma are set off from the other parts of the self.

Reprinted from the *Arts in Pyschotherapy, 14*, 7-14, 1987 with permission from Elsevier Science.

The attempt to preserve a sense of the good self, characterized by safety, control, and gratification, leads to an encapsulation and elimination of all aspects of the traumatic situation from consciousness. While most of the time in the posttraumatic period the person is unaware of the trauma, and often has amnesia for the events, these split off parts of the self may suddenly break through into consciousness. This leads to the biphasic nature of psychological trauma, in which profound denial alternates with uncontrollable intrusion of the traumatic events through nightmares, flashbacks, hallucinations, and unconscious reenactments of the trauma (Horwitz, 1976; van der Kolk, 1987). Paradoxically, these anxiety provoking intrusions reinforce further attempts to keep the trauma at bay. The result of this splitting off of the self leads to an overall reduction in the person's ability to attach words to feelings, symbolize, and fantasize, since any link of affect with cognition may lead to the reexperiencing of the trauma. A depletion in the complexity and richness of one's inner world results. This state of psychic numbing (Lifton, 1983) or alexithymia (Krystal, 1979; Sifneos, 1975), presents tremendous obstacles for any kind of psychotherapeutic intervention that seeks to uncover traumatic memories and foster reintegration.

Second, the interpersonal effects of trauma paradoxically reinforce the victim's attachment to the victimizer. Lindemann (1944) has defined psychological trauma as "the sudden, uncontrollable disruption of affiliative bonds." The sudden loss of secure attachment leads the victim to seek any attachment. If none can be found, then a complete withdrawal from others occurs. So complete is the loss of control experienced in the trauma that victims will redefine themselves as being helpless and having no control, and evidence signs of depression, hopelessness, and learned helplessness. However, if the abusing person remains available after the abuse, the victim will often seek comfort from them, resulting in clinging, dependent relationships with the abuser. Victims have an intense need for control over themselves and others, and avoid any situation in which they may not be in total control. These sadomasochistic relationships are especially likely to occur among sexually abused children, battered women, and prisoners of war (Jaffe et al., 1986). At the same time that the victim succumbs to the abuser out of fear of abandonment, the victim may also seek to transcend or overcome the situation through identification with the aggressor. In modeling oneself after the abuser one seeks psychological safety. Unfortunately, this switch in role ensures the continuation of abuse in future relationships, where victim becomes abuser. In either case, victims of trauma often find themselves repeatedly reenacting abusive relationships throughout their lives. Indeed, it was in the study of such disorders that Freud (1959) first described what he called the "repetition compulsion."

Finally, the third major result of psychological trauma is the feeling that one's humanity has been severely compromised, that one is cut-off from the community of people, that one has been forever soiled, marked as an out-cast, or turned into a beast. The victim of trauma senses that something is gone, and only an emptiness remains. To not be whole means one is no longer a member of the human race, and therefore cannot be forgiven.

The result of these psychological, interpersonal, and social processes may include (1) hallucinations and flashbacks that appear to be schizophrenic reactions, (2) dissociative states including conversion reactions, multiple personality disorders, fugue states, or other hysterical symptoms, (3) violent outbursts and manic behavior, (4) psychosomatic symptoms, (5) addictive behaviors, or (6) social withdrawal, passivity, and depression (van der Kolk, 1987). These symptoms are often misdiagnosed as psychological illness rather than delayed manifestations of traumatic experience, leading to misguided treatment for these patients.

Diagnosis and Treatment

The diagnosis of posttraumatic stress responses from childhood physical and sexual abuse or war trauma has been problematic. In many cases, due to the profound denial and dissociation at the time of the trauma, the patient does not remember the event. Second, in cases where the patient does remember, she/he often doesn't want to admit it because it is humiliating, frightening, or may have a harmful effect on loved ones (such as the abusive parent). Third, many of the symptoms do not emerge for months or even years (Figley, 1985; van der Kolk, 1987). Most therapists look for the precipitating events in the preceding several months, and tend to attribute current symptoms to current events. Thus, reports of traumatic stress responses are interpreted as signs of standard psychological illnesses such as schizophrenia or affective illness. Many Vietnam veterans with posttraumatic stress disorders, for example, were initially diagnosed as schizophrenic or depressed when they presented themselves to VAs in the early 1970s. Fourth, even when the traumatic event is clearly reported, therapists may underestimate its importance. Many therapists have been influenced by Freud's reinterpretation of traumatic processes as expressions of unconscious fantasies and wishes, rather than actual traumatic events (Freud, 1959; Masson, 1984). Thus a patient's report of sexual abuse by her father may be interpreted as a normal expression of oedipal longing, or an expression of the positive transference to the male therapist. Another reason that therapists minimize the possibility of actual trauma, other than allegiance to Freud, is that the acknowledgment of an actual traumatic event places a limit on the therapist's ambitions: if your patient's condition is caused only by unconscious wishes and misguided thoughts, it can be alleviated by insight and interpretation. If the pain is caused by an actual event, however, there is nothing you can do in psychotherapy to erase what happened, whether it be a sexual assault or a Vietnam atrocity. Awareness of the wide range of symptoms that can be produced by traumatic events and persistence in exploring the possibilities of trauma are necessary for the proper assessment of traumatic conditions. Only then can treatment begin.

Stages in Treatment

Treatment of victims of psychological trauma involves a three stage process: First, the patient needs to gain access in a safe and controlled way to the traumatic memories, to overcome his denial or amnesia for the events. Second, the patient needs to engage in a lengthy working-through process in which the trauma can be acknowledged, reexamined, and conceptualized, resulting in a modification of its intensity. The trauma is transformed from an intrusive reliving of the event into a memory that can be recalled when one wishes. Third, the patient needs to rejoin the world of others through interaction with other trauma victims, to find forgiveness from others for what happened, and to be able to go on with one's life.

Let me discuss how the creative arts therapies can make unique contributions in each of these stages.

Stage 1: Gaining Access to the Traumatic Memories

Due to the dissociation of the memories of the traumatic experience, and the resulting disruption of the patient's ability to translate feeling states into words (i.e., alexithymia), gaining access to traumatic events is exceedingly difficult. Nevertheless, this difficulty may not only be due to these psychological defenses, but may in fact also be due to the nature of the neurological processes responsible for the coding of the event. One of the truly remarkable facts about traumatic memories is that when they erupt in flashbacks or nightmares they are often an exact replica of the event, down to every detail, as if they were photographed (van der Kolk et al., 1984). Unlike other memories which vary slightly each time they are recalled, traumatic events are recalled exactly the same each time. Neuropsychologists have established that certain people have "photographic memories" (Gardner, 1974; 1982), and brain researchers such as Penfield and Perot (1963) have found that electrical stimulation of the brain can reproduce these kinds of photographic memories. Much evidence suggests that humans have two forms of memory encoding: one is a primitive visually-based memory that records an event as a whole, in exact detail. The problem is that such coding is very cumbersome and inflexible: one memory is completely separate from the next, and access to it is dependent upon similarity of sensory stimuli.

The second form of memory is based on coding experience according to a hierarchical system of constituent parts, so that each memory is really a reconstruction from common elements. This type of memory develops as the child's cognitive capacity increases, and is more flexible and based on associative links among phenomena. For example, a specific memory may be encoded under "summertime," "on vacation," "at the beach," and "sunburn."

It is likely that at times of overwhelming stimulation and terror in the moments of trauma, that the more highly developed cognitive system is bypassed and the event is recorded in photographic form, as a global record, unintegrated conceptually with other memories through normal associative links. It therefore is not available to be processed, worked through, and continually transformed as are other aspects of our memories. It is a fragment that emerges as a whole whenever stimulated by similar sensory input (e.g., startle responses of combat veterans to loud noises). Much of our early childhood experience relies on this type of coding, which may be responsible for our amnesia of our early years. The process of splitting may in fact be the psychodynamic equivalent of this neuropsychological shift in memory encoding.

Aside from the highly visual aspects of these memories, they have strong sensorimotor qualities. Schimek (1975) has noted that unconscious mental representations may in fact be events recorded in sensorimotor form, with strong visual and kinesthetic qualities. Reliance on verbal and discursive forms of thought interferes with access to these unconscious thoughts, which is why techniques such as hypnosis, dream-work, and free association are used in psychoanalytic therapy. Indeed alexithymia is the inability to translate these representations at the visual and sensorimotor levels into meaningful symbolic and verbal representations.

The Special Role of Art Therapy. Art therapy has a special role in gaining access to traumatic images and memories. Because the encoding of traumatic memories may be via a "photographic," visual process, a visual media may offer a unique means by which these may come to consciousness. In fact, reports of clinical and research efforts in the areas of child abuse have often used patient drawings (Greenberg & van der Kolk, 1987). Though traumatic memories can also be generated by particular sounds or intense body exercise, these modalities may overwhelm the patient (Kolb, 1984). The art work, by being distanced from the body of the patient, seems to provide a safer media for expression of traumatic images (Golub, 1985).

For example, V. was a Vietnam veteran who had been hospitalized for psychosis. He was given a diagnosis of schizophrenia. V. never spoke about his experiences in Vietnam, and his war experiences were essentially overlooked by the treatment team. When in an art therapy group he drew the picture shown in Figure 3 in response to the theme of "the Armed Services," the therapist was alert enough to ask him more about the threatening image. For the first time he divulged the fact that he had lost several of his close buddies in a misguided attack by our own airforce, or "friendly fire." In other drawings following this, V. demonstrated that the war had been a major factor in his decompensation.

Another Vietnam veteran with posttraumatic stress disorder had frustrated the staff because of his refusal to talk about the war, in which he had seen much combat. On other topics he was quite talkative and intelligent. In art therapy he began to draw pictures such as the one in Figure 4, directly recording the killing of Vietnamese, though he or the American forces were always half off the picture. He continued to refuse to speak about these incidents, though he kept drawing more pictures. Only through the artwork was his fear contained enough to be able to express what happened.

Figure 3

Figure 4

Many treatments of trauma victims utilize techniques such as hypnosis and sodium amytal interviews that attempt to induce a dissociative state, in order to access the trauma (Kolb, 1984). The problem with these approaches is that the patient's sense of control is compromised. In art therapy, the dissociation occurs between the self and the content of the picture, but without impairment to the patient's state of cognition. The sense of personal control and integrity, so important in treatment, is therefore better preserved.

Stage 2: Working Through

The purpose of the working-through phase is to change the coding of the traumatic event from a global, all or nothing representation to one that is integrated into the rest of the personality, is connected via associative links to other thoughts and feelings, and is therefore brought under the client's control. Intrusive reliving of the event is transformed into mere remembering.

As van der Kolk (1987) notes, verbal therapists encounter many problems with this phase of therapy. First, there is the danger of too rapid disclosure, leading to greater fears of being overwhelmed, embarrassed, and feelings of being out of control. Second, clients are often incapable of presenting "symbolic" forms of thought requested by the therapist such as dreams, fantasies, or transference feelings. Third, presenting alexithymic individuals with a situation in which feelings are evoked, when they are not capable of articulating them, will in fact stimulate an intensification of their somatic, addictive, and avoidant symptoms. Fourth, intimacy with the therapist is threatening because either they anticipate reenacting the traumatic event, or if they disclose what they have done, the therapist will be disgusted with them. The direct relationship with the therapist becomes fraught with too great intensity, leading to avoidance, greater denial, and termination of therapy.

> Karl was a 32 year old Vietnam veteran who was hospitalized after trying to shoot himself with a shot gun. He had been a medic in Vietnam and had had substantial experience with combat. He had tried to kill himself several times, suffered from flashbacks and intrusive imagery of Vietnam, and had become alcoholic. He was misdiagnosed as having major depression and spent two years in therapy without discussing his Vietnam experience. When as his therapist I finally began to inquire about his horrifying experiences in Vietnam, he began to miss sessions, became more paranoid and suspicious of our relationship, and began to drink more heavily. As I became more convinced of the importance of his traumatic experiences in Vietnam, I pressed him harder to discuss them. He then brought in a number of books, articles, and poems about the war "for you to read." I interpreted these actions as defensive intellectual maneuvers, and encouraged him to be more direct. He responded by a marked regression which included quitting his job, going on a drinking binge, and getting into a serious fight in a bar in which he was hurt. I finally gave up my insistence on discussing Vietnam, and we returned to other subjects.

> If I had understood his giving me books and poems about combat as an attempt to establish a safe transitional space within which to talk about Vietnam, rather than as an avoidant maneuver, I might have been more successful in helping him.

Normally, dreams, fantasies, and the transference provide a transitional space in which the therapist and patient can safely play with ideas and feelings that emerge in the process of discovery (Winnicott, 1971). What the creative arts therapies offer is a concrete and impersonal transitional space of the artwork, music, role-play, or poetry, that is more safe than the abstract and personal one of the transference. The need to disown and deny the affects and memories of the trauma, and to remain in control of them, are more effectively accomplished when these images arise on paper, in a dance, or in playing music.

In this way, the patient can play out, at arm's length, the gamut of feeling and impulse, and be helped by the creative arts therapist to modulate the directness and intensity of expression. Thus the creative arts therapies provide an externalized structure for transitional phenomena for which the patient is not wholly responsible. Instead of the discussion of a feeling, one has a discussion of a picture of a feeling, a less threatening situation for the patient because the picture is concrete and external to the self. All of the creative arts are effective in this stage of treatment because each allows a reworking, over and over again, of traumatic experience, at times indirectly, at times directly.

Stage 3: Rejoining the World

In addition to being cut-off from oneself, and from the therapist, the traumatized individual often feels a sense of alienation from the world. Becoming fully cognizant of the past and accepting the fact that it happened does not eliminate his/her feelings of personal disgust and self-hatred. It is therefore not surprising to find that after gaining access to memories of the traumatic event, and spending some time working them through, group therapy with other trauma victims has been the most effective treatment (van der Kolk, 1987). Group therapy provides what individual therapy with a nonabused therapist cannot—an understanding that one is not alone, that one is still human, and that one can give to others, despite what happened.

While all the creative arts therapies as well as verbal rap groups can be effective in this stage, theatrical forms of drama therapy have particular promise, for theatre's basic structure and purpose is to express the communal aspects of traumatic experience (Cole, 1975; Chapter 12). Empirical evidence for this view comes from the large number of groups that have used theatre as a forum for public confession, a means of "coming out," and for raising consciousness about their particular disability or unique experience. Prisoners, Vietnam veterans, ex-psychiatric patients, drug addicts, physically handicapped, and adult children of alcoholics have formed troupes to present aspects of their lives to public audiences (Johnson, 1980; Emunah & Johnson, 1983). The importance of performance before an audience cannot be underestimated in the treatment of victimized patients.

> Transformation of self-image is heightened in these self-revelatory performances... Self-revelation by cast members affects the misconceived images a public audience often has of mental patients, presuming their problems to be foreign and bizarre. A kinship is established between the audience and actors. For the group members, who perceive themselves as alien, the audience's identification with their struggles brings about a sense of belonging to the larger community rather than exclusion from it. The self, already part of a small group, now becomes part of the world. (Emunah & Johnson, 1983, p. 238)

An example of the power of theatrical performance comes from an inpatient unit at a VA hospital, where a rap group for Vietnam veterans had been meeting for many months:

The veterans had gained a great deal from the discussions about the war, their feelings of self-loathing, their anger at the world and other Americans, and their acknowledging the horrible events in which they had participated. Naturally, they continued to go over and over these subjects. Finally, one veteran said, "We understand what happened to us. But when are we going to be able to tell THEM?!" Since several patients were simultaneously in a drama group on the ward, the idea of presenting a play was suggested. The play, titled *"A Nam Vet's Family Album,"* was developed from improvisations of its members and rehearsed over a period of three weeks. It was performed initially on the ward to the staff and a visiting congressman. Then the group performed the play in a large auditorium for the entire hospital, where it was videotaped, and then again for the public at a local festival.

These performances had a profound impact on the veterans, who felt, many for the first time, that they had been accepted for what they were. One veteran invited his daughter to the performance, and afterwards when she told him that she was proud of him, he cried and said, "This is the first time my daughter has seen me doing something worthwhile—the first time she has seen who I can be." The play was a rite of passage for these veterans, a "coming out" as victims of a tragedy that simultaneously signified their transcendence of its effects.

The very nature of drama as a more verbal media suggests its particular importance in the later stages of treatment, after the existence of the trauma has become conscious and the patient has achieved some degree of personal tolerance. Drama, as well as poetry, become preferable modes of expression for the patient wishing to communicate directly with the world, represented either by members of a small group or a public audience. The desire to confess, to share, and to warn others of the consequences of the trauma is a deeply felt one. Beyond this desire lies the hope that through such confession one will receive forgiveness, and be brought back into the communal embrace.

Conclusion

Thus the creative arts therapies can be useful as diagnostic and psychotherapeutic tools for victims of psychological trauma. Unique aspects of these nonverbal media are applicable at each stage of treatment: initially gaining access to traumatic memories, working-through and integrating the split-off parts of the self, and finally in rejoining the world of others. Due to the manner in which the trauma may be neurologically encoded in visually dominated forms, art therapy has a special place in the assessment and early stages of treatment. In the later stages of treatment, due to the need for reintegration with one's community through direct communication, confession, and education, drama and poetry in group or performance formats seem to be especially useful.

Yet why do the creative arts therapies have such an intimate tie to trauma? In this paper, I have explored several cognitive, developmental, and psychodynamic reasons. But perhaps there is a more basic link. It is probable that art originally developed as a means of expression of, and relief from, traumatic experience. Art, song, drama, and dance in primitive times were motivated by a need for catharsis and for gaining control over threats to the community or to the individual. The arts abound at times of nightfall, death, birth, war, and natural disaster, for they help to encapsulate terror. If psychological trauma is the origin of art, is it any wonder that the creative arts therapies hold so much promise as a reparative force?

Chapter 14

CREATIVE ARTS THERAPISTS AS CONTEMPORARY SHAMANS: REALITY OR ROMANCE?

Shamanism has taken on new interest among mental health practitioners in recent years (Harner, 1982). It is common to see workshops and presentations devoted to the comparison of psychotherapy with shamanism. Nevertheless, the relationship of the creative arts therapies to this age old tradition has been the subject of some debate. The terms of this debate center on whether the comparison of creative arts therapists to shamans is an illuminating and helpful one, or rather a romantic reach into the past in order to bolster our current status.

Joseph Moreno (1988), a music therapist, has proposed that creative arts therapists are in fact contemporary shamans, and would benefit from more closely following shamanic principles, which he views as profoundly more holistic and integrated than current practices. He underscores the continuities between the arts therapies and shamanic traditions, including the use of multiple arts media, rhythm, enactment, relaxation and trance, guided imagery, and therapist participation. Acknowledging these parallels, he believes, will enhance our understanding of relationships among the creative arts therapies, and between them and other psychotherapies. Moreno contrasts the shamanic tradition with the compartmentalization of professional fields in modern society. He concludes by noting the absence of understanding of the cultural bases of our work, and encourages us to avoid insularity by learning about the arts in other cultures and during other historical times.

Shaun McNiff (1979; 1981; 1988), an art therapist, has for many years endorsed the importance of shamanic values in the practice of creative arts therapies. He asserts that modern culture's repression of the religious instinct and the values of the spirit and the soul is responsible for the renewed inter-

Reprinted from the *Arts in Psychotherapy, 15*, 269-270, 1988 with permission from Elsevier Science.

est in shamanism. He declares that specialization will not work and calls for the integration of the creative arts therapy disciplines. The value of the image of the shaman for creative arts therapists today is that it helps us "to access the deeper centers of the spirit and bring back the abducted soul" (p. 291). He uses the shamanic metaphor in practice through action-oriented methods using body movement, rhythm, storytelling, dreaming, free vocal expression, and image making. Believing that "the creative arts therapies are unconscious manifestations of indigenous religious impulses," he holds a conception of the therapeutic process as sacred and spiritual, consistent with shamanic traditions that view illness as a loss of soul.

Claire Schmais (1988), a dance therapist, counters these arguments by pointing out the many differences between shamans and creative arts therapists in their social contexts, notions of illness, role of the healer, and nature of interventions. Shamans have a unique social status as inspired religious figures, attained through an initiatory illness, as opposed to creative arts therapists who are one of many "practitioners," trained in standardized programs, and who perform their role for personal monetary gain. Shamans usually initiate the treatment process through self-intoxication with drugs, and then perform possession rituals in which they call upon the ancestral spirits, *for* the patient. Such a model clearly departs from actual practice of most creative arts therapists, revealing the comparison with shamanism as a *metaphor*. This metaphor is surely linked as much to the purportedly esteemed *role* of the healer in society as to actual therapeutic practice. In contrast to Moreno and McNiff, Schmais views the differentiation among the therapies and between areas of experience as useful. She warns of the potential dangers of fusing the arts and religious experience within the shamanic tradition, and reminds us of the need for in-depth training in each art form.

At heart, this is a debate not of facts but of values. The question is not whether creative arts therapists *are* contemporary shamans, because clearly there are many differences, but whether they *should* be. One's position stems I believe from one's attitude to the prevailing direction of our cultural development—toward greater specialization and differentiation of functions. Art, religion, and medicine are now clearly differentiated. Some view this as progress. Others, as regrettable. For the latter, shamanism is part of the antidote to this compartmentalization of life, and the creative arts therapies are seen as serving a potentially healing influence in the overall resurgence of human spirit. In this sense, the figure of the shaman is proposed as an ideal toward which we should strive, as opposed to other models such as teacher, servant, scientist, or good mother. To those who view the increased differentiation as progress, the refusion of science and spirit is clearly a retreat to the past, and the ideal of the shaman an unnecessarily exalted one, serving only to soothe our frustrations in competing in a world of research and quality assurance. Clearly, one's setting may have significant impact on one's view: as a private practitioner or faculty member in a training program, one is free to make inspiring associations to shamans; in a traditional hospital or clinic, one is more likely to keep such comparisons to oneself.

If neither the current situation of trying to clone ourselves as psychiatrists or analysts, nor seeking our culture's shadow side in the tribal shaman, seem satisfactory, (indeed both seem to be symptoms of a subtle grandiosity or search for power), then what are we to do? Eleanor Irwin (1988), a drama therapist, in commenting on this debate, gently reminds us of the essential elements of psychotherapy, which, more than techniques, are the therapist's presence, warmth, genuineness, and positive regard. Fundamentally, the arts therapist "must be good at relating, naming, and teaching, and be the sort of person others want to confide in and learn from" (p. 296). Irwin believes that it is a matter of personal preference whether one uses a shamanic or clinical model.

The center of this debate probably lies beyond the disciplines of creative arts therapies, at the level of helping professionals in general, or even of the broader culture. I agree with McNiff that the interest in shamanism is being driven by the repression of creativity in the wider culture, rather than by specific anthropological or theoretical considerations. Shamanism has in fact become a code word for anything that stirs passions or relates to the spiritual world—a use so broad that everything from psychotherapy to rock and roll are seen as shamanic. Recently even the Internet has been imbued with shamanic power, through which the average soul can travel through virtual realities, and access transcendent spaces. As we increasingly orient ourselves to the commodified experiences presented to us through mass media, as life becomes an arrangement of surfaces, the need for a structure within which we may recover the particularity of our own depths becomes stronger. I believe this debate signals the need to achieve a higher form of integration between these contrasting sensibilities of surface and depth, an integration we have not clearly glimpsed yet.

My own continued excitement about being a creative arts therapist is that this field, perhaps more than any other, is where this integration is going to take place. In fact, the vision of creative arts therapists as embodying both science and soul, logic and magic, is really a vision of what we hope for *all* human beings. Surely both orientations are steps on the way toward finding out who we are and how we can contribute meaningfully to the suffering members of our society. Clearly our commitment to the shamanic identity will always be circumscribed and mediated by many other simultaneously-held identifications.

So I ask you: how are we to preserve the subtlety of our emotional and spiritual lives in the midst of a world ever more external, quantified, and demystified? How does one integrate the transcendent gaze of the shaman with music from the compact disk player; the timelessness of the spirit world and marking the end of the session with the beep from one's digital watch?

We are only beginning to find our way.

Chapter 15

A GENDERED PROFESSION

What is the relationship of the creative arts therapies to women? Why are 90–95 percent of creative arts therapists women? Why is the percentage of men higher in the "more verbal" creative arts therapies of drama and poetry? Are these gender issues relevant to the challenges facing our profession in establishing our identity or legitimacy?

Much of the difficulty that our field has encountered may, in fact, be explained by the way our sexist culture views women, health care, and the arts. Women predominate in most of the positions in health care, most of which are underpaid compared to those in industry, business, and administration. Women are also the people who continue to take care of our children: *single parent families* is really a euphemism for families headed by women. Women, and men with a stronger feminine identification, make up the majority of people trained in the arts. Most of the psychotherapy clients in the country are women, and mothers are the only parents who show up at child guidance clinics with their children. Men are more likely to stay away from therapy, from the arts, from expressing their feelings, from exploring their internal worlds. Men prefer to control the arts, control the health care field, and prepare to do battle...

Sunday morning: it was early and thankfully still quiet on my wooded suburban street. Soon it began. As I looked through the window in my living room, I could see them coming. Dressed in green battle fatigues, armed with grenades, rifles, machine guns, and combat equipment of great variety, the latency age boys in the neighborhood edged forward. Since there was no enemy, they soon turned on each other. Blaaaaa! Craasshh! Screaming and bashing and then hitting for real. Crying and then running home to mommy. Then back for more. Their pistols are electronic now.

Later in the day, the male teenagers emerged from their parents' garages with their motorcycles and motorbikes: Grassssstt! Rrrrummm! Up and

Reprinted from the *Arts in Psychotherapy*, "Introduction to the Special Issue on Women and the Creative Arts Therapies," *16*, 235-238, 1989 with permission from Elsevier Science.

down the street. Blaaa. Rrreeeee! Until they fell off and got hurt. Then home to be given bandages, advice, and soup by their mothers.

Finally the fathers emerge. Yes, with their chain saws, symbols of their fierce determination to defeat some tree, two-by-four, or rockpile. Blaasssst! Churrrerer! Cutting. Hammering. All day. Until they are tired. "Honey, will you bring out a beer? *Bgruuhtiyty.* Honey, when will dinner be ready? *Blaaaaa.* What I can't hear you. *Blaasss.* Not that again. *Churrerer!* All right, I'm coming."

Where in all this noise is the impulse for caring? for aesthetic value? For introspection? Not to be found. Yet I must mediate my criticisms of my own gender.... (I am aware of the irony of my writing about a female profession of which I, as a male, am a member.) There are some characteristics—beyond design of machinery and road repair—that men do offer society. Women's attunement to interpersonal connection often expresses itself in closely-knit and therefore smaller social units. Men are attuned to larger social organizations and their hierarchical structures, and are usually less threatened by expressions of competition. Occasionally, these attributes are adaptive. For example, there are less than a dozen orders of monks which have remained stable over many centuries, in contrast to literally hundreds of orders of nuns, who keep splitting off from one another.

Yet, let not these observations minimize the obvious differences between women and men. When we mention *spouse abuse*, we really mean men beating their wives; when we mention *child abuse*, we usually mean men sexually molesting their daughters; when we talk of *sex between therapist and client*, we mean male therapists using their power to sexually abuse their female clients. When we talk of *violent crimes* in this country, we are really talking about things men do. Women are taking care of other people in our culture, are taking incredible abuse, and are doing so at very low wages. Men are in control, being better paid, but are emotionally lost, whether they are in prison or out.

All of our efforts as creative arts therapists to document our contributions, to develop our training programs, and to write sophisticated, scholarly articles, are constrained by the greater value our society places on control vs. empathy, external vs. internal concerns, managing vs. caring, aggression vs. understanding, business vs. the arts, ... men vs. women. In this sense, our struggle is part of a larger and perhaps even more important struggle, not merely that of the women's movement, but supporting the values that women have come to represent. This is a struggle to which all of us arts therapists, male and female, can contribute. A number of creative arts therapists have made such contributions in scholarly form.

For example, Ellen Handler Spitz (1989) summarizes recent advances in psychoanalytic theory by two female French analysts, Janine Chasseguet-Smirgel and Joyce McDougall, who attempt to articulate an autonomous theory of female sexuality not derivable from male sexuality, particularly the primacy of the phallus. They point out that the primacy of the phallus is linked to the questionable emphasis on sight over other senses (tactile, olfactory, kinesthetic) in the development of the child's representational world. Spitz discusses the relationship of perversion to artistic expression, and points out important implications for creative arts therapists. Such revisions in theory are necessary if women are to gain equal recognition in scholarly arenas.

Mary Lynne Ellis (1989) has examined the effects of cultural gender-specific expectations on women, particularly the emphasis on beauty and the idealized female images of the "little girl," Miss America, or sex idols that "denies women authentic reflections of themselves." The painting, in art therapy, can be viewed as a form of reflection to the self, and as such, may have an important healing influence in helping women find such authentic glimpses of their true identities. Ellis describes three women's journeys that illustrate how the painting becomes a territory over which the woman has control, within which she can explore unique images of herself outside of cultural pressures.

Susan Sandel (1989), in *On Being a Female Creative Arts Therapist,* examines the issues of unequal pay, low self-esteem, sexual harassment, dress, and mothering and emphasizes the challenges these present to female creative arts therapists, who must learn "to forgive one another for our need to survive in a less-than-perfect world." Sandel reminds us not to underestimate the intensity of the projection and fantasy that our work attracts, nor our efforts to minimize our subsequent distress. She suggests, for example, that the term "erotic transference" may at times be used to describe events that are closer to being sexual harassment by colleagues or clients.

Marlene Talbot-Green (1989) presents a strong feminist critique of the continuing sex bias in scholarship by universities, among professional journals, and in research, noting the relative absence of articles with a feminist perspective in creative arts therapy journals and in conference presentations. She questions the attempt by creative arts therapists to imitate uncritically the forms and structures of the physical sciences, and asserts that concepts of objectivity, neutrality, and quantification are the results of a primarily patriarchal perspective that need not be followed in rigorous scholarship. Indeed, she points to evidence that these methods actually cover up other types of bias. She calls for the development of new methods of research not so dependent upon these male models. Finally, she notes the "personal inability to acknowledge and incorporate the feminine, the soft, the vulnerable, into the psyches of individual researchers and therapists."

Harriet Wadeson (1989) also questions whether male pressures are shaping the female arts therapy profession. She raises the concern that in our attempt to fit in with the male establishment and male-dominated research traditions, we may be short-circuiting ourselves. Wadeson refers to Carol Gilligan's (1982) work on differences in male and female moral values, contrasting male adherence to principles and rules with the female's maintenance of connection and personal responsibility to others. Wadeson encourages us to assert the images of connection rather than quantification, and in so doing "become the architects of our own work."

Beyond the feminist critique of dominant cultural biases, creative arts therapists are turning their attention to the treatment of conditions unique to women. In *Empowering Women with Premenstrual Syndrome through the Creative Process*, Rebecca Phillips and Marcia Rosal (1989) review the literature about this poorly understood condition and then describe how art therapy can be helpful to women with PMS. They emphasize the importance of providing support and teaching coping strategies. Art therapy can be particularly helpful in improving self-esteem, teaching relaxation, gaining a sense of personal control, and in understanding the personal and interpersonal dimensions of the experience. Phillips and Rosal demonstrate the need to use our methods for uniquely female problems that have traditionally been minimized by male-oriented practitioners.

Nora Swan-Foster (1989) describes how art therapy can deepen the experience of prenatal bonding, separation through childbirth, and postpartum bonding in pregnant women. She utilizes a series of four pictures focusing on self, fear, transformation, and closing mandalas, and examines them for color, content, and placement in an assessment of psychological problems that may be developing during the pregnancy. Her carefully presented case descriptions illustrate how negative emotions are diffused and how women can become more receptive and tolerant of the progress of their pregnancies.

Barbara MacKay (1989) addresses the drama therapy of sexual assault. Using face painting, story-telling, dance-drama, and performance, MacKay helps her clients to access traumatic memories, modify their intensity, and rejoin the world by discovering forgiveness and communal bonding among fellow victims. Issues of self-blaming, denial, and the potential for the assault issues to overwhelm other important ones are discussed.

Barbara Sang (1989) illuminates the special psychotherapeutic needs of women artists. She describes how women are more often expected to be caretakers of creative artists than creators themselves. The low self-esteem that can develop among female artists results from not being taken seriously and not being given recognition. She believes that it is important as a therapist to show real interest in the artwork of her artist-clients, and even to attend exhibitions, performances, and to ask them to bring in their artwork. She supports women's efforts toward autonomy, including addressing physical and financial issues in the therapy.

Ellen Levine (1989) presents a series of reflective dialogues with her clients in a women's art therapy group. From their voices comes a powerful message of caring and growth, tied closely to what is best in the female spirit. Levine emphasizes the quiet, holding, female environment of the group setting, in which the therapist remains emotionally present but unintrusive. Levine reminds us that much of therapy is the "being there," beyond any specific techniques or interventions.

Creative arts therapists must grapple with the inevitable tangle between gender and other aspects of our professional life. This dialogue is critically important to our development as a mature profession, for it is important to be able to differentiate gender issues and the arts therapies. Are the principles of logic and the scientific method really male? Are beauty and caring really female? Or have these aspects of life become associated with gender as a byproduct of a more fundamental struggle among symbols and power? I think so. Rigorous thinking is not male. Ethical practice is not female. Standards of scholarship need not be altered for sexual politics.

And yet, it is hard to ignore the influence of gender. Each of us must confront the meaning of being one sex or the other: to challenge the unnecessary limitations that strong biological and cultural expectations place on us, and yet to accept and make peace with the uniqueness of our instincts. For myself, this means the search for an appreciation of who I am as a male—past the political stereotypes, the guilt about our sexist culture, the fear of women's annihilating powers, and discovering what my body already knows and remembers: the comfort in being part of a team, the reassurance in the physical contact of sports, the deep instinct for protecting the home when I cut firewood or patrol the perimeter of my yard, and the thrill of adventure when I have looked out of my tent at the cold night, far from home, stars beckoning the hero, fearless, a thrill made possible by being once removed from the earth, by being a man.

An open, public dialogue concerning the burdens that our sexist culture has placed on women in the creative arts therapy profession will draw out the resources of our mutual support, and, paradoxically, free up other, still unheard, voices among us, particularly those of male and gay/lesbian creative arts therapists.

I am proud and grateful to be a male creative arts therapist. I have found a profession that has been healing for me, where my male instincts have been both legitimized by, and subordinated to, a process in which I play and dream, act silly or cry, with people who are suffering, helping them as best I can. In these basic ways, our work transcends the distinctions made by either men or women.

Chapter 16

THE ARTS AS PSYCHOTHERAPY

The arts have always been used to express the strong personal feelings of pain, fear, and joy, to communicate to others about the world, and to celebrate the acts of one's community. When we were put to sleep as infants by our mother's soft singing, it was healing; when we wrote forlorn poetry late at night during our adolescence, it was healing; and when we danced together in the midst of our family at our wedding, it was healing. In the last thirty years, a new profession—the creative arts therapies—has developed that attempts to build on the natural healing of the arts to create a therapeutic tool with a scientific and psychological basis.

The creative arts therapies are the intentional use of art, music, dance/movement, drama, and poetry by a trained therapist in psychotherapy, counseling, special education, or rehabilitation. There are approximately 15,000 trained creative arts therapists in the United States, and several thousand in other parts of the world. Creative arts therapists are trained in specialized university programs, either four year bachelor's degrees, or two year Master's degrees. Several Ph.D. programs also exist. All therapists are required to have substantial training in the particular art form before beginning their training, either in university courses or through professional experience as an artist, dancer, actor or musician. Then they study psychology, learning theory, psychotherapy, and are trained in the special techniques, methods, and theories that have been developed to integrate the art forms with the healing process. Each therapist learns how to analyse the client's behavior in their particular art media: the art therapist learns what different colors, lines, forms, patterns, and placements mean; the dance therapist learns how to assess different types of movement patterns, energy levels, and use of body parts; and the music therapist learns how rhythm, harmony, pitch, timbre, and meter reflect different personality characteristics. Each discipline has developed sophisticated assessment procedures that give the therapist important information about different clients with different diagnoses.

Creative arts therapists work in many different settings. Many work in institutions such as psychiatric hospitals or outpatient mental health clinics where they serve as members of the treatment team. In some locations, their services may be part of the daily activities of the treatment, and in others they are specifically referred and the client is separately billed. Creative arts therapists also work in special education settings for the emotionally disturbed and mentally retarded, where they may be one of several adjunctive services offered the client. Increasingly, creative arts therapists are being employed in physical rehabilitation settings, working with the traumatic brain injured, physically handicapped, or substance abusers. Many creative arts therapists also work in nursing homes and geriatric centers. Finally, creative arts therapists are increasingly working independently in private practice where they offer their services for a fee, and act as primary therapists. Creative arts therapists are credentialled by their national associations and are referred to as registered or certified. In some states, they are also licensed as professional counselors.

Increasingly, creative arts therapists are doing clinical research. Scholarship from the faculty of over 100 universities is regularly reported in the eight professional journals in the field, including for example studies comparing creative arts therapies with traditional treatments; identifying markers of suicidial potential in artwork; measuring the impact of music therapy on heart rate, blood pressure, and hormone secretions; assessing the effects of drama therapy on flashbacks in Vietnam veterans; and identifying signs of sexual abuse in body posture and gesture.

History

Creative arts therapies as a profession began during the 1940s when a number of psychotherapists and artists began collaborating in the treatment of severely disturbed clients. The introduction of psychoanalysis into the United States, with its emphasis on the unconscious and appreciation for art as a sublimation of inner life, stimulated many psychotherapists to study the artwork of their patients. Since many severely disturbed patients were unable to utilize the highly verbal modality of psychoanalysis, nonverbal forms of communication seemed to hold much promise. Emigres from Europe who brought their rich traditions in both psychiatry and the arts became leaders of this new field. Creative arts therapies were nurtured in a few long-term psychiatric hospitals such as St. Elizabeth's in Washington, DC, the Menninger Clinic in Topeka, Kansas, and Chestnut Lodge in Rockville, Maryland, and by psychiatrists such as Jacob Moreno who had introduced action-oriented techniques into psychotherapy. The war also created the need for many services for returning veterans who sat in veterans hospitals with nothing to do. At the same time, the field of occupational therapy had moved away from psychiatry toward a more medicalized approach, creating a need in many settings for meaningful daily activity.

These factors led to the development of the field of activities therapy in the 1950s. A music therapy association formed in 1951. During the 1960s, the general atmosphere of social consciousness, the Vietnam War, and the dearth of jobs in the artistic field, brought a number of artists into the health field. By the late 1960s, the field of creative arts therapies was in full swing with university programs developing rapidly. The dance therapy association was formed in 1966, the art therapy association in 1969, and finally the drama and poetry therapy associations in 1979.

By this time, the creative arts therapies had diversified their interests well beyond psychoanalysis into behavior therapy, special education, and humanistic approaches, and had become integrated into the mainstream of health care. Now all of these associations have joined together as the National Coalition of Arts Therapy Associations (NCATA). Despite their similarities, the creative arts therapies developed relatively independently from the encounter group or New Age movements, and should not be confused with them.

A Typical Session

What is one to expect when one goes to a creative arts therapist? Of course, there is a wide range of approaches and styles, but a few basic elements can be described. Generally, a typical session, whether with an individual, family, or group, begins with discussion about how the client is doing and what problems they have been facing or are concerned about. Then, instead of exploring these issues by continued verbal discussion, the therapist guides the client into the use of a particular art media, such as painting, dancing, role-playing, or listening to or making poetry or music, as a means of working on the problem. Often the therapist will lead the client in warmup or relaxation exercises in order to help the client prepare for the work. For example, in art therapy, the client may be asked to draw or scribble randomly on a sheet of paper; in dance/movement therapy the client may be guided through slow breathing exercises, stretching, or even running around the room; in music therapy by listening to music, singing a familiar song, or making random noises on an instrument. These activities typically open up and relax the client, and indicate to the therapist the client's mood and level of tension. In the art therapy session, for example, the therapist may then ask the client to look at one of his scribbles and see if it reminds him of anything, and then to develop a picture from it.

The main part of the session is spent participating in the arts media. Sometimes the therapist participates with the client or group. Sometimes they do not. Sometimes the problem is worked on directly, as for example when a man is having trouble dealing with his boss, the drama therapist takes on the role of his boss, and they role-play the scene. At other times, the client merely draws, sings, or improvises, and the work of the therapist and client is to see what comes out. For example, the art therapist may ask the client to draw a picture of his mother, or a picture of his feeling of anger, or his perception of his cancerous tumor. The music therapist may help the client to produce a *Song of Myself,* or using the blues modality, create a song such as *Been Down So Long Since My Divorce Came Through.* The poetry therapy client may write and then read a poem written as a letter to a dead buddy in Vietnam, or to his father in heaven. In each of these activities, in addition to the conscious thoughts that arise in the client about the subject, the presence of the rhythms, melodies, colors, and actions of the arts media enhances the possibility that new aspects of the situation will emerge.

Often the therapist will leave it up to the client to make observations about how she/he is feeling and what the artwork means. At other times, the therapist may facilitate the client's exploring and asking questions about the poem, artwork, or song. Some therapists will in time offer their own ideas about what the artwork might mean for the client, and attempt to point out hidden meanings in what the client has produced. In doing so, these therapists will be guided by their particular theoretical framework, such as psychoanalytic, cognitive-behavioral, or gestalt.

In institutions, the course of therapy will be determined by the length of stay of the client. In outpatient situations, or in private practice, the creative arts therapy may be a brief one such as 6 to 8 weeks, when a particular problem can be focused on, or it can be a long-term commitment of 6 months to several years.

While many creative arts therapists are familiar with several arts media, generally each therapist specializes in one or two. In most cases, the selection of the particular media is based on the client's preference - some people like to draw, some to sing, some to act roles. However, in institutions where creative arts therapies work in teams, more sophisticated assessments have been developed that help the team select the best modality for the client, and suggest shifts from one to another. For example, in working with people with post-traumatic stress disorder such as Vietnam veterans or the sexually abused, art is the best modality to begin with because the drawings will elicit the visual aspect of the repressed images. Drama or poetry therapy are preferrable in the later stages of therapy, when the client has become aware of the traumas and wishes to rejoin the world by expressing to others what happened.

Aims of Creative Arts Therapies

Art was never really "invented;" rather it emerged naturally out of who human beings are. Even though today we think of art as belonging to a talented few, in early civilization dancing, singing, enacting stories, and drawing were common means of communicating and healing. Not only tribal shamans, but entire peoples, found that these ways of expression were able to help them cope with their fears, disappointments, and triumphs, and they found themselves moved by and changed through participation in these rituals.

Nowadays, the creative arts therapies are conceptualized with greater precision, but essentially are being used for the same purposes. Like all psychotherapy and counseling, creative arts therapies attempt to (1) alleviate distress, (2) increase understanding, (3) improve relationships, and (4) change physiological responses.

Alleviating Distress. Much of healing involves simply helping the person express his pain, fear, anxiety, or disappointment. The need to get it off your chest, to confess, to unburden yourself is strongly felt by most of us. For many people, merely talking to a friend, clergy, or verbal psychotherapist is sufficient. For others, however, this is not so easy. Perhaps the pain is cut off and hidden from the person, who doesn't even know it is there. This is often true of people who were sexually abused or victims of posttraumatic stress disorder. Perhaps they cannot use words well. This is particularly true of people with learning disabilities, schizophrenia, mental retardation, or Alzheimer's Disease. Or perhaps they are so good at words that they talk all around the distress but can't seem to feel it. This is true of very intellectual and otherwise high-functioning persons.

Because the art work involves the use of one's unconscious, the creative arts therapies can help people express their inner pain. This is why, for example, sexually abused children often "tell" first through their pictures, or in their puppet play. Putting something into physical action helps to achieve this catharsis of feelings.

Example: Mary is a ten year old girl who came to the child guidance clinic for learning problems, angry and negative behavior at home, and frequent crying spells. She refused to speak with her counselor, and instead looked apathetically at the toys in the room. She was referred to the art therapist, with whom she also refused to speak. The art therapist put a sheet of paper in front of her. She immediately drew a picture of a girl on top of a mountain. The art therapist, a male, asked, "What is her name?" and without speaking she wrote "Sandy" on the page. The art therapist said, "I'm Sandy, and I'm on top of the mountain!" Mary immediately threw the sheet on the floor and began drawing another picture, with Sandy on top of the mountain and a boy, a very ugly boy, being thrown off the mountain. She wrote "Bozo" next to the boy. The therapist said, "Oh, no! I'm Bozo, and Sandy just threw me off her mountain! Ahhhhhhh!" Mary laughed out loud, and gleefully began another picture. For several weeks, Mary and the therapist interacted through these pictures, dozens in each session, in which Sandy subjugated many people and triumphed over the world. Soon Mary joined in the narration of the stories, which increasingly centered on Sandy's abuse of a little girl named Marie. Within a few months, the full story of Mary's physical abuse by her mother emerged. The art therapist and Mary continued to use pictures and words for the entire year of therapy, even after Mary was able to talk about her life directly.

Increase Understanding. The creative arts therapies help clients understand themselves better because they increase a person's awareness of themselves. Instead of just talking with the client, creative arts therapists ask the client, "Show me." Then the client makes a picture or a poem, or dances, or makes up a song, or acts out a miniplay. The conflict or issue now is *out there.* In this way, the person's internal experience—otherwise so shifting and murky—is made real. It is easier to see what is going on, to get a handle on it, and try to solve the problem. The client gains the perspective on the problems by becoming his own audience. For patients with schizophrenia or psychosis in particular, this can be extremely helpful.

Example: Daniel was beset by conflicting thoughts that often left him paralysed. When asked how he was feeling, he only said, "Zigzag." The therapist then asked him to show through a movement or gesture what he zigzagged between. One motion was rigid and tense, the other soft and swaying. The therapist divided the room into two parts and had the patient move between them. One side Daniel named "Uptight," the other side he called "Loving." The clear spatial separation of these feelings helped Daniel control his thinking. Daniel was able to talk about how the uptight feeling was related to his father, who had called and told him that he was divorcing his mother. The Loving side represented his mother, and the marriage before it had broken up, which Daniel felt his illness was responsible for. Seeing it laid out like this allowed Daniel to talk very clearly without any psychotic thinking for the entire session.

This approach can also be crucial for highly verbal people who, while they say one thing, do another.

Example: John was a 35-year-old lawyer who had tried three different verbal therapists with little effect in improving his self-esteem or in getting to the roots of his depression. As a highly intellectual person, who understood psychoanalytic theory, he had talked endlessly about his childhood traumas, his passive aggressive interpersonal style, and his tremendous need for approval. After reading an article about dance/movement therapy, he decided to give it a try. Though at first he felt awkward, he grew to enjoy moving around the room, sometimes to music he selected, at other times in silence. He developed "dances" that expressed his depression, his intellect, his father, and mother. He continued to be able to analyse in detail every nuance of these dances with the therapist. His Dance of Depression was a striking one, full of tense, angular movements, lurching forward, with arched back and twisted neck. He said he felt particularly uncomfortable doing it. The therapist then decided to dance it for him to see. As she moved, he became visibly upset, and then he said that he suddenly remembered how his mother had looked getting out of the hospital bed when she had had a serious illness when he was a child. His dance of depression was just like it. He said he felt sick to his stomach, just as he had as a child watching her emaciated body. The therapist asked him to dance it again, and he did, this time with great intensity, silence, and emotion. He observed later, "My God, she is still with me." His improvement during the six months of this dance/movement therapy was continuous and rapid.

Improving Relationships. Many people come to therapy because their relationships with other people, particularly their family, are poor and seem stuck in the same old patterns. A husband and wife become so familiar with each other's styles, arguments and counterarguments, that their interactions can become like broken records. All that is positive in the relationship seems to have been drained out of it. The creative arts therapies help these problems in several ways. First by engaging couples or groups in the arts media, they place people on unfamiliar territory, where they are no longer assured of their own or the others' behavior. Second, the arts bring up unconscious material that had previously been hidden, that let each person know that there is much more to the other. Finally, since the creative arts therapies often involve spontaneity, humor, and play, they tend to illustrate to people how positive they can be for each other. All in all, the creative arts therapies provide new opportunities for clients to air their frustrations and take some distance on their relationship to see what is happening.

Example: Bob and Trish came to the drama therapist for couples therapy. They had been married for fifteen years, had two children, and were fed up with each other. Since the two children were born, Bob had distanced himself from Trish, and Trish had become increasingly angry and critical of him. She wanted a more intimate relationship and felt Bob had lost energy and was not interested in her sexually. Bob felt that she was too demanding and that he couldn't do anything to please her. So he tried to stay out of her way, which enraged her. In the initial session with the therapist these problems were amply demonstrated: Trish attacked Bob mercilessly, and Bob sat quiet, refusing to interact, while making indirect demeaning comments about her to the therapist. Discussion of their problems inevitably resulted in this repeated pattern. The therapist asked them to role-play several situations. They first played themselves and no matter how benign the situation, they soon turned it into the same old arguments and stances. They noticed this and agreed they were locked in a pattern. The therapist then asked them to play these scenes with reversed roles. Each of them exaggerated the other's position so much (Trish playing a wimpy inarticulate man, and Bob playing a monstrous, teeth-knashing Amazon) that they would alternatively interrupt the scene with "That's not fair!" or break out laughing. The therapist helped them to give names to the various stances that they took ("Wimp City," "Man-Eater"), and soon their interactions and arguments became much more playful. The therapy sessions provided a place where they could exaggerate their relationship beyond believablity. Finally, the therapist encouraged them to role play improvisational scenes as entirely different characters, such as animals or supreme court justices. In one scene, Trish played a dwarf who found a huge egg (Bob). She sat on it until it hatched, and Bob, as a giant Godzilla, emerged and stomped around the room decimating villages and office buildings (like the one where he worked), and then came back and picked up Trish (now a beautiful maiden) and carried her off. Both of them expressed tremendous relief that these treasured parts of themselves had only been suppressed, and not lost, in their marriage.

Change Physiological Responses. Changing bodily responses to stress, infection, and pain has become increasingly more important in therapy today. The use of relaxation and imagery techniques to lower stress, to reinforce new positive behaviors, and possibly to strengthen the body's autoimmune response have received more attention from many sources. Creative arts therapies, especially music and dance/movement therapies, have been used as a means of impacting on the body's ability to relax, self-regulate, and retrain one's thinking toward more positive imagery. These skills are particularly helpful in the control of high blood pressure and symptoms of certain chronic physical conditions such as lupus and arthritis.

Music and dance/movement therapies have also been used with traumatic brain injured people. In addition to basic physical stimulation used in traditional care, these therapies utilize rhythmic and melodic pathways toward healing. It is possible that these modalities are processed by different hemispheres or through different neural pathways than verbal or purely physical stimulation, and may at times offer a means of intervention. This has also been studied in dementia, where certain aphasias have been caused by damage to the left (dominant) hemisphere. Since music and other spatial processing is conducted largely by the right hemisphere, sometimes it is possible to improve an elderly persons' understanding through the use of music, art, or gesture.

Example: Ann is a 78-year-old woman with a left hemisphere stroke, severe aphasia, memory loss, lack of concentration, and depression. She was referred for music therapy in the nursing home where she lives. The music therapist first made a comprehensive assessment of her communication abilities and her music preferences, and discovered that she responded to music with particular rhythm, pitch, and meter, in addition to familiar songs from her past. Due to her disabilities, Ann often sat in her wheelchair with her head down muttering nonsense words. After a few minutes in the music therapy group, she became far more responsive, lifting her head up and enjoying the music of the others. The therapist utilized physical objects (such as scarves, mirrors, and fruit) and holding hands to stimulate attention and awareness during the songs. Whenever certain songs were sung, Ann was able to sing along, using the correct words. After each song, she said, "Thank you." Another time, she said, "You see, I'm not crazy." During the treatment it became clear that she was suffering from a depression that was making her cognitive impairments worse, for she was increasingly able to verbalize appropriately during the music structured by the music therapist. The therapist then attempted to build on this foundation. Ann loved the song, "Oh, Susanna," and after singing it several times, the therapist sang, "Oh, Oh, Anna, now don't you cry for me, For you've come from far away, with a smile upon your face." Ann grinned broadly and applauded. The therapist then asked her to sing, one line at a time, which she did: "Oh, Oh, Anna, now don't you cry for me; I'm just an old, old hag, with nothing left to say." Following this method, the therapist was able to get Ann to speak on several topics, most of which confirmed her low self-esteem. As a result of the therapy, Ann was begun on antidepressant medications which helped somewhat, and continued in music therapy. Her level of participation increased, as did her level of orientation and alertness.

Summary

The creative arts therapies are powerful primary and adjunctive treatments that are now available to the public. However, they are not a wonder treatment. As in all rehabilitation, the best results come from a client who is very motivated to change, a therapist who as a person is warm and understanding, and a good match between them. Nevertheless, the creative arts therapies have an important element to them that differs from other forms of treatment: the nonverbal and aesthetic modes of expression. Engaging in the spontaneity of creating, telling a story, playing with puppets, drawing, making a clay sculpture, or writing a poem, the client must draw new things from within himself. This process, while at times anxiety provoking, is usually enlightening and relieving. The demons inside are revealed to be merely parts of the self. Like the shamans of old, creative arts therapists help clients grow and solve problems by reaching the source of their own creativity and inner life. Unlike the shamans, creative arts therapists are guided by scientific and scholarly principles, are schooled in rigorous training programs, and function as members of the team with other health care professionals.

Chapter 17

CREATIVE SPIRITS: THE ARTS IN THE TREATMENT OF SUBSTANCE ABUSE

Drugs appear to give an enormous impetus to the creative intuition.
Alan Watts (1962)

No one can look upon God's face and live.
Henrik Ibsen, in *Peer Gynt*

The treatment of substance abuse with the creative arts therapies is confronted with a paradox: the creative arts and mind-altering substances are not entirely antagonistic forces; in fact they share close ties. Both have been hailed as methods of opening the "doors of perception," as Aldous Huxley (1954) proclaimed. Festivals and celebrations, such as Mardi Gras, are characterized both by intoxication and the arts, as are many central figures of mythology, religion, and literature, such as Dionysus, Bacchus, or Alice in Wonderland. Creative artists have often used stimulants to help access their inner images, as well as sedatives to numb the intensity of their psychic visions. Shamans, who are often cited as models for creative arts therapists, generally used psychoactive substances to enhance their healing powers (Harner, 1980).

So how can it be said that creativity is an antidote to substance abuse, when the two seem to occur so often together? When so many creative artists become addicts, like James Joyce, Eugene O'Neill, or Alvin Ailey? One might argue that the healing power of both the creative arts and psychoactive substances is derived from the same source. For example, Carl Jung took this stance when he told Bill W. that a person's use of intoxicants ("spirits") may be motivated by a spiritual quest, that is, a search for God that also underlies the arts (Jung, 1974). The questions are, Do creative expression and addiction support each other? Or can creativity become a replacement for addiction, as a kind of homeopathic alternative?

Reprinted from the *Arts in Psychotherapy*, "Introduction to the Special Issue on Creative Arts Therapies and Substance Abuse," *17*, 295-298, 1990 with permission from Elsevier Science.

132

Aldous Huxley defended the use of drugs to help people "get in touch" with their inner unconscious images, which societal dictates often suppress. Likewise, the creative arts therapies allow for the expression of essential aspects of self by circumventing the rigid censorship of the superego. However, in conditions characterized not by an overly rigid superego, but a weak one, perhaps a different approach is needed.

A large body of evidence indicates that primarily externally-focused, suppressive, and supportive approaches to substance abuse, such as found in Alcoholics Anonymous (AA), have been the most successful. These approaches advocate a focus on the disease, not on the self; on the present, not on the past; on the search for contact with a higher power, not resources within the self. An emphasis is placed on naming feelings, not examining them. In general the intent is to distract the addict from the self and direct his or her attention toward other people and the battle with the disease. Introspection leads to self-preoccupation, which leads to relapse. How can the creative arts therapies, which stimulate an inner-directed state, fit in with this approach?

Substance abuse programs also advocate avoidance of emotional arousal, as arousal leads to bodily tension that leads to relapse when addicts try to numb themselves. The emotional arousal offered by the creative arts therapies, stimulating clients' bodies, sights, and imaginations, is well-known, and has been identified as the key element in the treatment of other diagnoses, particularly depression and dementia. We all know of the "high" accompanying a truly creative achievement, followed by the "down." One study of drama therapy noted increased acting out and substance abuse following an intense and successful performance experience (Johnson, 1980). How can the creative arts therapies be used to contain, rather than evoke, emotions?

These potential criticisms of creative arts therapy treatment of substance abuse have also been leveled against insight-oriented psychotherapies. Perhaps the creative arts therapies, like psychotherapy in general, can help substance abusers feel better about themselves and give them increased courage and hope to go on, but are not primary treatments for the condition. It is therefore likely that successful creative arts therapy treatments for substance abuse will be tied closely to the principles of AA or relapse prevention models, rather than the psychodynamic models utilized with other psychiatric populations.

Substance abuse provides a real challenge for creative arts therapists because we cannot simply apply treatment models developed for other populations. We must design new treatment approaches to match the unique needs of substance abusers. In this way, the practice of creative arts therapy will be stretched and tested. After all, AA has done well, why get in its way? The fundamental question then becomes: What can the creative arts therapies add to the 12 Step process? I can point to four areas where creative arts therapists are making special contributions.

Step 1: Overcoming denial and shame, and admitting to oneself that one's life is out of control. Creative arts therapies can be helpful in treating shame because they ease the way for suppressed feelings and thoughts about the self to be acknowledged publicly. Lynn Johnson (1990), in a moving essay, identifies shame over exposure of the flawed self as a primary obstacle in addictions treatment. She demonstrates how poetry therapy helps to name this shame, how art therapy facilitates the realization that there is a problem, how drama and dance help to release the inner dragons and provide catharsis, and how music and drama performances help the addict bear witness to others. She emphasizes the importance of forgiveness in the treatment of the abuser, concluding, "creativity is an antidote to shame." Janet Reiland (1990) has developed a movement therapy intervention that targets dependency and shame issues among alcoholic women, largely by helping the clients differentiate body states from feeling states. Bonnie Fisher (1990) uses movement therapy to address the issue of powerlessness on the body level, in order to help patients find ways of achieving self-control. Discovering their own bodies can have profound effects on clients' self-confidence and perseverance against the disease.

Step 2. Imagining one's Higher Power. Many people have difficulty finding or seeing a higher power because they rely on traditional religious stereotypes that fail to capture their hearts. The creative arts therapies can provide other ways of imaging a Higher Power that are unique and meaningful to the client. Lynn Johnson (1990) finds the addict's need for a spiritual rebirth to be the essence of the healing task. "The role of the arts therapist to help patients regain their lost spirit through creative self-expression" (p. 300). Jude Treder-Wolff (1990) attempts to access the healthy self behind the addict to increase a sense of flexibility and awareness. Vocal and guitar improvisations, song writing, and musical games give voice to the addict's troubled, yet deeply human, inner world.

Step 4. The "searching moral inventory" can be deepened and enriched by having patients draw, dance, or sing presentations of their strengths and weaknesses. Kathryn Cox and Karen Price (1990) use drawings of negative incidents to help break through denial and shame among adolescent abusers. The art medium often allows for a more complete and honest representation of the pain, destruction, and loss accompanying these incidents than shame-filled verbal confessions do. Rebecca Milliken (1990) uses dance/movement therapy from a psychoanalytic perspective to help the client identify and tolerate feelings, develop trust in oneself, acknowledge losses, and explore more adaptive responses to the environment. The therapist's empathic and tolerant stance gives room to the client to face their situation, in the freeing context of expressive movement.

Step 12. Bearing witness to others. The creative arts therapies can greatly expand 12th Step work, particularly through dramatic and musical performances, art shows, and poetry readings that communicate to the public about substance abuse (Johnson, 1990). Louis Moffett and Liliana Bruto (1990) use theatrical performances as a means for clients to educate others about their illness, and to give testimony to their own courage in battling addiction. "Dramatic methods offer the therapeutic advantage of using the immature person's defenses of projection and acting out in the service of personal growth" (p. 347). They highlight the positive impact these performances have on the addict's immature defenses and coping behaviors.

In addition, the creative arts therapies can support goals consistent with cognitive-behavioral treatments of substance abuse, such as helping patients gain a sense of control over themselves, find substitute gratifications, and become educated about the illness. For example, Jerome Bump (1990) uses a variety of bibliotherapeutic methods to engage students in substance abuse education. Small group experiential exercises, journal writing, and selected reading of fiction facilitate spontaneous self-disclosure and emotional expression, which then lead to deeper understanding of the deeply complex issues facing substance abusers.

Supporting all of these helpful interventions is probably the creative arts therapies' efficacy in treating alexithymia, that is, the inability to translate bodily tension states into images and then representations of feelings. Unable to express themselves, addicts release tension through angry behavior or numb themselves through alcohol or drugs. The creative arts therapies help to regenerate the intermediate realms of symbolic representation between kinesthetic and verbal levels. Bodily tension then is given another outlet via the image. As one of my patients described it, "Whenever I get tense now, I pull out the pastels and draw, instead of going to the bar."

As creative arts therapists struggle to "find a path" to contribute to the treatment of substance abuse, the larger question remains: can the creative arts therapies be the "doors of perception" for addicted individuals without stimulating their desire for drugs? Transforming our usual perspectives will require a great deal of rigor, specificity, and modesty among developers of creative arts therapy treatments. Nevertheless, I believe we will not diminish ourselves by embracing an allegiance to those who have been fighting substance abuse for years, well before creative arts therapists joined the ranks. The hard learned lessons of the courageous men and women of AA and NA: the importance of abstinence, the power of the group, the regeneration of faith, and family intervention in the treatment of the disease, deserve our respect. Let us find our place with them. Let us do what we can.

Chapter 18

THE FAMILY, THEY SAY, IS DYING

The family they say is dying. The family has been blended, extended, enmeshed, disengaged, and torn apart. The nuclear family has had a meltdown. The average person's sentient feelings are increasingly attached to images of products, processes, and news from their work setting or the mass media. The ongoing sagas of "Dallas," or "Thirtysomething" may have more immediacy to us than our own families, whose members often live far apart. We return to family gatherings fueled by warm hopes, only to find tension, worn out traditions, and disappointment. Perhaps we are experiencing the transition to a new form of human communion, and the family should be cautiously let go. Or perhaps we are witnessing the breakup of human bonding that will lead to an even larger increase in crime, drug abuse, perversion, alienation, and suicide. In response to these threats to its integrity, some families have retreated into rigidified systems with overly-controlled interactions with the environment. Even those families within the normal range too often constrain their own members in narrowly defined roles that resist alteration or expansion. The delicate balance between integrity and transformation appears to be difficult to achieve.

The death of the intergenerational transmission of family stories, myths, and images contributes to the death of the family as a powerful source of meaning in our lives (Sandel, 1991). The interest recently in discovering our "roots," in term of genealogy, is a symptom of this alienation from our family. However, we also need to find our roots in the present, to find nourishment from our membership in our family now. The creative arts therapies may be an effective method for accomplishing this task.

What do families do together? Most eat, share chores, drive each other to events, argue, talk about problems, worry about each other, and go to movies or miniature golf. Some families take walks, some play sports together, some go to church. Creating art, role-playing, singing, or dancing are less common activities. Playing together may be a rare, if often most remembered,

Revised from the *Arts in Psychotherapy, 18*, 187-190, 1991 with permission from Elsevier Science.

moment a family life can treasure. Creative arts therapists should be able to help the family to play: bring greater intimacy to a disengaged family, more freedom and spontaneity to the rigid or enmeshed family. Increasing the integrity and flexibility of the family is essential in maintaining it as a supportive environment for individuals' growth, instead of as an incubator of psychopathology. Many families have lost the ability to serve as a transitional space for their members.

Family therapists have discovered that to impact on the complex family system, powerful and often intrusive techniques are required. They have welcomed action-oriented techniques such as rituals, tasks, or sculpting, approaches consistent with the creative arts therapies (Satir, 1967). Given the fact that the creative arts therapies are successful at overcoming and circumventing strong defenses, bringing unconscious or covert ideas to the surface, their application to family therapy should hold a great deal of promise. Yet, despite these synergies, the creative arts therapies have not to date had a significant impact on the practice of family therapy. It is not clear if this is due to creative arts therapists' lack of access to families, to inherent resistances of families to the arts media, or even our own resistances to families. This latter reason deserves special attention, since it is within our power to change. What is the relationship of creative arts therapists to our own families? Perhaps we became creative arts therapists out of identification with family members who were involved with or supported the arts. For many creative arts therapists, our childhood served as the source of our creative journey. We took on this arduous journey because someone we loved gave our artistic expression value, just as now we affirm our patients by giving value to their artistic creations. On the other hand, perhaps we discovered the arts as a means of solacing ourselves from the pain our families caused us, as a compensation rather than identification. In such a case, our reluctance to work with families would not be such a mystery.

In my own case, I began my adolescence performing skits with my brothers for my parents and their guests. I do not know why, for neither parent was a thespian or artist. I do remember my grandmother's joy in improvising stories for me, but I followed my physician-father into the sciences and entered college in physics. My turn to theatre began at that time, as the shadow of my father's alcoholism fell over my family and my happiness. I immersed myself in improvisational drama and found my way to drama therapy as my family faltered, and then lost its way. Seventeen years later, after my family was forced into family therapy as part of my father's treatment, were we able to play again....my brothers and I, and our wives, performing improvised skits for my parents, just as I performed skits with my patients for the staff and families at my hospital. Not surprisingly, my interest in treating families blossomed, and I found them much less resistant to drama therapy than I had before my father's treatment.

Other creative arts therapists, however, have found no reason for hesitance in working with families, and have made important contributions. Helen Landgarten (1987) and Hanna Kwiatkowska (1978) have based their careers on establishing family art therapy as a significant area for creative arts therapists. Their work has been extended by others such as Arrington (1991), Horovitz-Darby (1991), and Carey (1991). Eva Leveton (1991) has applied many psychodramatic techniques to family therapy, noting the significant overlap in these action-oriented methods. Anthony Decuir (1991) has been a strong advocate for music therapy applications in family therapy. Comparing the family to a concerto, with the identified patient as the soloist amongst the orchestra, Decuir suggests that the music therapist's job is to hear the unsounded chords, that is, the background to the patient's experience, often beclouded by the collusive family dynamic. He concludes that "facilitating communication among family members seems to be the most common use of music in family treatment" (p. 199). Steve Harvey (1991) has developed an integrated expressive arts approach to families that targets attachment behavior, through the use of movement games, drama, storytelling, and artwork. He begins by establishing an interactive expressive activity with the entire family, which is extended until repeatable patterns are identified, and then helps the family understand these themes. Harvey's work builds on other dance therapists' efforts (Bell, 1984; Meekums, 1991).

Creative arts therapists need to direct their energies, clinical talent, and scholarship toward the family. Many pressures—both internal and external to the family—are deadening family life. The creative arts therapies can help the families of the future reassert their family identity through creative and collective acts. We have much to offer them in their search for inspiration—because through the creative arts therapies what appears to have died can come alive; what seems to have been lost, can be found again.

Chapter 19

ON THE THERAPEUTIC ACTION OF THE CREATIVE ARTS THERAPIES: THE PSYCHODYNAMIC MODEL

Diverse theoretical models have been proposed to explain the therapeutic action of the creative arts therapies. The *psychodynamic model*, derived from psychoanalytic theory, developmental psychology, and object relations theory, proposes that inner states are externalized or projected into the arts media, transformed in health-promoting ways, and then reinternalized by the client. A thorough reading of creative arts therapy theory, across all modalities, reveals wide use of this model, even among nonpsychodynamic practitioners. This model contrasts with a behavioral model, which posits therapeutic effects from the client's accessing and then practicing new behaviors (e.g., assertive, relational) through the arts media, expanding their personal repertoire of imagery, movement, or roles. The psychodynamic model is also distinct from other creative arts therapy models, including humanistic, spiritual, narrative, and aesthetic approaches (Blatner, 1991). If an integrated psychodynamic theory of the creative arts therapies is possible, then clear articulation of its model of therapeutic action will be essential. This article will attempt to explicate this psychodynamic model, by identifying its basic assumptions, critiquing its inconsistencies, and proposing clarifications that hopefully strengthen its explanatory power. This theoretical discourse will suffer from the limitations inherent in the reductive process of model-building, and in the boundaries set by psychodynamic theory.

The Psychodynamic Model

The psychodynamic model of the creative arts therapies relies foremost on the process of *projection*, whereby aspects of the self are expressed in artistic products and processes (i.e., play). The concept of projection provides the

Reprinted from the *Arts in Psychotherapy, 25*, 85-99, 1998 with permission from Elsevier Science.

basis for asserting that the arts reveal personal material, which presumably is required in a psychotherapy. Projection has been viewed both as determining the content and form of the artistic expression, suggesting a causal process linking art and psyche, or as an attributional process in which the artwork is imbued with personal meaning after the artwork has been created. Second, the model utilizes the concept of *transformation*, in which personal material, in the form of artistic expression, is then altered, worked through, or mediated. Creative arts therapists have debated whether this transformative process occurs naturally, is reliant on the therapist's interventions, or results from unique aspects of the artistic media. Finally, the model relies on the concept of *internalization*, whereby the transformed personal material is reintegrated into the client's psychological state. Creative arts therapists also differ on the importance of verbalization in this reintegrative phase.

Creative arts therapists from all disciplines have justified the therapeutic value of their work with this model (e.g., Bruscia, 1987; Cavallo & Robbins, 1980; Dosamantes, 1992; Emunah, 1994; Grainger, 1990; Leedy, 1969; Naumburg, 1966; Rubin, 1984; Siegel, 1984, among others). For example, Helen Landgarten, an art therapist, writes, "Using an art form which is a natural primary process is a valid method of externalizing and concretizing an individual's imagery. After a person has done this, the art therapist can help bridge the gap between nonverbal expression and verbal communication. In this way, both repressed and potential material can be discovered and explored" (Landgarten, 1975, p. 65). Richard Courtney describes a similar process in drama: "Dramatic play in children, like dreams with adults, is an expression of the unconscious. The deep unconscious drives are the latent meanings of play which are turned into symbols and result in symbolic thought... In this sense, play is a projection of the child's inner world, it is the microcosm to the greater macrocosm and is the child's way of turning passivity into activity" (Courtney, 1968, pp. 93-94). Likewise, Stephanie Volkman, a music therapist, writes: "The instrument/music acts as a transitional object, bridging internal and external worlds as well as past and present..... Music reflects and acts as catalyst to the already active integrating force within the individual, combining cognition, affect, and kinesthetic action in a fluid form that allows repressed material to surface and be fully expressed and resolved" (Volkman, 1993, p. 250).

Penny Lewis succinctly states the psychodynamic perspective: "External representation of the unconscious is vital....expressive arts therapy focuses on making the preverbal explicit through the transference/countertransference relationship, expressive reexperiencing, and symbolic enactment within the transitional space of playing" (Lewis, 1987, p. 330). Shaun McNiff notes that this process may be characteristic of healing in general: "In all forms of psychotherapy and shamanism, there is an externalization, or symbolic acting out, of the inner feelings and changes that the person is experiencing. The healing relationship thus appears to be a dramatization that not only gives tangible form and clarification to private feelings but which also precipitates insight and emotional adjustment" (McNiff, 1981, p. 11).

Thus, the psychodynamic model suggests that psychotherapeutic change occurs, first, through projection or externalization of unwanted or unknown parts of the self onto play objects and behaviors; second, through the client's rearrangement or transformation of these parts during the play within the imaginal space and in the presence of the therapist; and finally, through an acceptance or re-internalization of these parts back into the self. Implicit in this model is a movement outward (externalization) of the unknown (unconscious), followed by their transformation in the therapeutic playspace, and finally a movement inward (internalization) of the known (conscious). Figure 5 illustrates the basic process of the model.

Figure 5

Basic Model of Therapeutic Action in the Creative Arts Therapies

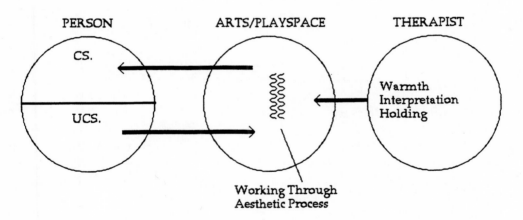

Working Through
Aesthetic Process

This model is explicitly derived from psychodynamic models of verbal therapy in which clients project aspects of themselves into, and then retrieve them from, the therapist. For example, Ogden (1982) describes this model from an object relations perspective: "The therapist learns from (in fantasy, 'takes in qualities of') another person on the basis of interactions in which the projector (patient) ultimately takes back (reinternalizes) an aspect of himself that has been integrated and slightly modified by the recipient (therapist)" (Ogden, p. 40). Note that in this conceptualization, the therapist serves as the arena for transformation, not the arts media. "The role of the therapist is to make available to the patient for reinternalization that which was the patient's to begin with, now slightly modified as a result of having 'reposed' in the therapist" (Ogden, p. 73). Thus, in psychoanalysis, projection occurs into the therapeutic space created by the privacy of the room and the transference to the therapist, and alteration of these projections occurs through the therapist's receptivity, holding capacity, and interpretations. The creative arts therapies expand the possibilities of this therapeutic space by inclusion of an aesthetic space between the client and therapist (Robbins, 1989).

This psychodynamic model in its various versions is so widely held among arts therapists that certain conceptual problems have not been adequately addressed. First, the model may inadvertently support criticism of the arts therapies as reliant on projective and externalizing defenses similar to those of acting out. Clearly, this criticism needs a response. I will reexamine the concept of externalization *as a defense*, and differentiate it from the *behavioral process of expression* in an arts media. Second, the nature of the important transformation that occurs within the arts media has remained vague. I will attempt to describe this process with greater specificity, critiquing the role of empathy in the healing process, and the role of mastery as a therapeutic function of play. Finally, the stage of reinternalization has received comparatively little scholarly attention, and is often equated with the task of closure or verbal processing. I will attempt to highlight the importance of this stage by examining its links to mourning and reparation.

A Critique of the Psychodynamic Model

Definition of Key Terms

The basic concepts of a psychodynamic model of therapeutic action in the creative arts therapies include: internalization, externalization, transitional space, accommodation, and assimilation. Despite widespread use, their definitions vary considerably from author to author.

Internalization and Externalization. These concepts have been discussed and debated since the beginning of psychoanalytic theory. Certainly there is not room here for a comprehensive analysis. Schafer (1968) in his book, *Aspects of Internalization*, defines internalization as "all those processes by which the subject transforms real or imagined regulatory interactions with his environment, and real or imagined characteristics of his environment, into inner regulations and characteristics" (Schafer, p. 9). Internalization includes the processes of incorporation, introjection, and identification. Kernberg (1976) has carefully differentiated these according to developmental stages. *Incorporation* is a primitive experience of taking in the other whole, becoming merged (in fantasy) with the object. *Introjection* is a form of internalization that occurs later in development, when aspects of the external environment are joined with the self, but maintain a degree of autonomy. The superego, for example, is built up of parental introjects. In moments of regression, these introjects may split off again, and either be experienced as alternate ego-states, or projected onto others (Schafer, 1968). *Identification* occurs even later, when the self has differentiated itself from the environment, and involves a mature alteration of the ego in line with the loved object. Incorporation, introjection, and identification are entirely psychological processes, and should be differentiated from *imitation*, which refers to behavior that might or might not reflect internalization.

The complementary concept is externalization, which involves fantasies of expelling unwanted aspects of self into objects in the environment. Externalization includes the subprocesses of projection and projective identification. Projection reassigns a quality of the self to another person or object, usually in the service of protecting the ego from anxiety or pain. Projective identification is a more primitive projective process that involves the fantasy that a part of the self has entered another person and controls them (Ogden, 1982).

In early object relations theory, processes of externalization were sometimes described as if parts of the self literally (rather than in fantasy) exited the body and entered external objects or people (e.g., "part-objects are projected into the therapist, where they repose.") The development of the concepts of self- and other-representations, however, provided a better understanding of how these dynamics occur (Sandler & Rosenblatt, 1962). Specifically, each person builds over time the notion of a self, and a corresponding notion of others (objects). These representations of self and world of course remain inside the body/mind of the person. Psychological processes such as defenses act through altering the differentiation and integration of these representations; internalization and externalization alter the boundaries between self- and other-representations. Thus, externalization can be defined as the process by which the location of a lived experience shifts from the representation-as-self within the person, to a representation-as-other. What "goes between" one person and another is behavior, which presumably is shaped by—but not identical with—these internal representations. I will use the term "Other" to mean these other—representations inside the person —entirely psychological entities; and "others" or "persons" to denote actual people.

Unfortunately, the term externalization is often used to describe overt expression in concrete behavior: e.g., "the child externalizes his feelings in the play." This use of the term confuses the behavioral with the psychological dimensions of the concept, leading to a misleading association of behavior with projection, and thinking with internalization. It is this inaccuracy that links play with defenses such as acting out. The mental and behavioral meanings of externalization need to be differentiated. I therefore propose the term *expression* be used to describe the behavioral manifestation of an internal state, either in verbal or nonverbal form. The complement to expression is *imitation*, that is, the behavioral manifestation of an external state, either in verbal or nonverbal form. These relationships are illustrated in Figure 6. Thus, a person can express (behaviorally) in play either an internalized or an externalized representation, or both at the same time, as for example when a child plays out a scene between a monster puppet and a scared little animal puppet. In fact, any picture one draws, any dramatic scene that one plays, is likely to include elements of both self- and other-representations, and therefore have both internalized and externalized elements.

Figure 6

Psychological Arenas within the Psychodynamic Model

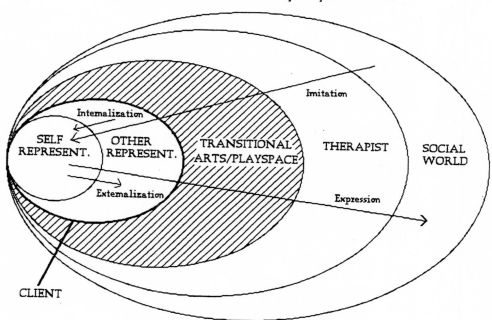

Assimilation and Accommodation. Expression and imitation as defined above parallel Piaget's analysis of the behavioral manifestations of cognition, which had a significant impact on developmental object relations theory, particularly through the work of Margaret Mahler (1975). Piaget (1962) defined assimilation as the application of already existing schemas (i.e., patterns of thinking, perceiving, or behaving) to external objects or activities. For example, when a child puts a toy truck in a baby carriage, the child is assimilating the truck into the schema of caring. Assimilation is perceiving and behaving toward the world according to one's own ideas: that is, assimilation is the outward expression of an inner state. Piaget notes that play is the condition where assimilation predominates over accommodation. Too often writers use the term assimilation when they mean accommodation (e.g., "the client assimilated the split-off traumatic imagery.") *Accommodation* is the altering of one's own previous schemas in accordance with the qualities of the external object. For example, when a child discovers by accident that a toy makes a ringing sound when she shakes it, she begins to shake it again, and then picks up another toy and shakes it. Accommodation leads to learning new schemas, while assimilation leads to new uses of objects. Accommodation represents the primacy of the external world over the internal, and is accomplished largely through imitation. Work is an adult activity that emphasizes accommodation by the person to the demands of the roles and tasks established by the organization. Assimilation on the other hand represents the primacy of the internal world over the external, and is accomplished largely through play and fantasy. Imagination and creativity are adult activities that rely on assimilation.

Successful adaptation occurs when these two processes are relatively balanced, providing what Piaget identifies as "mobility and reversibility of thought" (Piaget, 1962, p. 289). The balanced interaction between self and environment allows for both to be transformed in ways that provide integration of experience, as for example in the development of comprehended language. The elements of language (i.e., letters, words, grammar) are learned through imitation (i.e., accommodation), but are given meaning by linking them to personal associations and images (i.e., assimilation). The result is that one person can communicate inner states of feeling and thought to another.

Piaget's developmental concepts had a profound impact on psychodynamic theorists, who applied them to interpersonal dimensions, particularly the interaction between mother and child. The optimal interpersonal environment for the child is one that provides him/her with an opportunity to experiment with both accommodating to the external world and assimilating objects into the play. If the mother either does not allow the child room to play, or alternatively is too responsive to the child's every need, then the situation becomes imbalanced, and the safety and flexibility of this holding environment is reduced. This intermediary realm between mother and child has been named the transitional space (Winnicott, 1953).

Transitional Space. No concept so permeates the literature of the creative arts therapies as transitional space. Winnicott (1953) describes transitional phenomena as "the intermediate area of experience, between the thumb and the teddy bear, between the oral eroticism and true object-relationship, between primary creative activity and projection of what has already been introjected, between primary unawareness of indebtedness and the acknowl-edgement of indebtedness" (p. 90). Winnicott did not actually use the term transitional space, referring only to "potential space," largely because he focused on the interpersonal interaction (Winnicott, 1971). Creative arts ther-apists, however, have embraced the concept in its spatial meaning, for the notion of transitional space provides an excellent description of the environ-ment that is re-created in the creative arts therapy session; that is, an aes-thetic, imaginal, metaphoric space in which inside and outside, self and other, are mixed. Creative arts therapists have relied on related concepts such as ritual space (McNiff, 1981), playspace (Johnson, 1991), liminal space (Lewis, 1993), or therapeutic space (Robbins, 1989) to delineate the mode of interaction within our modalities. I propose the general term, *arts/playspace*, for the transitional space in which the arts media are employed. The arts/playspace is therefore an extension of the transitional space because it broadens the possibilities of interaction between client and therapist.

Now that I have described these key terms, I would like to address two conceptual problems in this model of therapeutic action, both of which are due to an overemphasis on the early phases of treatment rather than the entire breadth of the therapy process. These involve the role of discrepant interaction and identification with the Other.

Role of Discrepant Interactions in the Transitional Space

Creative arts therapists place an emphasis on the therapist's receptive and mirroring stance toward the client. Clinical principles of empathic reflection, mirroring, attunement, listening, and holding are central to many therapists' technique, and rightly so. However, this emphasis often underestimates the role of discrepant, or challenging, interactions in the client's development and growth. As I will attempt to demonstrate, it is the balance between con-cordant and discrepant interactions that gives rise to the possibilities of trans-formation in the psychodynamic model.

The processes of internalization and externalization work cooperatively to develop mature identifications: identifications that correspond enough to the outside world and yet are infused with personal meaning for the individual. Assimilation occurs when the mother responds to the child's desires, and accommodation occurs when the mother introduces discrepant responses to the child. A consensus exists that healthy development and adaptation are characterized by both processes. First, the child needs to experience an envi-ronment highly responsive to his/her needs; then slowly, the child should be challenged by increasingly new elements to which she/he must accommo-date.

Winnicott refers to unchallenged assimilation as an *illusion* "that there is an external reality that corresponds to the infant's own capacity to create" (p. 93). Yet he writes, "...the mother's main task (next to providing opportunity for illusion) is *disillusionment*"(p. 94). For only through disillusionment will the child internalize the mental image of the good-enough mother, to carry her inside, and therefore make a step toward greater self-reliance.

Stern (1985) describes the concordant process between mother and child as *attunement*, in which the mother matches the infant's energy, rhythm and needs. Yet he notes the importance of *purposeful misattunement*: "In purposeful misattunements, the mother intentionally over- or under-matched the infant's intensity, timing, or behavioral shape. The purpose of these misattunements was usually to increase or decrease the baby's level of activity or affect. The mother "slipped inside" of the infant's feeling state far enough to capture it, but she then misexpressed it enough to alter the infant's behavior but not enough to break the sense of an attunement in process" (p. 148).

Behrends and Blatt (1985), in their comprehensive review of the concept of internalization, conclude that internalization occurs through (a) the establishment of a gratifying involvement followed by (b) the experience of incompatibility of this involvement. Thus, the discrepant elements in an otherwise empathic, concordant relationship are essential to propel the person to take in what is being lost, that is, the Other. The transitional space appears to be the most flexible arena for internalization to be accomplished.

The creative arts therapy clinical literature rarely describes examples of purposeful misattunement; instead we are consistently presented with evidence of the therapist's attunement to the client through empathic responses. However, a balance between these types of interaction is needed in order for transformation to occur. Robbins (1988) agrees: "The aesthetics of the transitional space become a very important factor in aiding the process of identification between patient and therapist, with the identification process itself representing a delicate balance between gratification and frustration. .... Gratification exists in the form of a deep mirroring resonance, a oneness reminiscent of both the artist's merging with his medium in one phase of creation and also the early relating of mother and child.... Frustration arises in the form of separateness—the disruption of the resonance with interpretative interventions to give form and definition to the therapeutic communication" (pp. 7-8). Robbins reminds us also that the client identifies not only with their own images projected into the therapist, but with the therapist as a real person, whose capacity to tolerate a wide range of feeling helps to moderate the intensity of the client's inner world. Though Robbins emphasizes interpretation as a source of discrepancy in the therapeutic session, other forms of discrepancy may be introduced through the unique characteristics of art materials, requirements of aesthetic form, or personality of the therapist when engaged in the play. For example, Zierer (1987) deliberately adds what she calls "push strokes" on her client's work in order to disturb the aesthetic balance, so that the client is challenged to achieve a higher level of aesthetic integration. Grinnell's (1980) approach to music therapy, "developmental therapeutic process," explicitly utilizes Piaget's framework in providing *optimal mismatching* in the musical communication between therapist and client. Penny Lewis (1993) emphasizes the importance of discrepant interactions in dance/movement therapy, when the client is exploring the differentiation phase of the separation process. She utilizes specific rhythmic, dramatic, and spatial interventions. Similarly, I introduce what are called *divergent elements* in the improvisational play with the client in order to deconstruct repetitive role patterns (Johnson, 1991).

The delicate transitioning between attunement and misattunement, between assimilation and accommodation, in the therapeutic process may best be described as alternations between expressions of Self and Other, *both* of which interpenetrate the play, artwork, or puppets. The sense of simultaneity and cooccurrence that results provides the creative impetus for the turns and surprises, shifts and reversals, required by the process of change. Healing may begin when clients recognize themselves in the art, but continues when they confront the Other revealed to them in the liminal space.

The implications of such a perspective have been explored by Shaun McNiff (1991, 1993), when he has advocated for the "autonomy of the image." He suggests that the artwork, role plays, images, or poems revealed through the creative process should be viewed as independent beings, and dialogued with, as the Other, to free them from the client's well-worn schemas. While not denying "that a picture or dream is closely associated with the inner life of its maker or dreamer," he argues that it is the otherness of the image that contains much of its power to heal. "In order to practice imaginal dialogue, it is necessary to respect the image as an animated thing that is capable of offering support and guidance" (1993, p. 6-7). He recommends having other group members or the therapist play with the client's images to more fully explore the possibilities of Otherness. The moment when one lets go of *producing* the artwork, as if it were a thing under our control, and instead *receives* it, opening oneself to another realm, is the moment of transformation we have been seeking to describe. "Suddenly we find ourselves elsewhere; the music moves us..... I began to play as if the bow itself were making the music, and my job was simply to stay out of its way" (Nachmanovitch, 1990, p. 140). The healing transformation in psychotherapy, we will find, has the same structure.

These considerations lead us to the conclusion that essential to the stage of transformation in the psychodynamic model is the client's accommodation to discrepant information introduced by the therapist or arts media;

assimilation and empathic mirroring, on their own, will not produce the transformative moment.

Role of Identification with the Other in the Arts/Playspace

Internalization is stimulated by the disillusionment occasioned by a discrepancy between inner and outer worlds, usually in the form of pain/loss/disappointment/abuse/conflict experienced in relation to others. These misattunements, discrepancies, and incompatibilities with the world of external objects stimulate internalization because the person attempts to minimize the discrepancy by accommodating his/her schemas to the Other. In the best case, the person develops mature identifications with the Other, in which these discrepant elements are integrated into more complex views of the world. However, in situations of greater conflict, the person may take in the Other in unintegrated form, carrying the aggression implicit in such disillusionments. This process has been termed identification with the aggressor when a power differential is a prominent feature, and identification with the lost loved object when loss predominates (Kernberg, 1976). These are essentially the same mechanism, which I will term *identification with the Other*.

Identification with the aggressor is often a result of traumatic events, which force the victim to accommodate to the threatening Other, that is, the perpetrator. Paradoxically, when the perpetrator has had a previous gratifying relationship with the victim, as in incest or domestic violence, the resulting identification can be even stronger. Identification with the aggressor attempts to distance the person from pain by directing the hostility toward others who represent the vulnerable Self, resulting in the development of various disturbances of interpersonal relations.

Identification with the lost love object is a means of adapting to loss or death. In normal mourning, the person at first introjects the lost loved object (i.e., the cause of pain), and then slowly lets go of it (Freud, 1924). In pathological mourning, the person holds onto the Other, distorting their object relations. "The shadow of the object falls upon the ego, and the latter is henceforth judged as though it were an object, the forsaken object" (Freud, p. 252). Thus, with this defense, the person directs their hostility toward the Other disguised as oneself, giving rise to a condition of low self-esteem or depression.

Early scholars of play were impressed with the frequency with which children portrayed these identifications with the Other in their play (Erickson, 1940; Peller, 1954; Waelder, 1932). A consensus developed that through play, children often turned passive into active in order to gain mastery over painful life events, a rationale that was extended further as a basis for the therapeutic role of play. The following is the classic example of this rationale.

The Dentist

A six year old child is taken to the dentist for an exam, which includes a rather long procedure in which the dentist has to scrape a tooth, causing much discomfort for the child. When the child comes home, she initially is desultory and throws a toy, but soon engages in play as a doctor, examining her dolls with a stick. She says "open your mouth" over and over. She then engages her parents as patients, and looks into their mouths. The parents playfully say, "Ahhh," and "That hurts!" to which the child responds, "I'll give you a lollipop when it's over."

In this example, play behavior follows a situation in which the child is forced to accommodate to the world: the dentist inflicts pain. The child comes home and applies her schemas of the event by reversing roles: the child plays the dentist and performs painful operations on dolls or parents, imitating the "perpetrator." The child avoids the feelings of danger engendered by the vulnerable, passive, victimized experience, and therefore gains pleasure through avoidance and displacement of pain onto others. This example has been universally used to illustrate the healing power of play, in which the child learns to master his/her experience by *turning passive into active* (Gould, 1972). But should *mastery over pain* be the basis of the therapeutic endeavor? The child may have lowered her experience of pain, but now identifies with the aggressor. The Self has now been infiltrated with the abusive/lost Other. Surely this is benign in the case of a dentist, but considerably less so in the more malevolent situations that bring our clients into treatment. Continued experiences of abuse or abandonment, if internalized, lead to a personality shaped either by the need to dominate others, projecting the vulnerable, weak parts of the self onto others, or by self-recrimination, low self-esteem, and interpersonal withdrawal (Kernberg, 1976). Is not the preferable therapeutic goal for the child in the example above to be able to acknowledge her vulnerable self, thereby restoring the Other as Other?

Identification with the Other may be a necessary stage in the processing of painful experience, but it should not be the final one. Our clients arrive in the therapeutic setting having already internalized the persecutory or abandoning Other, and having externalized vulnerable aspects of self, both of which may be simultaneously expressed in the artistic media. They have turned passive into active, Self into Other. As long as they flee the acknowledgement of this "passive" self, they cannot come to terms with it, and will endlessly repeat the problematic scene and its derivatives. Repetition compulsion may be the result of this lack of transformation from identification with the Other to reclaiming the hurt Self. Such a reclaiming will necessitate resuming the aborted process of mourning.

In attempting to articulate the psychodynamic model of the creative arts therapies with greater precision, I have highlighted these three points: (1) a client's expression in the arts/playspace should be differentiated from the psychological process of externalization; (2) the therapeutic action within the arts/playspace is facilitated by discrepant as well as concordant interactions with the therapist and the play materials, and (3) the therapeutic process involves a critical transformation of the client's relation to the Other. These points will now be integrated into the following presentation of the psychodynamic model.

The Course of Therapeutic Action: A Psychodynamic Model

The psychodynamic model of therapeutic action is schematized in Figure 7. In this model, the person alters their inner world in order to adapt to painful life experience. If normal methods of support, mourning, and reparation are not successful, the person may seek the path of creative arts therapy. I will conceptualize the therapeutic process as a continuous operation of three Movements. Though these may also be called stages, steps, or phases, such references evoke a linearity that does not occur in actual therapeutic practice, where each may overlap, weave around, or occur simultaneously with each other.

Figure 7

Model of Therapeutic Action in the Creative Arts Therapies:
Three Movements in the Healing Process

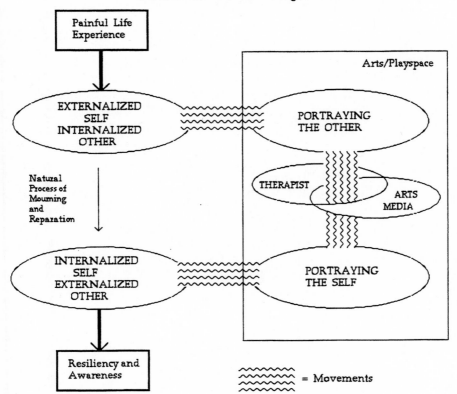

A Movement from Being the Other, to Portraying the Other: Entering the Arts/Playspace

This Movement involves the engagement of the client in the arts/play-space, not simply for the technical reason of initiating the arts experience, but more importantly on the psychological level, where the client makes a commitment to the possibilities of change. Resistance to engagement not only derives from discomfort with the arts media, but more centrally with the demand to loosen one's hold on the Other and its reality in order to allow room to play with, and ultimately transform, them. Thus, the transformation of "real" behavior into "pretend or imaginative" behavior is an act of internalization because the client shifts from being the Other, to portraying the Other; that is, from acting out to pretending. This shift implicitly requires the client to put his/her own conflicts in perspective; and perspective gives space for alternatives. The challenge is that once the door is open, alternatives of one's choosing as well as those unknown, present themselves. Let us examine this movement in more detail with the following example of a child's play behavior provided by Piaget (1962).

> On the same day I knocked against J.'s hands with a rake and made her cry. I said how sorry I was, and blamed my clumsiness. At first she was angry as though I had done it deliberately. Then she suddenly said, half appeased, "You're Jacqueline and I'm daddy. There! (she hit my fingers). Now say: "You've hurt me. (I said it.). I'm sorry, darling. I didn't do it on purpose. You know how clumsy I am (p. 133).

In this example a child replays a painful incident, reversing roles, and playfully inflicting, rather than receiving, pain. Presumably one motivation to move into the playspace is to avoid pain through role reversal (identification with the Other). Note, however, that at first Jacqueline became angry for real (as did the child in the Dentist example, who first threw a toy prior to playing). A different child might have reversed roles and actually struck back at Piaget. Jacqueline struck back within a playspace, that is, in a way that did no harm to the adult. This illustrates that the unique component of the playspace is not role reversal (i.e., turning passive into active), but rather is a *constraint against doing harm*. Such constraint differentiates play from the actual event, where there is no protection from pain. Perhaps it is this "protection" within the arts/playspace that eventually draws the client, who recognizes the possibilities for relief.

Emunah (1985) describes helping a resistant adolescent enter the play-space:

> One day I spontaneously approached a 14 year old client, Tom, who insisted he wouldn't budge from his chair. In a playful tone, I said, "try as hard as you can to stay in the chair." Gently, I took hold of Tom's hands and attempted to pull him to a standing position as he struggled to remain seated. His aggressive and hostile stance transformed into a playful one, and through the physical contact, a relationship was established between the two of us. Another client, seemingly delighted at witnessing this match, grabbed my place, claiming that he could lift Tom. Soon all the clients were pairing off with each other, alternating roles which represented resistance and surrender. (p. 74)

Emunah is effective in transforming the adolescent's anger at authority into a game, allowing him to enter the playspace. Why does he enter? Apparently he gains pleasure, as demonstrated by his laughter and delight, in defeating her authority. But this is not really defeating her; in fact he submits to her. It is likely that his resistant stand originated in painful interactions with another authority. Thus, he could comply with Emunah (the therapist), because he was able to preserve the resistance to the abusive authority in the roleplay. At this moment, these authorities of the past and present became differentiated, and placed in fantasy and reality, respectively. What is remarkable is that Emunah, janus-faced, becomes both at the same time.

Another aspect of the playspace that results from the constraint against harm is that painful interactions can be more fully expressed. In the real confrontation of adolescent and group leader, the original abusive interaction with the parent is replayed, in displaced form. The leader considers her options, the client anticipates possible punishments and coercions. Neither wants a full confrontation and so the situation becomes tense, they hesitate, wary of the possible physical struggle to come. The client's desire to play this through (i.e., his *act hunger*, Moreno, 1946) is thwarted. Emunah's invitation to the client to enter the playspace allows this physical struggle to take place, releasing the pent up energy, and more fully revealing the degree to which the client feels abused and wishes to fight back.

These considerations allow us to claim that the arts/playspace is a moral space: its morality derives from the constraint against harm that remains one of its defining conditions. Yet, this constraint against harm is not linked with the suppression of the evil intention, rather, the moral constraint exists simultaneously with the representation of evil/pain. The canvas, the dance, the song, the drama, and the poem reveal the evil that could be chosen, but is not. At its essence, the constraint against harm *is* the transitional space; and thus *play can be defined as the internalization of a moral constraint.*

The Boys Group

A group of 7–9 year old boys come to a clinic for a group therapy session. In the waiting room, they are quiet as they sit with their mothers. When the group leaders open the hallway door, they come rushing through and begin to yell and hit each other. In the group session the boys are out of control, running around the room, hitting and making fun of each other. The two group leaders are forced to yell at them to be quiet, grab them to prevent them from fighting, force them to sit down and lecture them about bad behavior. The boys ignore these attempts at limit-setting.

Several weeks later, as the boys are running down the hall toward the group room, one leader suddenly squats down, looks furtively from side to side, and whispers, "What? Do you hear it?" The boys instantly become quiet and gather around the leader. The leader says, "I think that there is a dangerous animal hiding around here, waiting to leap out and grab me. Shhh! I think I hear it! The boys move close to the leader, looking at him. The leader says, "Follow me, but be very quiet, so the animal does not hear us. You'll protect me, won't you?" The boys then quietly tiptoe down the hall behind the leader into the group room. The other leader then becomes the monster, whom the boys playfully kill, saving the first therapist. Throughout the session, they continue to play out various stories with little disruptive behavior.

In this group, unruly and out-of-control behavior stimulated strong (if unsuccessful) limit-setting and angry feelings on the part of the therapists. The entrance into the playspace resulted in the boys triumphing over a monster, whom they attacked and killed over and over. The boys identified with the powerful Other, avoiding representations of being vulnerable, frightened, or deficient, which they reserved for the therapists' characters. However, the constraints of the playspace provided the distance that changed the representation of the Other from a real behavior into an imagined one, and more importantly, changed the representation of the vulnerable self from an entirely projected external object into one that was available for imaginative transformation. Thus for these boys the interiority of experience had been increased, simultaneously with its expression in the arts/playspace.

The goal of this movement had been achieved: they had shifted from being the Other, to portraying the Other. The flexibility and range of possibilities in their experiential world had significantly increased. The contentious struggle between them and the leaders had transformed into a collaboration in which real harm would not be done. The next movement involves the transformation of self- and object-representations.

A Movement from Portraying the Other to Portraying the Self: Transforming Representations

This movement of the therapeutic action occurs as the representations transform from portrayal of the Other with whom the client has identified, to the portrayal of the Self, which was weakened when the client accommodated to the painful experience. The imagery/play will now reveal representations of the originally hurt, vulnerable parts of the self. This transformation is a critical movement in the healing action of the creative arts therapies. An examination of almost any case study in our literature reveals the outlines of this process. For example, Horovitz (1981) describes the art therapy of a five year old, autistic boy, who had been shot at age two. At first he had difficulty engaging with the art materials, using them to smear or mixing them up haphazardly. Then he used clay to fashion "googily-gook" monsters, whales, and alligators. Two-headed dinosaurs slaughtered objects created by the therapist. [These images suggest identification with the Other and the portrayal of the perpetrator.] He then began to create people and houses. He eventually recreated the trauma scene and, significantly, had the therapist play his mother who bit him, as he portrayed himself clinging to a lifeboat, calling for help. Later he painted a picture of "me bleeding." [These images indicate the transformation into portraying himself as a victim of the Other]. Horovitz reports that the child made significant improvements in his functioning over the course of treatment.

As the play transforms, clients allow themselves to experience the self-in-danger, and reexperience the Other as Other. Self and Other are therefore restored to their original positions, within the boundaries of the arts/play-space. Let us return to the example of the boys group:

> Several months later, every session begins with the boys tiptoeing down the hall, and the leaders begin a dramatic play as soon as the group enters the room. There is no destructive behavior in the sessions. The boys now look forward to playing the characters who are hurt, tortured, or killed. For example, the boys take turns as lost babies, being swung in a blanket by the two leaders as the other boys act as friends from the forest, bringing food and feeding them. They need protection from the "bad parents" who left them outside to die.

In this group, the boys transform from being strong men who attack and kill the evil monsters (played by the therapists) to lost children needing food and protection. The shift in play occurred simultaneously with a reduction in their acting out behavior, interpersonal violence, and distress outside the session. As the transformation progressed, the boys showed total involvement in the playspace. It is likely that these moments of transformation in the play correspond to the moments of catharsis in psychodynamic psychotherapy, where previously repressed feelings are released.

The important shift during this movement reestablishes the boundaries between Self and Other, though the evil/abandoning Other is expelled into, and thereby revealed in, my world. This process illuminates how identification with the Other protects the person from anxiety: becoming the Other is a way to unconsciously locate and control it. Releasing control over the image of the Other provides it with the autonomy and freedom to strike again. "Often we are stunned and disturbed by images, especially in dreams where they come upon us without our conscious participation. ... Demons have a way of digging deep into avoided depths" (McNiff, 1993, p. 8). As the transformation to portraying the Self occurs, the "released" monsters and demons are often portrayed by the therapist in the interactional play, or concretized in the various art forms, both of which help to delimit their freedom and reassure the client.

This (often cathartic) release of the Other has been compared to shamanic healing rituals by David Cole (1975), who names the critical turning point as the *rounding*. Many forms of magic and ritual utilize this natural human process of calling forth the Other (e.g., the use of amulets, religious icons, channeling). Fables of toys coming to life, or of Frankenstein, reflect experiences of the rounding, when the Other, in its freedom, presents itself. Even walking alone on a dark night illustrates this: at first one hears the night noises and considers, then easily puts aside, thoughts about potential danger; suddenly, however, despite one's own intellectual awareness, the rounding occurs, and the same noises become animated with danger and immediacy, filled with the projected perpetrator, now present; one runs anyway, chagrined though possessed by the spirit, "spooked."

Yet it is not clear what conditions are required in order for this transformation from *active back to receptive* to occur. What motivates this movement toward internalization? I propose that this internalization is stimulated by the client's confrontation with discrepant interactions with the arts media or the therapist's behavior, propelling the reidentification with the vulnerable Self. The source of the discrepancy is likely to be the emergence of the Other in the arts media or the therapist. Due to their autonomous nature, the arts media or the therapist produce stimuli that are beyond the bounds of the client's projections, presenting the client with colors, sounds, postures, or words that are unknown, foreign, discrepant. These discrepancies then serve as the ground within which the client perceives the eruption of the Other, initiating the process of transformation.

In these moments, the therapist and/or the arts media contain aspects of both self- and other-representations, in a simultaneous presence filled with contradiction and imbalance (Dintino & Johnson, 1996). The therapists in the boys group, for example, needed to hold the potential for either victim or bad parent; the arts media in Horovitz' case had to represent both dinosaurs and "me bleeding." The client eventually resolves this state of imbalance and flux by reversing identifications and retrieving the vulnerable Self. The arts media clearly provide the rich environment that can contain the simultaneity and contradiction needed for the client's transformation. The therapist strives to meet the same criteria, whether through verbal interpretation, participation in the artistic activity, or mere presence. The therapist's own imaginative capacities to hold simultaneous yet contradictory images may be his/her single most important personal quality, far more than empathy, insight, or knowledge of the world (Rothenberg, 1988).

A Movement from Portraying the Self to Being the Self: Resuming Mourning and Reparation

This movement involves reflecting on the life within the playspace and its relation to life in the world, and acknowledging one's painful/conflictual experiences. In psychodynamic theory, this movement involves resolving the transferential relationship as the client invests in new interpersonal relationships. Many creative arts therapy approaches conceive of this phase as helping clients exit the playspace and return to the nonliminal world, utilizing the notions of closure, group processing, or deroling (Emunah, 1994; Lewis, 1993; McNiff, 1981). However, I believe that the work of this movement extends beyond closure and resolving transference, beyond diminishment of affect and psychological distancing. The optimal goal of this movement is for the client to integrate the transformed experiences made possible by the therapeutic process into a renewed sense of self. This important reinternalization occurs as the processes of mourning and reparation resume. As in many of the great rite-of-passage fables, (e.g., Alice in Wonderland, Peter Pan, or the Wizard of Oz), the return home and departure from the imaginary world are tinged with a wistful grieving.

As in mourning, the process of this movement allows recognition of the boundary between the playspace and the present to be felt, over and over again. Thus rituals of death and burial (e.g., the wake) serve to present mourners with evidence that their loved one is out there, not inside them; the image of the lost person arises, but then collides with presence of the coffin or grave (Bowlby, 1961). The therapeutic process serves a similar function. Through the transformations within the arts media, the Other is revealed and the vulnerable Self is retrieved. However, now the focus shifts from Other to Self. The work of this movement is to place the identification with the victimized self in perspective, by marking the boundaries of time and space separating the original harm from the current burden. This differentiation occurs when the client experiences the representation of the vulnerable Self as a *portrayal*, that is, an image within the arts/playspace. During the original experience of pain or loss, the client was forced to accommodate to the Other; there was no room to maneuver. The replaying of the vulnerable Self in the arts/playspace is fundamentally different: the client's painful experience is now contained within the imaginal realm, with its greater flexibility and constraint against harm. Therefore, the differentiation between the remembered experience and the playspace propels the recognition of the boundary between past and present, resulting in a sense of being freed from the chains of a previous reality. The freed Self is now available for reparation, in which the objects that were lost can be rediscovered in new objects and activities. The truth of conflict and pain has been irrevocably inserted into one's world; but one rejects mastering it via externalization and repetition; rather, one knows evil or loss, yet chooses to do good and seek reparation.

Many therapists view verbalization as an essential component of this movement, perhaps because verbalization promotes direct communication concerning the state of their progress through these stages. However, reflection and mourning may be either verbal or nonverbal processes. For example, the Jewish ritual of *sitting shiva* after a death is surely both, with meditative silence holding the grief over the loss, and the presence of others a reassurance that life will go on. Thus it is likely that the essential processes of mourning may also take place in a movement, brushstroke, or song, and are not dependent upon verbal reflection. Through this therapeutic process, whether verbal or nonverbal, the client—like the mourner—may achieve solace for the remembered loss, and awe at the largeness of human experience.

Though there are few detailed examples of this later stage of psychotherapy in creative arts therapy literature, the processes described here are often very evident. For example, Elaine Siegel (1984) offers a case example of an adult man with obsessive-compulsive disorder in dance-movement therapy. In the initial phases of therapy, he demonstrated rigid, arrogant, grandiose and denigrating behavior, including sarcastic attacks of the therapist. During the transformation, he shifted to portraying a pitiful, lonely boy, swaying in a fetal position, singing: "Alone, all alone, I play by myself" (Siegel, p. 210). Through these portrayals, he recovered a number of memories of childhood losses. In the later phases of therapy, "he created dances in which the mourning for his early abandonment and the death of his father were expressed" (Siegel, p. 211). He preferred to dance to recorded funeral marches. His compulsive rituals had nearly disappeared.

What helps the person tolerate the burden of a remembered loss is the discovery of good objects (i.e., the good parent prior to their death, the good self prior to the rape) in other people and activities in the world, and engagement in a renewed attachment to these good objects (Klein, 1937). The creative arts therapies offer the client tangible evidence of the possibility of reinvestment in new objects, for the results of creative products and performances within the playspace come to stand for the previously lost or damaged good objects (Emunah, 1994). In verbal psychotherapy, reparation is initiated through the positive transference to the therapist, who, unlike the creative products, cannot leave the session with the client. The therapist must eventually interpret the client's attachment as a healthy reparation, but then redirect them to external activities and people. The emphasis on mental activity within the therapeutic arena must be translated into action in the real world. Creative arts therapists offer an intermediary realm that can more concretely represent the client's new investments in the world, and therefore provide greater flexibility in the client's transition from therapy to real life. This intermediary realm is inextricably linked to the physical action of the body and its extension into the physical products of the arts media.

The departure from the therapeutic arts/playspace is made over a bridge between past and future, built out of the simultaneous presence of similarity and difference, continuity and discontinuity. The creative arts therapies provide such a bridge through the multiplicity inherent in the arts/playspace: being both imaginal and embodied, of the Self and the Other.

Conclusion

A psychodynamic model of therapeutic action in the creative arts therapies is presented, critiqued, and clarified. The therapeutic arts/playspace is brought to bear when painful life experience is unable to be transformed through normal processes of recovery such as mourning and reparation, and instead emerges as repetition compulsion, symptomatic expression, and interpersonal strain. The creative arts therapies act through overlapping, at times simultaneous, movements of entering the arts/playspace, transforming self- and other-representations, and resuming the processes of mourning and reparation. Each movement reflects an essential component of the free flow of consciousness during the therapeutic process, creating journeys filled with entrances and exits, reversals and repairs. This model of therapeutic action of the creative arts therapies is fundamentally a model of internalization, recollection, and moral constraint, and as such, serves as a powerful antidote to processes of externalization and acting out. What is learned in the arts/playspace hopefully may serve as a model for mature thinking and feeling in general: being the capacity to experience and remember without the compulsion to reenact the original harm. The therapeutic playspace serves as a moral imperative to do no harm, though one has been harmed. The psychodynamic model offers a path toward truth and personal responsibility—rather than Mastery—through which suffering can be transformed into resilience.

Chapter 20

REFINING THE DEVELOPMENTAL PARADIGM IN THE CREATIVE ARTS THERAPIES

The developmental paradigm has been one of the most significant theoretical frameworks utilized by creative arts therapists to understand the relation between the arts and healing. Most clinicians and scholars in the field utilize insights and concepts from various developmental theories, even when their theory or method is not explicitly developmental. Due to the wide dissemination and influence of developmental paradigms, a careful examination of the implications for the creative arts therapies is needed. Presumably, general principles linking the arts to development and then to healing will be one of the cornerstones of an integrated theory of the creative arts therapies.

The purpose of this chapter is to elucidate the developmental paradigm in the creative arts therapies. I will review the developmental models that have been proposed for individual modalities as well as those that integrate all the arts media. By developmental model, I am referring to models of creative arts therapies that are based on a developmental theory of human development, rather than stage models of treatment, in which treatment strategies are organized sequentially.

In order for a developmental framework to be clinically useful in the creative arts therapies, the relationship between the arts and development needs to be clearly understood. A number of propositions will need to be explored. For example, it has been proposed that the arts are both developmentally less mature (Piaget, 1951) and developmentally more advanced (Kris, 1952) forms of expression, in comparison to verbal interchange. It has also been proposed that the various arts media lie on one developmental continuum, from dance and music at the lower end, to drama and poetry on the higher end. In analyzing these ideas, I will attempt to differentiate those aspects of the arts that are indeed developmental from those that are not.

The second critical issue I will address is the nature of the process of development itself. It is not sufficient simply to lay out the developmental stages that children or clients are apt to transverse; we must have an idea of how the person moves through these stages. I believe there is sufficient information to be able to propose a theoretical model of such a mechanism of development as it relates to the arts.

Before proceeding to these issues, I will first review the main characteristics of the developmental paradigm, summarize the major principles of development, and then describe the major developmental approaches of creative arts therapists.

The developmental paradigm has a number of strengths. First, it provides a powerful framework for understanding the process of psychotherapy. The identification of stages provides a means of assessing major issues and then tracking their progress in therapy. The therapist is aided in sequencing interventions and in predicting upcoming themes. The developmental model helps both client and therapist "locate" themselves on a "path" toward greater health and functioning. Second, the developmental paradigm maps abnormal behavior onto a normal or natural course of development, suggesting that by removing the obstacles, or freeing a blockage, then clients will resume their previously normal journey. Disturbing symptoms are thereby reframed as merely departures from the normal course of development, a course presumably the same for all human beings. In contrast, the existential and behavioral paradigms, for example, do not make the assumption that all people are traveling on a similar course, and therefore define deviation in more individualistic terms.

On the other hand, developmental models are inherently linear, in that human development is mapped onto the sequentiality of time. The inevitable series of "stages" presented in a developmental model fails to capture the obviously multidimensional complexity, even convolutedness, of the human condition. Therefore, it is common for developmentalists to offer a disclaimer that each stage subsumes those prior to it, that each person may show aspects of different stages simultaneously, or that stages may not even emerge in the predicted order. Strictly speaking, however, the developmental paradigm relies on just such linear orders.

Another problem with developmental models is the implicit primacy of "higher" or "later" forms. The imagery of developmental models nearly always includes movement from lower to higher, from earlier to later, and from primitive to mature, forms, deeply linking value-laden perspectives with developmental stages. When the highest rung on the ladder is labeled "integrated," "creative," or "self-reflective," the prescriptive emphasis is unmistakable. This fallacy of the primacy of higher forms underlies the view that verbalization is a higher (and therefore preferred) form of expression over artistic expression. Developmental models have had difficulty conceptualizing the autonomous functions of earlier stages within later stages of development. Erickson utilized the term *epigenetic* to describe the integration of earlier conflicts within later stages of development, but does not describe what he means in great detail. Too often it is assumed that earlier skills, functions, or behaviors need to be let go or given up, rather than developed into independent arenas of functioning and communication. For example, playing ball is a child's game, but becoming a professional basketball player entails tremendous amounts of discipline, self-sacrifice, concentration, intelligence, perseverance, and tolerance of frustration. Clearly developmental "maturity" as an adult is measured by these latter qualities, not the act of playing with a ball. The error is locating the developmental process in the child's activity (ball, drawing, playacting) rather than in the organization of their activity. Thus there is verbalization that is global, aggressive, and foul, and movement that is highly abstract, complex, and articulated. The level of development is not contained in the media. Thus when we say it is important for clients to be able to "put it into words," we really mean achieving a degree of self-reflection, not merely the act of speaking. The linearity of most developmental theories tends to result in these types of conceptual confusion.

Developmental Theories

Development has been studied in physical, cognitive, emotional, social, and moral domains of experience; in infants, children, and adults; and across cultures. Developmental theory has emerged out of two interweaving traditions: an empirical tradition based on actual observations of human behavior, initiated by Piaget (1937; 1951), and including such authors as Vgotsky (1962), Levinson (1978), Singer (1966; 1973), Gesell (1943), and a clinical tradition based on developmental object-relations theory, including Freud (1905), Jung (1931), Erickson (1963), Klein (1932), Jacobson (1964), Winnicott (1953), Mahler (1975), Werner (1948), Kohlberg (1986), and Stern (1985). The complexity of such inquiry is staggering and perhaps it is best to assume we are only at the beginning of our understanding of human development. Nevertheless, despite many outstanding issues and controversies among developmental psychologists, there is a consensus regarding several major characteristics of human development. First, mental activity appears to develop out of kinesthetic (embodied) experience, and that language is at one end of a continuum of modes of representation that include sensorimotor, imagistic, and symbolic forms (Piaget, 1951; Werner & Kaplan, 1963). This continuum is characterized by increasing distance or separation between the *signifier* (word, gesture, sound) and what is being *signified* (the object, feeling, event), (Werner & Kaplan, 1963). Second, development leads to an increasingly stable distinction between experiences attributed to an external reality, and those attributed to an internal imagination or fantasy (Jacobson, 1964; Piaget, 1937). Third, development leads to the construction of representations of oneself and a world of others, characterized by increasing capacities to experience both autonomy and relatedness (Mahler, Pine, & Bergman, 1975; Stern, 1985). Fourth, development follows a continuum of increasing adaptability, characterized by responses to external demands that are increasing complex, flexible, controlled, and self-reflective (Werner & Kaplan, 1963; Winnicott, 1953; Mahler, Pine, & Bergman, 1975; Selman, Lavin, & Brion-Meisels, 1982). These capacities are the product of increasing differentiation and integration of the structure of the mind (Werner, 1948). Fifth, as a consequence of the above, it is believed that each stage of development focuses particular attention on specific conflicts, issues, and thought-contents (Erickson, 1963; Kohlberg & Lickona, 1986; Levinson, 1978; Piaget, 1951).

These principles have been found to be largely applicable to the development of play (Sutton-Smith, 1974; Singer, 1973; Erickson, 1940; Gesell, 1943; Peller, 1954; Gould, 1972; Klein, 1932), art (DiLeo, 1973; Goodenough, 1926; Levick, 1983; Lowenfeld, 1970), and mental imagery (Singer, 1966). The child's growing physical and mental capacities provide a welcome arena for the expanding scope and complexity of their play. Specific mileposts may mark important transitions in each media: for example, drawing of the circle or hands on the body in visual art; being able to role-play oneself, or knowing what a mask is, in drama; making a change in the rhythm, in music. Presumably creative arts therapists should be knowledgeable about these mileposts within their own primary media, since understanding the developmental sequencing of these skills is relevant to the expressions of both adults and children.

Developmental Models of the Creative Arts Therapies

The utilization of developmental models in the creative arts therapies appears to have been motivated largely for clinical reasons. Some authors were confronted with the need to understand the expected developmental stages of expression in order to know how to interpret meaningful deviations (Levick, 1983; Siegel, 1984). Some desired to shape their sessions according to a natural developmental sequence, on the assumption that clients' response to treatment would deepen and personal growth would be maximized (Jennings, 1993). Still others based their actual therapeutic interventions on their understanding of particular developmental processes (Grinnell, 1980; Johnson, 1982, 1986, 1991). Finally, as the field of creative arts therapies expanded, some authors became interested in how the various arts media were organized developmentally, and so proposed models that applied across the disciplines (Johnson & Sandel, 1977, 1996; Kagin & Lusebrink, 1978; Lewis, 1993).

Myra Levick (1983) has extensively researched the normal and abnormal visual art expressions of children, and documents their orderly sequence of development. Though her work has been particularly important for assessment, she notes that a developmental understanding allows the therapist to identify the types of artistic activities that might be most appropriate to introduce to the client, as well as allowing a more accurate interpretation of the conflicts and issues hidden within the artwork. Many art therapists have relied on information collected by Levick and other researchers such as DiLeo (1973), Gardner (1980), Lowenfeld (1970), and Winmer (1982) to provide a "map" of visual artistic expression that aids their clinical work with clients (see Malchiodi, 1998).

Elaine Siegel (1984) has proposed a model of dance/movement therapy based on psychoanalytic theory, largely derived from ego psychology and Mahler's theories of individuation. She has analyzed each stage of development (i.e., oral, separation-individuation, anal, and phallic) in terms of object relations, process of internalization, drive differentiation, defenses, and level of anxiety, and linked it with corresponding patterns of normal and symptomatic motility. For example, in the oral incorporative phase of normal symbiosis (8 weeks to five months), she notes the following: "Normal motility: holds up head, rolls over, can reach, clutch and scratch. When pulled to sit, there is no head lag. Head and spine are integrated..... Symptomatic motility: Hyperactivity or catatonia. Body distortions with and without fantasy content. Bizarre gestures. Head rolling. Rocking. Fusion of hips and torso. Fusion of head, neck and torso. Toe walking....." (pp. 43-44). Siegel uses this knowledge of the developmental stages of motility as a template for understanding the developmental level being expressed by her adult clients' movements in therapy sessions. The developmental stages with their accompanying nodal issues and themes becomes, as for Levick, a helpful assessment tool. In addition, Siegel gives numerous examples how this knowledge then shapes her therapeutic interventions (e.g., interpretations or instructions).

Sue Jennings (1993; 1994), a drama therapist, utilizes an embodiment-projection-role model of drama therapy derived from the work of Piaget (1951) and Courtney (1968). She notes that in normal development the child initially engages in sensorimotor play (embodiment) using movement and gesture, then engages in drawing, painting, and objects (projection), and then later engages in dramatic play and games (role). This paradigm is used for shaping and structuring sessions, in which stretching and body movements turn to play with objects, and then shift into role-playing. Implicitly,

Jennings' model suggests that dance, art, and drama lie on a developmental continuum.

Barbara Grinnell's (1980) model of therapy, called Developmental Therapeutic Process, utilizes music and play based on Piaget's model of cognitive development, especially the concept of equilibration between the processes of assimilation and accommodation (Piaget, 1951). In her largely improvisational and interactive approach to therapy, she engages the child in artistic expression, noticing when disequilibrations in their play occur. Often in these moments, the child will be playing things out according to his/her own inner schema, and not accommodating to the contributions of the therapist, due to too large a discrepancy between them in their play. In Grinnell's method, the therapist then alters the discrepancy so that it remains developmentally challenging yet within the integrative capacities of the child. For example, when working with a psychotic child who responds to a verbal interaction in the play with echolalia and blocking the therapist out, Grinnell shifted the play into a musical interaction without words, allowing the child to resume the interaction with the therapist. These purposeful discrepancies are intended to produce an *optimal mismatch* in the interpersonal relationship between client and therapist, very similar to Stern's (1985) concept of *purposeful misattunements* he observed in healthy mother-child interactions. Through the therapist's repeated interventions, the child-therapist relationship is maintained within a normative developmental process that Grinnell believes is in and of itself sufficient as a goal for therapy. Grinnell's model is clearly based entirely on developmental processes, and is not restricted to assessment or descriptive purposes.

David Johnson (1982; 1984; 1986; 1991; 1996) has proposed a developmental model of drama therapy, Developmental Transformations, based on Piaget (1951), Werner and Kaplan (1963), and Mahler (1975), that, like Grinnell's model, provides guidance for the interventions of the therapist while engaged in improvisational play with the clients. Five principles of development are described: (1) *Structure* (or the tolerance of ambiguity) refers to the degree to which the client needs boundaries or direction in their expressive activities. In drama, this emerges in the amount of verbal direction/instruction/leadership provided by the therapist. (2) *Media of expression* refers to the developmental sequence of movement, sound, imagery, and then verbalization. (3) *Complexity* refers to the number of different elements being played with in the task, space, and role dimensions of the session. (4) *Interpersonal Demand* refers to the degree to which clients have to take into account other participants in their interaction. (5) *Affect Expression* refers to how intense and personal the emotional content is in the play. In Johnson's model, the therapist's interventions follow these developmental principles, responding to the fluctuations in "flow" in the ongoing play. Disruptions of flow (the equivalent of disequilibrations in Grinnell's terms), are understood to be areas where the clients are experiencing difficulty, calling for a slight shift in the play by the therapist to allow for resumption of the flow. The therapist increases or decreases the structure, media of expression, complexity, interpersonal demand, or affect expression, rather than introducing an entirely different exercise. In general, the beginning of developmental transformations sessions are likely to be structured by the therapist, and involve unison sound and movement, low affect, and minimal interaction, and transform toward greater spontaneity and complexity, use of imagery and verbalization, more intense and personal affect, and greater interaction. The therapeutic goal of developmental transformations, however, is not to attain the "highest" levels, but to be able to transverse all levels freely, with minimal disruption, in the service of expressing one's inner thoughts and feelings.

Penny Lewis (1987; 1993) has integrated the developmental theories of Freud's (1905) psychosexual stages, Kestenberg's (1975) theories of movement, Mahler's (1975) object relations model, Erickson's (1963) psychosocial stages, and Jung's (1931) stages of individuation in a comprehensive model of creative psychotherapeutic treatment. In this model, she links stages of childhood development to common, critical themes in therapy, with specific arts media that are likely to allow for the fullest expression of these issues. "Awareness of the target developmental age for specific art media is important to have, not only when working with children, but also when working with any age individual who is exploring and reexperiencing earlier developmental phases"(1994, p. 32). For example, she lists the following for the developmental age of 0–6 months: "Phase: Oral; symbiosis; first maternal phase; uroboric pleroomic paradise. Themes: trust, merging, mirroring, dependence, nurturance, attunement, holding and handling, horizontal plane dominance. Art Media: sound (music and voice) and movement with an oral sucking and inner genital feminine rocking rhythm. Body awareness: inner and outer eye contact, breathing together; nonverbal dyadic drama" (1994, pp. 30-31). Lewis justifies the integration of these divergent theories by the psychotherapist's need to address multiple levels of experience with the client, including sexual, cognitive, relational, and cultural/archetypal. The principle is that a client's expression in a particular therapy session can be understood in terms of a developmental sequence, and that the therapist's interventions should be guided by an understanding of the developmental dimensions of their particular arts media.

Sandra Kagin and Vija Lusebrink (1978) were among the first to propose a developmental model of the expressive arts therapies, called the Expressive Therapies Continuum. In an early paper, they focused on their own particular modality of art therapy, but in a later work, the full ramifications of the model to all the creative arts therapies was made (Kagan &

Lusebrink, 1978; Lusebrink, 1991). Their model also follows Piaget (1951), Bruner (1964), Werner (1948), and psychoanalytic models, in proposing three layers of experience: Kinesthetic/sensory; perceptual/affective; and cognitive/symbolic. Each level is characterized by greater reflective distance and complexity than the one before. Each level serves to reveal potentialities in the client's self-expression, the first level through action, the second level through form, and the third through schema. Creative expression occurs at each level when all elements are balanced. Each level also has healing dimensions, that is, those aspects that can be brought to bear in the healing process (e.g., kinesthetic: energy release and rhythm; sensory: awareness of internal sensations); and an emergent function that leads naturally into the next higher level (e.g., for kinesthetic/sensory level: beginnings of internal and external form perception). Kagan & Lusebrink's model is very useful in analysing what they call the boundary properties of various arts media, which provide for the containment or expression of emotion and imagery. They demonstrate how each level is expressed within each art therapy modality, noting that this model demonstrates the commonalities among these therapies and provides a common language for practitioners. Indeed, Goldberg, Coto-McKenna, and Cohn, (1992) have incorporated the model into their group process evaluation tool.

Johnson and Sandel (1977; 1996) have proposed a developmental model of the arts therapies based on the mode of representation associated with each arts media. Nearly all observers of infant and child development have noted that cognitive development proceeds from purely kinesthetic and bodily movement expression, to imagistic and gestural forms, to verbal and linguistic forms of expression. Piaget, Bruner, and Werner have variously called these stages kinesthetic, enactive, imagistic, iconic, symbolic, and lexical. The kinesthetic level involves bodily feeling and the sounds and movements the infant can make as it responds to its internal and external environment. The enactive level involves bodily action or movement directed outward, toward objects, including calling out, pointing, and grabbing. The imagistic level emerges when these movements or sounds begin to have a shape to them that evokes an image, as when the baby calls for "maaa." The iconic level occurs when this image-making more strongly defines the expression, as when the baby cups its hand to represent a cup, or draws something that looks similar to the object. The symbolic level occurs when the expression represents the object more complexly, but is not an exact representation of the object, as a transition to the lexical level, when formal language is used to represent experience.

Johnson and Sandel point out that the various art modalities seem to line up with these stages, from movement to sound to gesture and art to drama and poetry and lexical speech, suggesting that dance/movement, music, art, drama, and poetry therapies may be aligned developmentally. See Figure 8. In a series of studies, Johnson and Sandel have explored the impact of different media and types of creative arts therapy intervention on the clinical process or therapeutic outcome (Johnson & Sandel, 1977; Johnson, Sandel, & Eicher, 1983; Johnson, Sandel, & Bruno, 1984). They found that more severely ill schizophrenic clients were able to engage more fully in movement and music than drama and poetry (Sandel & Johnson, 1974). Likewise, some adolescents attempting to avoid feelings of regression may avoid pure movement and favor more organized games (Johnson & Eicher, 1990).

Figure 8

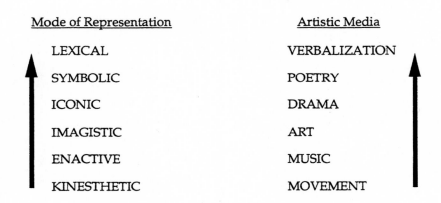

However, such a global conceptualization does not take into account the many forms of each of these therapies, which within themselves can vary tremendously in their levels of complexity, verbalization, or structure. Indeed, Johnson, Sandel, & Bruno (1984) themselves conducted a study that showed that changing certain aspects of the complexity or structure within a dance therapy session can have significant effects on the same population. Likewise, such a conceptualization does not reflect the variation that can occur within one client over even a brief period of time. In fact, it seems more likely that this developmental sequence (from kinesthetic to verbalization) could characterize the process within each arts modality. Many arts therapy sessions begin with a relatively unrestricted creative expression (movement, stretching, free sketch) out of which various images emerge which are then developed, and finally discussed near the end of the session. Such a process follows what Werner and Kaplan (1963) have termed the *microgenetic principle* (see Figure 9). This sequencing is the implication also of Kagan & Lusebrink's model.

Summary

An examination of the above clinical and theoretical attempts by creative arts therapists to incorporate developmental frameworks reveals that in general they have resulted from these authors' clinical experience. Specific differences in artistic media, therapeutic style, or theoretical interest are to some extent over-valued in comparison to the broader commonalities obvious among them. It therefore may be helpful to take a step back and address the fundamental questions linking all the arts modalities: what is the relationship between the arts and development? and how does the process of development occur within artistic media?

Figure 9

THE MICROGENETIC PRINCIPLE

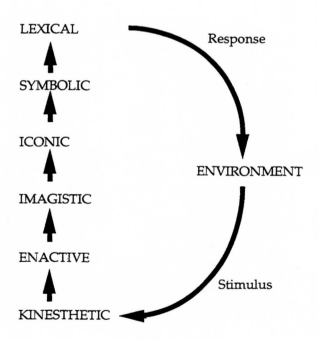

The Relationship between the Arts and Development

The beauty of the arts and creative pursuits is their complexity and resistance to intellectual reduction, so what follows is no doubt an egregious act of violence to their fundamental spirit. That said, I will now attempt to articulate how the arts fit into a developmental schema (outlined in Figure 10).

Figure 10: A Model of the Arts and Development

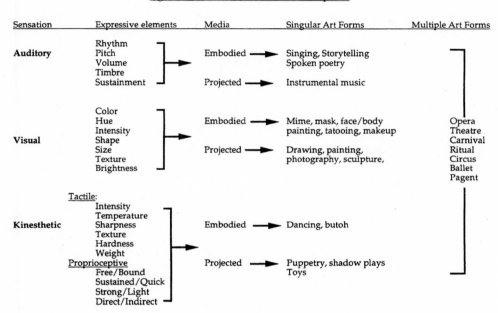

Sensation. The foundation of artistic expression is surely the human capacity for sensation. Without the capacity to sense, there can be no art for sensation provides for the perception of or input to experience. Each art form, therefore, should be easily linked to one or more of the five senses, auditory, visual, kinesthetic, olfactory, and gustatory. Taste and smell (whose art forms include cooking and cosmetics, respectively) have served secondary roles in what are known as the fine arts. Kinesthetic sensation may be further divided into tactile (touch) and proprioceptive (bodily awareness) forms. The artist's creativity is brought to bear through the expressive elements of each sensation.

Expressive Elements. Each sensation consists of different qualities, which through their variation, constitute the potential range of that particular sensation. For example, the auditory sensation has qualities of pitch, rhythm, and volume; the visual sensation has qualities of color, size, and brightness. I will call these qualities, *expressive elements,* since it is through their alteration and variation by the artist that the artwork is born. The major expressive elements are listed in Figure 10. It is important to note that expressive elements are not created by the artist, they are built-in characteristics of sensory perception. The artist has control only over their variation (e.g., what level of volume, how large the circle, how sharp the movement) and combination.

Variation. Artistic expression involves the purposeful variation of these expressive elements in order to communicate feelings or thoughts (Langer, 1953; Ehrenzweig, 1971). Qualities of variation include complexity, balance, harmony, style, accuracy, and integration. The artists' repertoire of variations will have been developed through years of playing as a child and then a period of serious study. These variations can retain a sense of playfulness, as in improvisational forms of artistic expression, or they can be crafted variations, as might be seen in meticulously worked out paintings, dances, or instrumental performances. However, every artistic creation has both play and craft, spontaneity and precision. Without some play, artistic expression becomes utilitarian and technical. Without craft, art loses its ability to communicate to others. Fundamentally, it is through the variation of expressive elements of sensation that the artist translates an inner state into an external form. The creative transformation lies here.

Media. These variations occur through the artist's action on objects in the world, that is, artistic media or materials. Media can be divided into *Embodied* forms, where the object of variation involves the human body (e.g., voice, hands, body movement, skin), and *Projected* forms, where the variations occur on external objects (e.g., canvas, paints, toys, stones, instruments). Piaget and others have noted that in children, embodied play emerges first, followed by projected play with objects. *Introjected* play occurs as mental imagery develops, leading to the "adult" forms of play such as daydreaming and creative thinking. Since art is an expression through action on objects in the world, there are no introjected art forms per se. However, introjected play, as the basis for all mental imagery and imagination, serves as the impetus for the artwork in the first place. Though playing and drawing may be the child's initial means of exploring the world, drama and art later become his/her means of expressing what was found. In this sense, art bridges the gap between the inner and outer worlds; the artwork is therefore an outward expression of an inward image. Indeed, this is the difference between sculpting versus building a stone wall, composing a letter versus typing someone else's letter. An artwork therefore returns to the world what had been introjected, evoking so often that uncanny feeling of familiarity in the midst of a new, creative act.

Singular and Multiple Art Forms. Through the exploration of these expressive elements, and learning and remembering the relationships among these elements, the artist gains greater control over their expression, and is able to utilize them in expressions of greater depth and power. As noted above, competent artists must both be able to tap into their inner imagery as well as having mastered the behavior of their artistic media or materials. Singular art forms are those that utilize one or a narrow range of media, such as painting, mime, poetry, sculpture, singing, or instrumental music. Multiple art forms are those that use a combination of artistic media, such as theatre, opera, ballet (See Figure 10). Historically, multiple art forms tended to develop first, since early communities found no reason to limit their range of expression (McNiff, 1980). Indeed, even arts based on smell and taste were integrated in these communal rituals/dances/enactments. Over time, interest in exploring artistic expression within the constraints of a singular art form has developed.

Summary

Thus, the arts can be defined as intentional variations of the expressive elements of sensation in external media, for the purpose of representing inner imagery and feeling. In this conceptualization, developmental process occurs only in the relation between mental imagery/feeling and the artist's variations. Neither the five senses nor their elements, nor types of media, are variable. Being constant, they are outside of a developmental paradigm. In this sense, I can conclude that the various art forms are developmentally equivalent; that is, they cannot be sequenced in one developmental continuum. Development is applicable in the expressive qualities the artist/client brings to the particular media, where what is being represented is either more or less differentiated, complex, accurate, integrated, harmonious, or interpersonal.

The Developmental Process of Artistic Expression

Development, then, is not to be confused with the series of steps, stages, or levels that are used to describe it. Development is not specific to particular art forms, art materials, or formats. Development must be an unfolding *process.* Describing clients by stages is like describing a race by the number of laps, rather than the process of running. So what is the developmental process of artistic expression? How do these expressive elements come to stand for human experience? How do they become infused with feeling and gather meaning? My answer to this question will be based on the concepts of differentiation and integration, and the notion of the self-other representation linked by an affective bond.

Heinz Werner, in a monumental work, *Comparative Psychology of Mental Development* (1948), proposed that development in general appears to proceed through stages of increasing differentiation and hierarchical integration. Thus, humans develop from one single cell, which divides into more cells that become differentiated into a wide range of forms and functions, ultimately composing a complex body. After each division, a specific relation is set up between the two entities that gives definition to each. When each of these divisions divide again, the resulting divisions have their own relationship to each other, but continue to be linked to the relationship established between their "parents." For example, a group of children at recess divide into two teams. Then each team meets and assigns roles of offense and defense. Then differentiated roles are assigned within the offense, and the defense. Differences increase within an organized whole (team). As two percepts are differentiated, they become hierarchically organized. Werner proposes that the instructions for development do not need to be complex; the developmental "operation" is always the same: a differentiation and integration of the new parts. Development then is a series of transformations in which the products of the prior events are acted upon by the same transformation. In this manner, complexity increases naturally even though governed by one fundamental operation. This is called a *recursive* process, which Figure 11 illustrates.

Figure 11

THE RECURSIVE PROCESS OF DEVELOPMENT

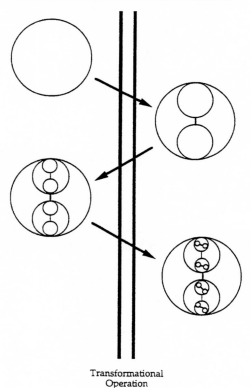

Transformational
Operation

Psychoanalytic object relations theory proposes that the person is a construction of representations of the self and others, and that, following Werner, through development, these become increasingly differentiated and hierarchically integrated. "The stages of development of internalized object relations—that is, the stages of infantile autism, symbiosis, separation-individuation, and object constancy—reflect the earliest structures of the psychic apparatus. Discrete units of self-representation, object representation and an affect disposition linking them are the basic structures of these early developmental stages, and will gradually evolve into more complex substructures..." (Kernberg, 1976, p. 17). The important contribution here is that the basic unit of human experience is a differentiated self-representation and other-representation, linked by an affective bond. This suggests that when this object relation was created, an original whole was differentiated into two parts, but remain integrated via the affective bond. That is, *the affect is the integrative element, and will be generated each time there is a differentiation.* As the inner world of the person is increasingly differentiated into parts, various affects are generated within each division, leading ultimately to an overall "mood" of the whole. Each affect contributes to this overall mood. In the example given above of the children at recess, this mood corresponds to the "morale" of the team. Each child will have a different feeling about their specific role, about their own team, and being a child at recess, yet all will participate in the general morale of the team. Such feelings are hierarchically organized, meaning they are simultaneously-held differences. For example, if I am asked "how are you feeling," after a moment of hesitation I can answer with my overall mood, but if asked, "how does your knee feel? how do you feel about your job? how do you feel about your sister?" I am likely to give different answers, despite the fact that presumably they had all been present when initially asked. Thus each self-other relationship is a complex of component moods, which give color, shape, depth, and tone to any given image or thought (Werner & Kaplan, 1963).

Linking Werner's recursive process of differentiation and hierarchical integration with the object relation's notion of affect as the integrative bond between differentiated percepts, I can now complete a model of the process of development of artistic expression. Development proceeds in a recursive fashion through a continuous series of transformations involving *perception* of distinctions in the environment, *affective response* to these distinctions, *animation* of the body and mind by the affect, and behavioral *expression* that alters the environment. Alterations in the environment inspire new perceptions and so the cycle continues. Within the context of artistic creation, the relevant environment consists of the artistic media, or arts/playspace (see Figure 12).

I will demonstrate this model with the following example: Let us begin with any random artistic act..... a brushstroke on the paper, or a steady beat on a drum. OK, I strike the drum. At first all there is, is noise. As I bring my attention to this noise, I hear the beat, and then I hear the silence. One cannot have a beat without a silence in between. That is, I differentiate the noise from the silence. There is now the beat and the silence. This differentiation brings with it an affect, small perhaps, but definitely present: a foreboding, a loss, anger. This affect, generated by the differentiation, now is present within me, and I allow it to influence my arm. That is, a loop is created between my perception and affective mood and my embodied action. In this case, feeling anger, I strike the drum harder. Another variation has been created, linking inner with outer. This cycle completes a primary artistic act. I notice the louder, sharper sound. Now there is the original beat, the silence, and the sharper beat. Another variation of affect is generated in comparing the sharper and normal beat. I am frightened; I am energized. This affect now influences my next beat, and perhaps I return to the normal beat. I then notice the phrase: normal beat, silence, sharper beat, silence, normal beat, which generates a new affect, let's say, pleasure. So I repeat the whole phrase. Over time, this familiar phrase becomes a piece of a self, or character. Added to other phrases, I soon construct a story.

Figure 12

THE MECHANISM OF DEVELOPMENT
IN THE CREATIVE ARTS THERAPIES

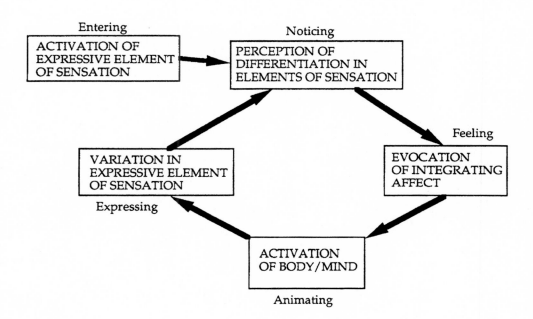

Through this process, random sounds or movements or brushstrokes come to be filled by feeling, and are then developed into meaning, then simple phrases, and then a picture, or song, or dance, or story. Indeed, as the artist pauses before beginning, and then presses a thumb into the clay or raises an arm, the deep attention to the nuance of feeling generated by that first artistic act, gives rise to the next. The artist's attention begins with note heard or color seen, but moves toward the *next* note or color sensed from within. The recognition of colors or postures or sound vibrations evokes feelings which then are looped back into expressive variations. These sets of variations and their affects become objects. The variations, affects, and objects become locations. The repetition of these situations create time (now and then), and space (here and there). Further development of these objects, in situations, spaces and times, creates story (real and imagined). The organization of stories creates the self and world. This, briefly stated, is the developmental process alive at the heart of artistic expression. The clinical implications for treatment of this perspective will now be described.

Implications for Treatment Process

A developmental model of any use should have implications for clinical practice. First, the above considerations suggest that the developmental process is independent of any specific arts modality, that is, developmental considerations are not so important between the various media, but *within* each one. Therefore, a basic developmental treatment process applicable to all the creative arts therapies should be possible.

Second, the above considerations de-emphasize the importance of stages and their attendant difficulties with linearity and prescription, and turn greater attention to the dynamics of variation, or expressiveness, brought to the work by the artist/client. By attending to elements such as the distance between signifier and signified, levels of autonomy and relatedness, stability in inner/outer distinctions, adaptability, and thought contents, the therapist is provided with a host of possible information about the ongoing progress of the client.

Third, these considerations suggest that appreciation of the fundamental developmental aspects of artistic expression will be congruent with any theoretical framework guiding the therapist's overall technique. However, embracing a purely developmental view would allow the therapist to eschew all other theory-based agendas and focus exclusively on facilitating the developmental process with the client. Grinnell's (1980) and Johnson's (1982) methodologies appear to be approximations of such approaches. Nevertheless, it seems possible now to sketch out what the basic principles of a purely developmental approach to the creative arts therapies might entail.

A Developmental Treatment Process

Entering. First, the client and therapist must enter the therapy space and have found a way into the imaginal realm, what I have called the *arts/play-space*, through some kind of warm-up activity (see Chapter 19). The client becomes engaged in the creative medium.

Noticing. The developmental process begins when the client differentiates a perception, often on his/her own. The therapist can, if needed, facilitate this process by using methods that bring the client's attention to the artistic expression. Essentially, the therapist poses the question, "What do you notice?" which of course can be asked verbally or nonverbally (by pointing, or looking at the artwork).

Feeling. When the client does notice something, a feeling or mood will arise in relation to it. Since so often these processes are happening rapidly, it is common for them to be passed over. A developmental therapist will, however, be specifically tracking them. The question, "what feeling arises?" can again be asked directly, or implied by nonverbal methods.

Animating. The next step is allowing that feeling or mood to animate the body/mind, that is, to let that feeling in. The therapist can facilitate this step if needed by direct methods, saying "tell me more about that feeling," "let that feeling in," "what does that feeling have to say?" or within the action of the art expression itself (e.g., providing a pause in action, looking at the client, modeling a movement). This step is very much an embodied one, of submitting to the feeling without predetermining its effect. If the affect is not listened to, the client's inner world is diminished, and they will have difficulty sensing what to do next. If the animation is directed into noncreative avenues, the client may engage in acting out or avoidant verbalization.

Expressing. The last step involves allowing the animation to express itself in the next creative act, whether that be the sound, movement, brushstroke, poetic phrase, or dramatic characterization. The therapist can be helpful in this step by altering the conditions available to the client for that expression: providing different materials, changing the structure of the group, or shifting instruments. Those who work intermodally can also allow a shift in media entirely, as in moving from drama to art, or movement to poetry. As the client expresses him/herself in a new way, the process moves back to the beginning by bringing the client's attention to that new expression.

Other Considerations. Verbalization and insights can occur during any one of these steps, however, if verbalization is viewed as an endpoint, or point of departure from this developmental process, then it should be avoided. For example, if when asked about how one feels, the client speaks about his family, then at some point the therapist should continue with the process of animating by having the client direct his feelings expressed about his family into his next creative expression. Verbalization should be incorporated into this process, not used to abort it.

The process above is written as if the therapist's role is as a guide or facilitator of the client's interaction within the arts/playspace. However, many therapists work interpersonally, where they are a full participant in the arts/playspace with the client. In such cases, the therapist will need to progress through these steps along with the client. This will tend to reduce verbalization and emphasize nonverbal interventions by the therapist as she/he responds to the client. In this case, what the client is asked to notice may be the therapist's behavior, not a sandtray or their own movement. Here the developmental process becomes an intersubjective one. In this approach, the therapist's own capacities for attending, feeling, animating, and expressing may become powerful healing factors for the client, and the therapist's difficulties with them may become interferences in the client's healing journey.

The process outlined above bears striking similarities to many well-established therapeutic approaches that utilize developmental ideas. Among these include Eugene Gendlin's (1981) focusing method and Fritz Perls' (1969) gestalt therapy. Many creative arts therapists follow similar approaches in their interactions with clients, even when they do not identify themselves as using a developmental model, as can be seen in many case examples published in the literature. My purpose in explicating this model is to highlight the essential elements underpinning the developmental process in the creative arts therapies, to point out it is not dependent upon the specific arts modality used, and to offer a simplified outline of a clinical method. I will end with an example of how such a process might occur, taken from my own method in drama therapy.

Clinical Example

This example is from an ongoing group of women who were in a developmental transformations group (see Johnson, 1986).

Entering: The eight women enter the room. The therapist asks them to form a circle and stretch their bodies. The therapist instructs them to raise their hands and pull down the drama therapy "curtain" and then one at a time enter the pretend space. The women do this easily and with energy.

Noticing. The group begins a warm-up exercise where each one leads the group for a moment with a sound and a movement, and then passes the leadership to the person on their left. As G. shook her hands and then moved them toward the center of the circle with a "Huh" sound, another member, B., made a much more tired sounding version of "Huh." The therapist could tell that other members noticed this difference. The therapist turned to B. and smiling, said, "Huuhh?" in a similar manner. B. responded playfully, "Huuuh, HUUUHHH." The group laughed with energy.

Feeling. The therapist then asked, "Well what kind of HUHH, was that?" and different group members responded with "tired," "exhausted," "frustrated," until one member A. said, "totally exasperated," whereupon most members exclaimed, "Yes!"

Animating. The therapist paused and said, "hmm, let that feeling come into your mind and body. Imagine not only what B. must be feeling but how you are feeling about it." The group members variously began small swaying movements, looked down in thought, or remained still.

Expressing. The therapist then asked the group to repeat the movement just as B. had presented it, in unison, aware that each member would be having her own associations to the action. The group burst into action as they said or shouted, "HuuuH!" repeatedly. Another member, L., began to be filled up with emotion as if she was thinking of a situation in her life that distressed her. She directed her arm movements toward another woman, M., across the circle from her, who began to respond back to her in a slightly different manner, almost an arrogantly uttered, "Yehhhh."

Noticing. The whole group's attention now focused on these two without the therapist having to say anything. She motioned for L. and M. to enter the circle and interact with each other. They immediately began to interact, making a variety of sounds and sneers at each other, as if L. were playing some kind of a victim trying to stand up to M.

Feeling. The therapist asked group members to say how this interaction was making them feel, and several feelings and images were mentioned....

This example hopefully illustrates how one methodology, in this case developmental transformations, might implement the process outlined above.

Conclusion

The developmental paradigm has been utilized by creative arts therapists for purposes of assessment and therapeutic intervention. In general, these attempts have been overly influenced by the particular modality and clinical styles of their authors, obscuring the fundamental connection between developmental process and artistic expression. An analysis of the arts in relation to development reveals that each art modality has the same relationship with developmental processes: development expresses itself through the structure and content of the artist's variations of expressive elements of sensation. Additionally, by focusing on the basic processes of development rather than stages, many of the weaknesses of a developmental paradigm (e.g., linearity, primacy of higher forms) can be avoided. A new model of developmental process is proposed, based on the concepts of differentiation, integration, and affective bond, that highlights development as a recursive transformation of perception, affect, and bodily expression. Such a model describes phenomena shared by all of the creative arts therapies, and thus contributes to a scholarship supporting their intimate connection.

Section IV
EPILOGUE

Chapter 21

THE OTHER ROOM

I have had a private practice in drama therapy since 1976. However, since 1980, when I became a clinical psychologist, I have seen clients both for drama therapy and verbal psychotherapy. My office has two rooms: one is set up like a traditional office with two chairs, a desk, a carpet, and file cabinets. The other room is a large carpeted room with almost no furniture in it —a pile of pillows, a stereo, a box containing puppets and props, two small chairs, a bench, and two wooden cubes. This is where I usually conduct drama therapy sessions.

Some clients will come to me specifically for verbal psychotherapy. In fact, they often do not know that I am also a drama therapist. When they enter my office, they have to pass through the other room first. Even though they look at this room with curiosity, not one of these clients has ever commented about it during the first session. Only later. Our conversation then goes something like this.

Act One

Client:	That's an interesting room.
DRJ:	Hmm, mm.
Client:	What's it for?
DRJ:	That is where I work with my clients in drama therapy.
Client:	Oh, you mean with children.
DRJ:	Adults, too.
Client:	That's interesting.

And then they drop the subject. That is okay with me, since I do not feel it is my job to get them to do drama therapy when they came to me for something else. Nevertheless, the other room apparently continues to bother them. A few sessions or months later, the client will ask again.

Revised from *Dramascope, 8,* 1992 with permission of the National Association for Drama Therapy.

Act Two

Client:	That's an interesting room
DRJ:	Hmm, mm.
Client:	What kinds of things do you do in there?
DRJ:	Well, we move around, role play different scenes, play, really..... not much more than that.
Client:	That sounds really creative.
DRJ:	People have a chance to try out different aspects of themselves in drama therapy.
Client:	I'm sure that's really helpful for certain types of people.
DRJ:	Hmm, mm.

And that will be all. We continue with our verbal therapy; we develop a strong alliance; I show genuineness and warmth; the client achieves new insights......Until, perhaps a couple of months later, the client will raise the subject again.

Act Three

Client:	You know, about that other room?
DRJ:	Yes.
Client:	If you were to work with someone like me, with issues similar to those that I struggle with, what would you do in that other room?
DRJ:	(I explain in more detail about improvisational roleplaying.)
Client:	That sounds really interesting.
DRJ:	Yes.
Client:	Not that I think we should do it.
DRJ:	Hmm, mm.

I can see their struggle—they are drawn to it as if they already know what is in that empty room—yet it is new and will require a reorganization. It means taking a risk......Finally, when they cannot take it anymore, when the traditional two chairs and a desk and filing cabinets are no longer enough; when their wish to find the freedom that has eluded them in hours of talk overwhelms them, they finally say:

Act Four

Client:	You know that other room?
DRJ:	Yes.
Client:	I think I would like to try doing drama therapy in there.
DRJ:	Let's think about it.
Client:	I'm tired of thinking about it. I want to give it a try, though I have no idea what we will do.
DRJ:	There is nothing special about that room. It will just be you and me, just like here.
Client:	Yes, I suppose. Even though there is nothing in there....it is open. I want to go.
DRJ:	Seems like an interesting idea. OK.

And we begin to work in that other room, the room that represents imagination, creativity, spontaneity, role—something other than, or beyond, the self. It is an empty room filled with freedom, with possibility, with drama: things that my clients came to psychotherapy to rediscover.

There is an Other Room beckoning creative arts therapists, an open room where we can be together. True, each of us has our own traditional room that is comfortable, known. This Other Room of a unified creative arts therapy profession is just next door—we see it each time we work together. Entering that room will also require a reorganization, will mean taking a risk. Even if no one enters it for a long time, it will always be there as a possibility. I must be patient.

This other room, this other Self, beckons. It has been hard for my clients to resist.

SELECTED BIBLIOGRAPHY ON THE CREATIVE ARTS THERAPIES

Books

Blatner, A., & Blatner, A. (1988). *The art of play.* New York: Human Sciences Press.

Feder, E., & Feder, B. (1981). *The expressive arts therapies.* Englewood Cliffs, NJ: Prentice-Hall.

Fleshman, R., & Fryrear, J. (1981). *The arts in therapy.* Chicago: Nelson Hall.

Gladding, S. (1992). *Counseling as an art: The creative arts in counseling.* Alexandria, VA: American Association for Counseling and Development.

Lewis, P. (1993). *Creative transformation: The healing power of the arts.* Wilmette, IL: Chiron Publications

McNiff, S. (1981). *The arts and psychotherapy.* Springfield, IL: Charles C Thomas.

McNiff, S. (1986). *Educating the creative arts therapist.* Springfield, IL: Charles C Thomas.

McNiff, S. (1992). *Art as medicine: Creating a therapy of the imagination.* Boston: Shambala.

Payne, H. (Ed.). (1993). *Handbook of inquiry in the art therapies: One river, many currents.* London: Jessica Kingsley.

Robbins, A. (1980). *Expressive therapy: A creative arts approach to depth-oriented treatment.* New York: Human Sciences Press.

Robbins, A. (1986). *The artist as therapist.* New York: Human Sciences Press.

Robbins, A. (1989). *The psychoaesthetic experience.* New York: Human Sciences Press.

Spitz, E. (1985). *Art and psyche.* New Haven, CT: Yale University Press.

Warren, B. (1984). *Using the creative arts in therapy.* Cambridge, MA: Brookline Books.

Weisberg, N., & Wilder, R. (1985). *Creative arts with older adults.* New York: Human Sciences Press.

Weiss, J. (1984). *Expressive therapy with elders and the disabled.* New York: Haworth.

Professional

Aldridge, D. (1993). Artists or psychotherapists? *Arts in Psychotherapy, 20,* 199-200.

Arnheim, R. (1990). The artist as healer. *Arts in Psychotherapy, 17,* 1-4.

Bruscia, K. (1986). A future together–The National Coalition of Arts Therapy Associations. *Arts in Psychotherapy, 13,* 95-100.

190   *Essays on the Creative Arts Therapies*

Cashell, L., & Miner, A. (1983). Role conflict and role ambiguity among creative arts therapists. *Arts in Psychotherapy, 10,* 93-112.

Dulicai, D. (1984). The challenge we face. *Arts in Psychotherapy, 12,* 247-248.

Dulicai, D., Hays, R., & Nolan, P. (1989). Training the creative arts therapist: Identity with integration. *Arts in Psychotherapy, 16,* 11-14.

Fink, P. (1988). The importance of the creative arts therapist in psychiatric treatment. *Arts in Psychotherapy, 15,* 175-176.

Fryrear, J., & Fleshman, R. (1981). Career information on the arts in mental health. *Arts in Psychotherapy, 8,* 219-224.

Gibson, G. (1989). Beyond creative arts therapies. *Arts in Psychotherapy, 16,* 219-222.

Irwin, E. (1988). Arts therapy and healing. *Arts in Psychotherapy, 15,* 193-296.

Jampel, P. (1991). Echoes of the 1990 NCATA Conference. *Arts in Psychotherapy, 18,* 459-462.

Knill, P. (1994). Multiplicity as a tradition: Theories for interdisciplinary arts therapies—an overview. *Arts in Psychotherapy, 21,* 319-329.

Landy, R. (1995). Isolation and collaboration in the creative arts therapies—The implications of crossing borders. *Arts in Psychotherapy, 22,* 83-86.

Lerner, A. (1984). The creative arts in therapy as an integral part of treatment. *Arts in Psychotherapy, 12,* 293-296.

Levick, M. (1980). Response to Connie Naitove—Creative arts therapist: Jack of all trades or master of one? *Arts in Psychotherapy, 7,* 261-265.

Levick, M. (1989). On the road to educating the creative arts therapist. *Arts in Psychotherapy, 16,* 57-60.

Levick, M. (1995). The identity of the creative arts therapist: Guided by ethics. *Arts in Psychotherapy, 22,* 283-297.

Lippin, R. (1985). Arts medicine: A call for a new medical specialty. *Arts in Psychotherapy, 12,* 147-151.

Lorenzetti, M. (1994). Perspectives on integration between arts therapy areas. *Arts in Psychotherapy, 21,* 113-118.

MacLean, B. (1991). Developing a meaningful quality assurance program. *Arts in Psychotherapy, 18,* 51-58.

McNiff, S. (1988). The shaman within. *Arts in Psychotherapy, 15,* 285-292.

Moreno, J. (1988). Creative arts therapist and contemporary shaman. *Arts in Psychotherapy, 15,* 271-280.

Naitove, C. (1980). Creative arts therapist: Jack of all trades or master of one? *Arts in Psychotherapy, 7,* 253-260.

Nijenhuis, A. (1992). Fieldwork and training in the development of the profession of creative therapy: A fruitful dialogue. *Arts in Psychotherapy, 19,* 93-98.

Nijenhuis, A. (1993). Arts therapy: The integration of art and therapy. *Arts in Psychotherapy, 20,* 201-204.

Robbins, A. (1982). Integrating the personal and theoretical splits in the struggle towards an identity as art therapists. *Arts in Psychotherapy, 9,* 1-10.

Robbins, A. (1985). Working towards the establishment of creative arts therapies as an independent profession. *Arts in Psychotherapy, 12,* 67-70.

Sandel, S. (1987). Moving into management. *Arts in Psychotherapy, 14,* 109-112.

Sandel, S. (1989). On being a female creative arts therapist. *Arts in Psychotherapy, 16,* 239-242.

Scavone, K. (1992). State creative arts therapies coalitions: Models and challenges. *Arts in Psychotherapy, 19,* 57-60.

Schmais, C. (1988). Creative arts therapies and shamanism: A comparison. *Arts in Psychotherapy, 15,* 281-284.

Smitskamp, H. (1995). The problem of professional diagnosis in the arts therapies, *Arts in Psychotherapy, 22,* 181-188.

Stark, A., & Warres, J. (1984). A working model for a conference on the creative/expressive arts therapies. *Arts in Psychotherapy, 12,* 279-282.

Vaccaro, M. et al. (1979). Mini-symposium: The interfaces of creativity in therapy. *Arts in Psychotherapy, 6,* 137-154.

Wadeson, H. (1989). In a different image: Are male pressures shaping the female arts therapy professions? *Arts in Psychotherapy, 16,* 327-330.

Weiss, B. (1988). The administrative journey. *Arts in Psychotherapy, 15,* 161-164.

Clinical

Adelman, E., & Castricone, L. (1986). An expressive arts model for substance abuse group training and treatment. *Arts in Psychotherapy, 13,* 53-60.

Adler, R. & Fisher, P. (1984). My self—through music, movement, and art. *Arts in Psychotherapy, 12,* 203-208.

Aldridge, A. (1993). Hope, meaning, and the creative arts therapies the treatment of AIDS. *Arts in Psychotherapy, 20,* 285-298.

Ambrogne-O'Toole, C. (1988). Exploring female sexuality through the expressive therapies. *Arts in Psychotherapy, 15,* 109-118.

Farrelly, J., & Joseph, A. (1991). Expressive therapies in a crisis intervention service. *Arts in Psychotherapy, 18,* 131-138.

Goldberg, F., Coto-McKenna, S., & Cohn, L. (1991). Creative arts group process evaluation tool: Implications for clinical practice and training. *Arts in Psychotherapy, 18,* 411-418.

Goldstein-Roca, S. & Crisafulli, T. (1994). Integrative creative arts therapy: A brief treatment model. *Arts in Psychotherapy, 21,* 219-222.

Harvey, S. (1991). Creating a family: An integrated expressive approach to adoption. *Arts in Psychotherapy, 18,* 213-222.

Johnson, C., Lahey, P., & Shore, A. (1992). An exploration of creative arts therapeutic group work on an Alzheimer's unit. *Arts in Psychotherapy, 19,* 269-278.

Kelly, C. (1988). Expressive therapy assessment. *Arts in Psychotherapy, 15,* 63-70.

Landy, R. (1987). The creative arts therapy workshop as form and function. *Arts in Psychotherapy, 14,* 279-284.

Lawlor, E. (1992). Creativity and change: The two-tiered creative arts therapy approach to codependency treatment. *Arts in Psychotherapy, 19,* 19-28.

Lyons, S., & Tropea, E. (1987). Creative arts therapists as consultants: Methods and approaches to inservice training in the special education forum. *Arts in Psychotherapy, 14,* 243-248.

Naitove, C. (1988). Arts therapy with child molesters: An historical perspective on the act and an approach to treatment. *Arts in Psychotherapy, 15,* 151-160.

Pulliam, J., Somerville, P., Prebluda, J., & Warja-Danielsson, M. (1988). Three heads are better than one: The expressive arts group assessment. *Arts in Psychotherapy, 15,* 71-78.

Turner, Y., & Clark-Schock, K. (1990). Dynamic corporate training for women: A creative arts therapies approach. *Arts in Psychotherapy, 17,* 217-222.

Theoretical

Aldridge, D., Brandt, G., & Wohler, D. (1990). Toward a common language among the creative arts therapies. *Arts in Psychotherapy, 17,* 189-196.

Arnheim, R. (1980). Art as therapy. *Arts in Psychotherapy, 7,* 247-252.

Blatner, A. (1991). Theoretical principles underlying creative arts therapies. *Arts in Psychotherapy, 18,* 405-410.

Bruscia, K. (1988). Standards for clinical assessment in the arts therapies. *Arts in Psychotherapy, 15,* 5-10.

Cavallo, M., & Robbins, A. (1980). Understanding an object relations theory through a psychodynamically oriented expressive therapy approach. *Arts in Psychotherapy, 7,* 113-124.

Diaz de Chumaceiro, C. (1995). Serendipity's role in psychotherapy: A bridge to the creative arts therapies. *Arts in Psychotherapy, 22,* 39-48.

Emunah, R. (1990). Expression and expansion in adolescence: The significance of creative arts therapy. *Arts in Psychotherapy, 17,* 101-108.

Fink, P. (1973). Art as a reflection of mental status. *Arts in Psychotherapy, 1,* 17-30.

Garai, J. (1979). New horizons of the humanistic approach to expressive therapies and creativity development. *Arts in Psychotherapy, 6,* 177-184.

Gorelick, K. (1989). Rapprochement between the arts and psychotherapies: Metaphor the mediator. *Arts in Psychotherapy, 16,* 149-156.

Grenadier, S. (1995). The place wherein truth lies: An expressive therapy perspective on trauma, innocence, and human nature. *Arts in Psychotherapy, 22,* 393-402.

Irwin, E. (1986). On being and becoming a therapist. *Arts in Psychotherapy, 13,* 191-196.

Johnson, L. (1990). Creative therapies in the treatment of addictions: The art of transforming shame. *Arts in Psychotherapy, 17,* 299-308.

Kagin, S. & Lusebrink, V. (1978). The expressive therapies continuum. *Arts in Psychotherapy, 5,* 171-180.

Knill, P. (1995). The place of beauty in therapy and the arts. *Arts in Psychotherapy, 22,* 1 - 8.

Landgarten, H. (1991). Family creative arts therapies: Past and present. *Arts in Psychotherapy, 18,* 191-194.

Landy, R. (1993). A research agenda for the creative arts therapies. *Arts in Psychotherapy, 20,* 1-2.

Landy, R. (1993). The child, the dreamer, the artist, and the fool: In search of understanding the meaning of expressive therapy. *Arts in Psychotherapy, 20,* 359-370.

Lewis, P. (1987). The expressive arts therapies in the choreography of object relations. *Arts in Psychotherapy, 14,* 321-332.

Lewis, P. (1988). The transformative process within the imaginal realm. *Arts in Psychotherapy, 15,* 309-316.

Lewis, P. (1992). The creative arts in transference/countertransference relationships. *Arts in Psychotherapy, 19,* 317-324.

Lusebrink, V. (1989). Education in creative arts therapies: Accomplishments and challenges. *Arts in Psychotherapy, 16,* 5-10.

Lusebrink, V. (1991). A systems oriented approach to the expressive therapies: The expressive therapies continuum. *Arts in Psychotherapy, 18,* 395-404.

McNiff, S. (1986). Freedom of research and artistic inquiry. *Arts in Psychotherapy, 13,* 279-284.

McNiff, S. (1987). Research and scholarship in the creative arts therapies. *Arts in Psychotherapy, 14,* 285-292.

McNiff, S. (1991). Ethics and the autonomy of images. *Arts in Psychotherapy, 18,* 277-284.

McNiff, S. (1993). The authority of experience. *Arts in Psychotherapy, 20,* 3-10.

Niederland, W., & Sholevar, B. (1981). The creative process—A psychoanalytic discussion. *Arts in Psychotherapy, 8,* 71-102.

Politsky, R. (1995). Toward a typology of research in the creative arts therapies. *Arts in Psychotherapy, 22,* 307-314.

Robbins, A. (1988). A psychoaesthetic perspective on creative arts therapy and training. *Arts in Psychotherapy, 15,* 95-100.

Robbins, A. (1992). The play of psychotherapeutic artistry and psychoaesthetics. *Arts in Psychotherapy, 19,* 177-186.

REFERENCES

Aldridge, D., Brandt, G., & Wohler, D. (1990). Toward a common language among the creative arts therapies. *Arts in Psychotherapy, 17*, 189-195.

Almond, R. (1974). *The healing community.* New York: Jason Aronson.

Arrington, D. (1991). Thinking systems—seeing systems: An integrative model for systemically oriented art therapy. *Arts in Psychotherapy, 18*, 201-212.

Behrends, R., & Blatt, S. (1985). Internalization and psychological development throughout the life cycle. *The Psychoanalytic Study of the Child, 40*, 11-39.

Bell, J. (1984). Family therapy in motion: Observing, assisting, and changing the family dance. In P.L. Bernstein (Ed.), *Theoretical approaches in dance/movement therapy.* Iowa: Kendall-Hunt.

Blatner, A. (1991). Theoretical principles underlying the creative arts therapies. *Arts in Psychotherapy, 18*, 405-410.

Bonny, H. L. (1987). Music: The language of immediacy. *Arts in Psychotherapy, 14*, 255-262.

Bowlby, J. (1961). Process of mourning. *International Journal of Psychoanalysis, 42*, 317-340.

Bruner, J. (1964). The course of cognitive growth. *American Psychologist, 19*, 1-6.

Bruscia, K. (1986). A future together—The National Coalition of Arts Therapy Associations. *Arts in Psychotherapy, 13*, 95-101.

Bruscia, K. (1987). *Improvisational models of music therapy.* Springfield, IL: Charles C Thomas.

Bruscia, K. (1988). Standards for clinical assessment in the arts therapies. *Arts in Psychotherapy, 15*, 5-10.

Bump, J. (1990). Innovative bibliography approaches to substance abuse education. *Arts in Psychotherapy, 17*, 355-362.

Carey, L. (1991). Family sandplay therapy. *Arts in Psychotherapy, 18*, 231-240.

Cashell, L., & Miner, A. (1983). Role conflict and role ambiguity among creative arts therapists. *Arts in Psychotherapy, 10*, 93-98.

Cavallo, M., & Robbins, A. (1980). Understanding an object relations theory through a psychodynamically oriented expressive therapy approach. *Arts in Psychotherapy, 7*, 113-124.

Cole, D. (1975). *The theatrical event,* Middletown, CT: Wesleyan University Press.

Courtney, R. (1968). *Play, drama, and thought.* New York: Drama Book Specialists.

Cox, K.L., & Price, K. (1990). Breaking through: Incident drawings with adolescent substance abusers. *Arts in Psychotherapy, 17*, 333-338.

Decuir, A. (1991). Trends in music and family therapy. *Arts in Psychotherapy, 18,* 195-200.

DiLeo, J. (1973). *Children's drawings as diagnostic aids.* New York: Brunner/Mazel.

Dintino, C., & Johnson, D. (1996). Playing with the perpetrator: Gender dynamics in developmental drama therapy. In S. Jennings (Ed.), *Drama therapy: Theory and practice, Vol. 3,* (pp. 205-220). London: Routledge.

Dosamantes, E. (1992). Spatial patterns associated with the separation-individuation process in adult long-term psychodynamically movement therapy groups. *Arts in Psychotherapy, 19,* 3-12.

Dulicai, D. (1984). The challenge we face. *Arts in Psychotherapy, 11,* 247-248.

Dulicai, D., Hays, R., & Nolan, P. (1989). Training the creative arts therapist: Identity with integration. *Arts in Psychotherapy, 16,* 11-14.

Ehrenzweig, A. (1967). *The hidden order of art.* Berkeley, CA: University of California Press.

Ellis, M.L. (1989). Women: The mirage of the perfect image. *Arts in Psychotherapy, 16,* 263-276.

Emunah, R. (1985). Drama therapy and adolescent resistance. *Arts in Psychotherapy, 12,* 71-79.

Emunah, R. (1989). The use of dramatic enactment in the training of drama therapists. *Arts in Psychotherapy, 16,* 29-36.

Emunah, R. (1994). *Acting for real: Drama therapy process, technique, and performance.* New York: Brunner/Mazel.

Emunah, R., & Johnson, D. (1983). The impact of theatrical performance on the self-images of psychiatric patients. *Arts in Psychotherapy, 10,* 233-240.

Erickson, E. (1940). Studies in interpretation of play. *Genetic Psychological Monographs, 22,* 134 - 201.

Erickson, E. (1963). *Childhood and society.* New York: Norton.

Fieffer, J. (1966). *Little murders.* New York: Pantheon.

Figley, C. (1985). *Trauma and its wake.* New York: Brunner/Mazel.

Fisher, B. (1990). Dance/movement therapy: Its use in a 28-day substance abuse program. *Arts in Psychotherapy, 17,* 325-332.

Forrester, A., & Johnson, D. (1995). Drama therapy on an extremely short term inpatient unit. In A. Gersie (Ed.), *Brief treatment approaches to drama therapy,* pp. 125-138. London: Routledge.

Frank, J. (1962). *Persuasion and healing.* New York: Basic Books.

Freud, S. (1905/1978). Three essays on the theory of sexuality. In J. Strachey (Ed.), *Standard edition of the complete psychological works, Vol. 7.* London: Hogarth Press.

Freud, S. (1920/1966). *Introductory lectures on psychoanalysis.* New York: Norton.

Freud, S. (1924/1978). Mourning and melancholia. In J. Strachey (Ed.), *Standard edition of the complete psychological works, 14,* 243-258.

Freud, S. (1920/1978). Beyond the pleasure principle. In J. Strachey (Ed.), *Standard edition of the complete psychological works, Vol. 18.* London: Hogarth Press.

Gardner, H. (1974). *The shattered mind.* New York: Random House.

Gardner, H. (1980). *Artful scribbles: The significance of children's drawings.* New York: Basic Books.

Gardner, H. (1982). *Art, mind, and brain.* New York: Basic Books

Geller, S., DePalma, D., & Daw, J. (1981). Developing art therapy services in a university counseling center. *American Journal of Art Therapy.*

Gendlin, E. (1981). *Focusing.* New York: Bantam.

Gergen, K. (1991). *The saturated self.* New York: Basic Books.

Gesell, A., & Ilg, F. (1943). *Infant and child in the culture of today.* New York: Harper.

Gilligan, C. (1982). *In a different voice: Psychological theory and women's development.* Cambridge, MA: Harvard University Press.

Goldberg, F., Coto-McKenna, S., & Cohen, L. (1991). Creative arts group process evaluation tool: Implications for clinical practice and training. *Arts in Psychotherapy, 18,* 411-418.

Golub, D. (1985). Symbolic expression in posttraumatic stress disorder: Vietnam combat veterans in art therapy. *Arts in Psychotherapy, 12,* 285-296.

Goodenough, F. (1926). *Measurement of intelligence by drawings.* New York: World Book.

Gorelick, K. (1989). Rapprochement between the arts and psychotherapies: Metaphor the mediator. *Arts in Psychotherapy, 16,* 149-155.

Gould, R. (1972). *Child studies through fantasy.* New York: Quadrangle.

Grainger, R. (1990). *Drama and healing: The roots of drama therapy.* London: Jessica Kingsley.

Greenberg, M., & van der Kolk, B. (1987). Retrieval and integration of traumatic memories with the "painting cure". In van der Kolk, B. (Ed.), *Psychological trauma,* (pp. 191-216). Washington, DC: American Psychiatric Press.

Grinnell, B. (1980). *The developmental therapeutic process: A new theory of therapeutic intervention.* (Doctoral dissertation, Bryn Mawr College, Bryn Mawr, PA). Available from University Microfilms.

Harlow, H., & Harlow, M. (1971). Psychopathology in monkeys. In H. Kimmel, (Ed.), *Experimental psychopathology.* New York: Academic Press.

Harner, M. (1982). *The way of the shaman.* New York: Bantam Books.

Harvey, S. (1991). Creating a family: An integrated expressive approach to adoption. *Arts in Psychotherapy, 18,* 213-222.

Horovitz, E. (1981). Art therapy in arrested development of a preschooler. *Arts in Psychotherapy, 8,* 119-126.

Horovitz-Darby, E.G. (1991). Family art therapy within a deaf system. *Arts in Psychotherapy, 18,* 251-262.

Horowitz, M. (1970). *Image formation and cognition.* New York: Appleton-Century-Crofts.

Horowitz, M. (1976). *Stress response syndromes.* New York: Jason Aronson.

Huxley, A. (1954). *The doors of perception.* New York: Harper & Row.

Irwin, E. (1977). Play, fantasy, and symbol: Drama with emotionally disturbed children. *American Journal of Psychotherapy, 31,* 426-436.

Irwin, E. (1986). On being and becoming a therapist. *Arts in Psychotherapy, 13,* 191-196.

Irwin, E. (1988). Arts therapy and healing. *Arts in Psychotherapy, 15,* 293-296.

Jacobson, E. (1964). *The self and object world.* New York: International Universities Press.

Jaffe, P., Wolfe, D., Wilson, S., et al. (1986). Family violence and child adjustment: A comparative analysis of girls' and boys' behavioral symptoms. *American Journal of Psychiatry, 143,* 74-77.

Jampel, P.F. (1991). Echoes of the 1990 NCATA Conference. *Arts in Psychotherapy, 18,* 459-462.

Jennings, S. (1993). *Introduction to dramatherapy.* London: Jessica Kingsley.

Jennings, S. (1994). The theatre of healing: Metaphor and metaphysics in the healing process. In S. Jennings (Ed.), *The handbook of dramatherapy,* (pp. 93-113). New York: Routledge.

Jernberg, A. (1979). *Theraplay.* San Francisco: Jossey-Bass.

Johnson, D. (1980). Effects of a theatre experience on hospitalized psychiatric patients. *Arts in Psychotherapy, 7,* 265-272.

Johnson, D. (1982). Developmental approaches in drama therapy. *Arts in Psychotherapy, 9,* 183-190.

Johnson, D. (1984). The representation of the internal world in catatonic schizophrenia. *Psychiatry, 47,* 299-314.

Johnson, D. (1986). The developmental method in drama therapy: Group treatment with the elderly. *Arts in Psychotherapy, 13,* 17-34.

Johnson, D. (1991). The theory and technique of transformations in drama therapy. *Arts in Psychotherapy, 18,* 285 - 300.

Johnson, D., Forrester, A., Dintino, C., James, M., & Schnee, G. (1996). Towards a poor drama therapy. *Arts in Psychotherapy, 23,* 293-306.

Johnson, D., & Eicher, V. (1990). The use of dramatic activities to facilitate dance therapy with adolescents. *Arts in Psychotherapy, 17,* 157-164.

Johnson, D., & Munich, R. (1975). Increasing hospital-community contact through a theatre program in a psychiatric hospital. *Hospital and Community Psychiatry, 26,* 435-438.

Johnson, D., & Sandel, S. (1977). Structural analysis of movement sessions: preliminary research. *American Journal of Dance Therapy, 1,* 32-36.

Johnson, D., Sandel, S., & Bruno, C. (1984). Effectiveness of different group structures for schizophrenic, character-disordered, and normal groups. *International Journal of Group Psychotherapy, 34,* 413-429.

Johnson, D., Sandel, S., & Eicher, V. (1983). Structural aspects of group leadership styles. *American Journal of Dance Therapy, 6,* 17-30.

Johnson, L. (1990). Creative therapies in the treatment of addictions: The art of transforming shame. *Arts in Psychotherapy, 17,* 299-308.

Jung, C. (1931/1960). The stages of life. *Collected Works of C.G. Jung, vol. 12.* Princeton, NJ: Princeton University Press.

Jung, C. (1954). *Collected works.* New York: Bollingen.

Jung, C. (1974). Letter to Bill W. In *AA Grapevine.* New York: Alcoholics Anonymous.

Kagin, S. & Lusebrink, V. (1978). The expressive therapies continuum. *Arts in Psychotherapy, 5,* 171-180.

Kaufman, G. (1980). *Shame: The power of caring.* Cambridge, MA: Schenkman.

Kernberg, O. (1976). *Object relations theory and clinical psychoanalysis.* New York: Jason Aronson.

Kestenberg, J. (1975). *Children and parents, studies in development.* New York: Jason Aronson.

Klein, M. (1932). *The psychoanalysis of children.* London: Hogarth.

Klein, M. (1937). Love, guilt, and reparation. In M. Klein & J. Riviere (Eds.), *Love, hate, and reparation,* (pp. 306-343). London: Hogarth.

Klein, M. (1955). The psychoanalytic play technique. In: *New directions in psychoanalysis.* London: Tavistock.

Kohlberg, L., & Lickona, T. (1986). *The stages of ethical development: From childhood through old age.* San Francisco: Harper.

Kohut, H. (1971). *The analysis of the self.* New York: International Universities Press.

Kolb, L. (1984). The posttraumatic stress disorders of combat: A subgroup with a conditional emotional response. *Military Medicine, 149,* 237-243.

Kris, E. (1952). *Psychoanalytic explorations in art.* New York: International Universities Press.

Krystal, H. (1979). Alexithymia and psychotherapy. *American Journal of Psychotherapy, 33,* 17-31.

Kwiatkowska, H.X. (1978). *Family therapy and evaluation through art.* Springfield, IL: Charles C Thomas.

Landgarten, H. (1975). Adult art psychotherapy. *Arts in Psychotherapy, 2,* 65-76.

Landgarten, H. (1987). *Family art psychotherapy: A clinical guide and case book.* New York: Brunner/Mazel.

Landy, R. (1982). Training the drama therapist: A four part model. *Arts in Psychotherapy, 9,* 91-99.

Landy, R. (1983). The use of distancing in drama therapy. *Arts in Psychotherapy, 10,* 175-185.

Landy, R. (1986). *Drama therapy: Concepts and practices.* Springfield, IL: Charles C Thomas.

Landy, R. (1993). *Persona and performance.* New York: Guilford.

Lane, R., & Schwartz, G. (1987). Levels of emotional awareness: A cognitive-developmental theory and its application to psychopathology. *American Journal of Psychiatry, 144,* 133-143.

Langer, S. (1953). *Feeling and form.* New York: Charles Scribner's Sons.

Leedy, J.J. (1969). *Poetry therapy.* Philadelphia: Lippincott.

Leedy, J.J. (1985). *Poetry as healer: Mending the troubled mind.* New York: Vanguard.

Leveton, E. (1991). The use of doubling to counter resistance in family and individual treatment. *Arts in Psychotherapy, 18,* 241-250.

Levick, M. (1980). Response to Connie Naitove. *Arts in Psychotherapy, 7,* 261-264.

Levick, M. (1983). *They could not talk and so they drew: Children's styles of coping and thinking.* Springfield, IL: Charles C Thomas.

Levick, M. (1989). On the road to educating the creative arts therapist. *Arts in Psychotherapy, 16,* 57-60.

Levine, E.G. (1989). Women and creativity: Art-in-relationship. *Arts in Psychotherapy, 16,* 309-326.

Levinson, D. (1978). *The seasons of a man's life.* New York: Ballantine.

Levy, F. (1988). *Dance/movement therapy.* Reston, VA: American Alliance for Health, Physical Education, Recreation, and Dance.

Lewis, H.B. (1971). *Shame and guilt in neurosis.* New York: International Universities Press.

Lewis, P. (1987). The expressive arts therapies in the choreography of object relations. *Arts in Psychotherapy, 14,* 321-332.

Lewis, P. (1993). *Creative transformation: The healing power of the arts.* Wilmette, IL: Chiron Publications.

Lifton, R. (1983). *The broken connection.* New York: Basic Books.

Lindemann, E. (1944). Symptomatology and management of acute grief. *American Journal of Psychiatry, 101,* 141-148.

Lowenfeld, V. (1970). *Creative and mental growth.* New York: MacMillan.

Lusebrink, V. (1989). Education in the creative arts therapies: Accomplishments and challenges. *Arts in Psychotherapy, 16,* 5-10.

Lusebrink, V. (1990). *Imagery and visual expression in therapy.* New York: Plenum.

Lusebrink, V. (1991). A systems oriented approach to the expressive therapies: The expressive therapies continuum. *Arts in Psychotherapy, 18,* 395-404.

MacKay, B. (1989). Drama therapy with female victims of assault. *Arts in Psychotherapy, 16,* 293-300.

Madison, J., Hamilton, A., & Jay, J. (1788/1987). *The federalist papers.* London: Penguin.

Mahler, M., Pine, F., & Bergman, A. (1975). *The psychological birth of the human infant.* New York: Basic.

Malchiodi, C. (1998). *Understanding children's drawings.* New York: Guilford.

Masson, J. (1984). *The assault on truth: Freud's suppression of the seduction theory.* New York: Farrar, Straus, & Giroux.

Maxmen, J. (1978). An educative model for inpatient group therapy. *International Journal of Group Psychotherapy, 28,* 321-337.

McNiff, S. (1979). From shamanism to art therapy. *Arts in Psychotherapy, 6,* 3.

McNiff, S. (1981). *The arts as psychotherapy.* Springfield, IL: Charles Thomas.

McNiff, S. (1986). *Educating the creative arts therapist.* Springfield, IL: Charles C Thomas.

McNiff, S. (1988). The shaman within. *Arts in Psychotherapy, 15,* 285-292.

McNiff, S. (1991). Ethics and the autonomy of images. *Arts in Psychotherapy, 18,* 277-284.

McNiff, S. (1993). The authority of experience. *Arts in Psychotherapy, 20,* 3-10.

Meekums, B. (1991). Dance/movement therapy with mothers and young children at risk of abuse. *Arts in Psychotherapy, 18,* 223-230.

Milliken, R. (1990). Dance/movement therapy with the substance abuser. *Arts in Psychotherapy, 17,* 309-318.

Moffett, L.A., & Bruto, L. (1990). Therapeutic theatre with personality disordered substance abusers: Characters in search of different characters. *Arts in Psychotherapy, 17,* 339-348.

Moreno, J. (1988). The music therapist: Creative arts therapist and contemporary shaman. *Arts in Psychotherapy, 15,* 271-280.

Moreno, J. L. (1946). *Psychodrama.* Vol. I. Beacon, NY: Beacon House.

Nachmanovitch, S. (1990). *Free play: The power of improvisation in life and the arts.* Los Angeles: Tarcher.

Naitove, C. (1980). Creative arts therapist: Jack of all trades or master of one? *Arts in Psychotherapy, 7*, 253-260.

Nathanson, D. (1987). *The many faces of shame.* New York: Guilford.

Naumburg, M. (1966). *Dynamically oriented art therapy.* New York: Grune & Stratton.

Nordoff, P., & Robbins, C. (1977). *Creative music therapy.* New York: Harper & Row Publishers.

Ogden, T. (1982). *Projective identification and psychotherapeutic technique.* New York: Jason Aronson.

Peller, L. (1954). Libidinal phases, ego development, and play. *Psychoanalytic Study of the Child, Vol. 9.* New York: International Universities Press.

Penfield, W., & Perot, P. (1963). The brain's record of auditory and visual experience. *Brain, 86*, 595-696.

Perls, F. (1969). *Ego, hunger, and aggression.* New York: Random House.

Phillips, R.A., & Rosal, M.L. (1989). Empowering women with PMS through the creative process. *Arts in Psychotherapy, 16*, 277-282.

Piaget, J. (1937). *The construction of reality in the child.* New York: Basic Books.

Piaget, J. (1951). *Play, dreams, and imitation in childhood.* New York: Norton.

Pratt, J. (1922). Principles of class treatment and their application to various chronic diseases. *Hospital and Social Services, 6*, 401-411.

Reiland, J.D. (1990). A preliminary study of dance/movement therapy with field-dependent alcoholic women. *Arts in Psychotherapy, 17*, 349-354.

Robbins, A. (1980). *Expressive therapy: A creative arts approach to depth-oriented treatment.* New York: Human Sciences.

Robbins, A. (1982). Integrating the personal and theoretical splits in the struggle towards an identity as art therapists. *Arts in Psychotherapy, 9*, 1-10.

Robbins, A. (1985). Working toward the establishment of creative arts therapies as an independent profession. *Arts in Psychotherapy, 12*, 67-70.

Robbins, A. (1988). A psychoaesthetic perspective on creative arts therapy and training. *Arts in Psychotherapy, 15*, 95-100.

Rothenberg, A. (1988). *The creative process of psychotherapy.* New York: Norton.

Rubin, J. (1984). *The art of art therapy.* New York: Brunner/Mazel.

Rubin, J. (1987). *Approaches to art therapy, theory, and technique.* New York: Brunner/Mazel.

Sandel, S. (1980). Countertransference stress in the treatment of schizophrenic patients. *American Journal of Dance Therapy, 3*, 20-32.

Sandel, S. (1989). On being a female creative arts therapist. *Arts in Psychotherapy, 16*, 239-242.

Sandel, S. (1991). Family stories. *Arts in Psychotherapy, 18*, 263-264.

Sandel, S., & Johnson, D. (1974). Indications and contraindications for dance therapy and sociodrama in a long-term psychiatric hospital. *American Dance Therapy Association Monograph, 3*, 47-65.

Sandel, S., & Johnson, D. (1983). Structure and process of the nascent group: Dance therapy with chronic patients. *Arts in Psychotherapy, 10*, 131-140.

Sandel, S., & Johnson, D. (1987). *Waiting at the gate: Creativity and hope in the nursing home.* New York: Haworth Press.

Sandel, S., & Johnson, D. (1996). Theoretical foundations of the Structural Analysis of Movement Sessions. *Arts in Psychotherapy, 23*, 15-26.

Sandler, J., & Rosenblatt, B. (1962). The concept of the representational world. *Psychoanalytic Study of the Child, Vol. 17.* New York: International Universities Press.

Sang, B.E. (1989). Psychotherapy with women artists. *Arts in Psychotherapy, 16*, 301-308.

Sartre, J.P. (1960). *Critique of dialectical reason.* Paris: Librairie Gallimard.

Satir, V. (1967). *Conjoint family therapy.* Palo Alto, CA: Science and Behavior.

Schafer, R. (1968). *Aspects of internalization.* New York: International Universities Press.

Scheff, T. (1979). *Catharsis in healing, ritual, and drama.* Berkeley, CA: University of California Press.

Schimek, J. (1975). A critical reexamination of Freud's concept of unconscious mental representation. *International Review of Psychoanalysis, 2*, 171-187.

Schmais, C. (1988). Creative arts therapies and shamanism: A comparison. *Arts in Psychotherapy, 15*, 281-284.

Selman, R., Lavin D., & Brion-Meisels, S. (1982). Troubled children's use of self-reflection. In F. Serafica (Ed.), *Social-cognitive development in context.* New York: Guilford.

Siegel, E. (1984). *Dance-movement therapy: Mirror of our selves.* New York: Human Sciences Press.

Sifneos, P. (1975). Problems of psychotherapy of patients with alexithymic characteristics and physical disease. *Psychotherapy and Psychosomatics, 26*, 68-75.

Singer, J. (1966). *Daydreaming.* New York: Random House.

Singer, J. (1973). *The child's world of make believe.* New York: Academic.

Spitz, E.H. (1989). The world of art and the artful world: Some common fantasies in creativity and psychopathology. *Arts in Psychotherapy, 16*, 243-252.

Spitz, R. (1965). *The first year of life.* New York: International Universities Press.

Stark, A., & Warres, J. (1984). A working model for a conference on the creative/expressive arts therapies. *Arts in Psychotherapy, 11*, 279-282.

Stern, D. (1985). *The interpersonal world of the infant.* New York: Basic Books.

Stone, A. (1992). The role of shame in posttraumatic stress disorder. *American Journal of Orthopsychiatry, 62*, 131-136.

Sutton-Smith, B., & Sutton-Smith, S. (1974). *How to play with your children.* New York: Hawthorn.

Swan-Foster, N. (1989). Images of pregnant women: Art therapy as a tool for transformation. *Arts in Psychotherapy, 16*, 283-292.

Talbott-Green, M. (1989). Feminist scholarship: Spitting into the mouths of the gods. *Arts in Psychotherapy, 16*, 253-262.

Treder-Wolff, J. (1990). Music therapy as a facilitator of creative process in addictions treatment. *Arts in Psychotherapy, 17*, 319-324.

van der Kolk, B. (1987). *Psychological trauma.* Washington, DC: American Psychiatric Press.

van der Kolk, B., Blitz, R., Burr, W., et al. (1984). Nightmares and trauma. *American Journal of Psychiatry, 141*, 187-190.

Vgotsky, L. (1962). *Thought and language.* Cambridge, MA: MIT Press.

Volkman, S. (1993). Music therapy and the treatment of trauma-induced dissociative disorders. *Arts in Psychotherapy, 20,* 243-252.

Wadeson, H. (1989). In a different image: Are "male" pressures shaping the "female" arts therapy professions? *Arts in Psychotherapy, 16,* 327-330.

Waelder, R. (1932). The psychoanalytic theory of play. *Psychoanalytic Quarterly, 2,* 15-35.

Washington, G. (1939). *Writings.* Washington, DC: Washington Press.

Watts, A. (1962). *The joyous cosmology.* New York: Vintage.

Way, B. (1967). *Development through drama.* London: Humanities.

Werner, H. & Kaplan, S. (1963). *Symbol formation.* New York: Wiley.

Werner, H. (1948). *The comparative psychology of mental development.* New York: Science Editions.

Winner, E. (1982). *Invented worlds: The psychology of the arts.* Cambridge, MA: Harvard University Press.

Winnicott, D. (1953). Transitional objects and transitional phenomena. *International Journal of Psychoanalysis, 34,* 89-97.

Winnicott, D. (1971). *Playing and reality.* New York: Basic Books.

Wurmser, L. (1981). *The mask of shame.* Baltimore, MD: John Hopkins University Press.

Yalom, I. (1975). *Theory and practice of group psychotherapy.* New York: Basic Books.

Zierer, E. (1987). Creative analysis involving multidisciplinary evaluations of a case study. *Art Therapy, 4,* 113-125.

AUTHOR INDEX

SUBJECT INDEX

A

Accommodation, 144–45
Activities professionals, 33
Adaptation, 145
Administration, 16, 18, 21
Aesthetic distance, 25, 44
Aesthetic theory of therapy, 24–25
AIDS quilt, 80
Alcoholics Anonymous model
  and group therapy, 78
  and shamed identity, 71
  and substance abuse, 133–35
  creative arts techniques, 134–35
Alcoholism and family dysfunction, 5
Alexithymia, 103, 105, 106, 108
Alzheimer's clients and musical communication, 22, 39
American Art Therapy Association, 55
American Dance Therapy Association, 55
American Music Therapy Association, 55
American Revolution
  linked to creative arts therapies unification, vi, 6, 38, 47–48
  founding fathers and Puritan work ethic valuation, 66, 77
American Society for Group Psychotherapy and Psychodrama, 55
Aphasic clients and musical communication, 22, 39
Art and community, 93–101
  cathartic experiences, 95
  creative expression and transformation, 23–24, 26–27, 37, 77, 94, 110–12
  creator, performer, audience, 24, 39, 95
  power and vulnerability, 96
  psychological trauma, 102–12
  religion, art, community, healing, 23–24, 95
  science and soul; logic and magic, 115
  transcendent, 23–24, 77, 94
  void, representation of, 26

Art and organization
  intrinsic organization of elements within art forms, 44
Art therapy, ix, 5, 8, 13
  psychological trauma, 102–12 (*see also* Trauma)
  science and soul; logic and magic, 115
  sexual abuse treatment, 39, 102–5
  trauma memories, 106–10
Artistic expression
  aesthetic fundamentals, 24–25, 39
  brain locality, 23
  creative expression and transformation, 23–24, 26–27, 37, 77, 94, 110–12
  play, 25–26
  religion, art, healing, 23–24, 95
  right brain activity, 22
Artistic reality modes, 24
  creator, performer, audience, 24, 39
  science and soul; logic and magic, 115
Artists, training, 25
Arts and culture
  benefits of arts education, 93
  communitas, 93–101
  cultural value of arts v. work, 66, 77 (*see also* Shame dynamics)
  funding for fine arts, 14
  psychological trauma, 102–12
  science and soul; logic and magic, 115
  societal view of arts and luxury/time, 66
Arts in Psychotherapy (journal), 7, 39
Assimilation, 144–45
Attitude of entitlement, perception of, 73
Attunement/misattunement, 147, 166
Autonomy v. isolation, 10

B

Balance, 24
Beauty, 24
  creative expression and transformation, 23–24, 26–27, 37, 77, 94, 110–12

208

HOW WE SEE GOD AND WHY IT MATTERS
A Multicultural View Through Children's Drawings and Stories

To Be Published 2001, 230 pages
Robert J. Landy
hard and paper

HOME IS WHERE THE ART IS
An Art Therapy Approach to Family Therapy

To Be Published 2001, 224 pages
Doris Banowsky Arrington
hard and paper

CREATIVE SPIRITUALITY FOR WOMEN
Developing a Positive Sense of Self Through Spiritual Growth Exercises

Published 2000, 180 pages
Iris St. John
$26.95, spiral (paper)

ESSAYS ON THE CREATIVE ARTS THERAPIES
Imaging the Birth of a Profession.

Published 1999, 228 pages
David Read Johnson
$45.95, cloth
$31.95, paper (displayed)

EXPRESSIVE ARTS THERAPIES IN SCHOOLS
A Supervision and Program Development Guide

Published 1998, 128 pages
Karen Frostig & Michele Essex
$21.95, spiral (paper)

THE DYNAMICS OF ART AS THERAPY WITH ADOLESCENTS

Published 1998, 260 pages
Bruce L. Moon
$55.95, hard
$41.95, paper

ART THERAPY WITH SEXUAL ABUSE SURVIVORS

Published 1997, 188 pages
Stephanie L. Brooke
$44.95, cloth
$28.95, paper (displayed)

CHARLES C THOMAS • PUBLISHER, LTD.
P.O. Box 19265, Springfield, IL 62794-9265
Call 1-800-258-8980 or 1-217-789-8980 or Fax 1-217-789-9130
Complete catalog available at www.ccthomas.com •
books@ccthomas.com

Books sent on approval • Shipping charges: $5.95 U.S. / Outside U.S., actual shipping fees will be charged • Prices subject to change without notice

ART THERAPY WITH STUDENTS AT RISK
Introducing Art Therapy into an Alternative Learning Environment for Adolescents

To Be Published 2001, 148 pages
Stella A. Stepney
hard

ETHICAL ISSUES IN ART THERAPY

Published 2000, 254 pages
Bruce L. Moon
$49.95, hard
$33.95, paper

THE ART OF DYING
A Jungian View of Patients' Drawings

Published 1999, 242 pages
Yvonne B. Williams
$31.95, hard

A LEAP OF FAITH
The Call to Art

Published 1999, 210 pages
Ellen G. Horovitz
$46.95, hard
$33.95, paper

THE ART AND SCIENCE OF EVALUATION IN THE ARTS THERAPIES
How Do You Know What's Working?

Published 1998, 398 pages
Bernard Feder & Elaine Feder
$79.95, cloth
$62.95, paper (displayed)

THE HANDBOOK OF SCHOOL ART THERAPY
Introducing Art Therapy Into a School System

Published 1997, 206 pages
Janet Bush
$50.95, cloth
$37.95, paper (displayed)

A THERAPIST'S GUIDE TO ART THERAPY ASSESSMENTS
Tools of the Trade

Published 1996, 164 pages
Stephanie L. Brooke
$36.95, cloth
$25.95, paper (displayed)

A CONSUMER'S GUIDE TO ART THERAPY
For Prospective Employers, Clients and Students

Published 1994, 112 pages
Susan R. Makin
$33.95, cloth
$19.95, paper (displayed)

ART AND SOUL
Reflections on an Artistic Psychology

Published 1996, 156 pages
Bruce L. Moon
$38.95, cloth
$27.95, paper (displayed)

DATE DUE

March 2906		
APR 0 5 2006		

GAYLORD   PRINTED IN U.S.A.